lonely planet

Best Road Trips

NEW ZEALAND

ASHLYN OSWALT, BRETT ATKINSON, ANDREW BAIN,
PETER DRAGICEVICH, MONIQUE PERRIN,
CHARLES RAWLINGS-WAY, TASMIN WABY

CONTENTS

SOUTH PACIFIC OCEAN
Cape Reinga
Bay of Islands
Tasman Sea
Kaitāia
Russell
Whangārei
Dargaville
Great Barrier Island
Wellsford
AUCKLAND & THE NORTH p53
Auckland
Whitianga
Papakura
Thames
Bay of Plenty
Hicks Bay
Tauranga
Hamilton
Whakatāne
Ruatoria
ROTORUA & THE CENTRAL NORTH ISLAND p87
Te Kuiti
Rotorua
New Plymouth
Taupō
Tūrangi
Gisborne
Wairoa
Tongariro National Park
Napier
Hāwera
Hastings
Whanganui
Palmerston North
Waipukurau
Dannevirke
Abel Tasman National Park
Marlborough Sounds
Levin
WELLINGTON & THE EAST COAST p113
Tākaka
Masterton
Karamea
Nelson
Picton
WELLINGTON
MARLBOROUGH & NELSON p133
Blenheim
Cook Strait
Westport
St Arnaud
Reefton
Hanmer Springs
Greymouth
Kaikōura
Tasman Sea
Hokitika
Arthur's Pass
Waipara
CANTERBURY & THE WEST COAST p159
Franz Josef Glacier
Fox Glacier
Mt Hutt
Christchurch
Lake Tekapo
Haast
Banks Peninsula
SOUTH PACIFIC OCEAN
Geraldine
Ōmarama
Timaru
Milford Sound/ Piopiotahi
Wānaka
Waimate
Fiordland National Park
Queenstown
Ōamaru
Alexandra
Te Anau
Palmerston
Manapōuri
Dunedin
QUEENSTOWN & THE SOUTH p207
West Cape
Winton
Gore
Tuatapere
Balclutha
Invercargill
Oban
Stewart Island/ Rakiura
0 200 km
0 100 miles

WELCOME TO NEW ZEALAND

New Zealand's extraordinary natural beauty needs no further promotion. The very fact you've picked up this book suggests you're already familiar with images of its majestic mountains, sparkling lakes, dramatic fiords and dazzling beaches. There's simply no better way to access those beautiful spots and get under the skin of the country than on a road trip.

The scenery changes continuously, swiftly moving from farmland to native bush, to steamy geothermal zones, to lakefront, to mountains, to coast. Even in the flattest parts of this island nation there's always a mountain on the horizon, and water's never far away either. Distances aren't huge, so you're always near the next town, where you can almost guarantee there'll be a petrol station, a bed for the night and a decent coffee.

Exploring New Zealand by road is easy. Flick through the 26 routes in this book and start planning.

Arthur's Pass National Park (p30)

NEWJADSADA/SHUTTERSTOCK

MY PERFECT ROAD TRIP

ASHLYN OSWALT

OTAGO HERITAGE TRAIL, p232

The unexpected vistas and charming settlements are why I love this drive. It's perfect in every season – burgeoning with blossoms in spring, roadside fruit stalls and refreshing lake dips in summer, brilliant colours in autumn, and a snowy wonderland in winter (though a 4WD and nerves of steel are required!). It's truly the road less travelled, full of surprises – perfect for history buffs, hikers and avid bike riders alike.

I VIEWFINDER/SHUTTERSTOCK, FILIP FUXA/SHUTTERSTOCK

Right: West Coast Road (p162)
Far Right: Clutha River/Mata-Au

BEST LONG DRIVES

1. **Northland & the Bay of Islands** Head north from Auckland to the very tip of the North Island at Cape Reinga, then loop back on the western coast.

2. **Waves & Caves** Take in the western side of the North Island from Auckland to Whanganui, stopping off at caves and beaches.

3. **Pacific Coast Explorer** A meander along the Pacific Ocean coastline of the North Island from Tauranga to Havelock North.

4. **West Coast Road** Keep the Tasman Sea on your right, taking in gorges and glaciers as you travel from Westport to Haast.

5. **Southern Scenic Route** Take the long (and scenic) way from Te Anau to Dunedin, including a detour to Stewart Island/Rakiura.

OUR PICKS

BEST MOUNTAIN DRIVES

SNOW CHAINS
Chains are required on some South Island mountain roads when there's a threat of black ice or heavy snow.

Mountains provide a backdrop to every New Zealand road trip, whether they are the stand-alone volcanic cones of the central North Island, the intimidating jagged peaks of the Southern Alps or the many other prominent ranges scattered across both islands. Many of New Zealand's most memorable drives head up and over alpine passes, sure to elicit gasps at every turn.

1 TWO PASSES

Loop through the Southern Alps between Christchurch and Greymouth via Lewis Pass and then Arthur's Pass. p178

2 INLAND SCENIC ROUTE

Skirt glacial lakes near the Southern Alps before crossing to Central Otago via Lindis Pass. p184

3 SOUTHERN ALPS CIRCUIT

Journey along both sides of the Alps, crossing them three times via famously beautiful passes. p198

4 MILFORD SOUND/ PIOPIOTAHI MAJESTY

Absorb magnificent scenery before you reach Fiordland National Park and an unforgettable final reveal. p210

5 CENTRAL OTAGO EXPLORER

Circle past popular ski fields and four highly photogenic lakes on this impressive highland loop. p218

Lewis Pass (p179)

LEFT: JAMIE FARRANT/SHUTTERSTOCK
RIGHT: KLANARONG CHITMUNG/SHUTTERSTOCK

ROAD CLOSURES

Some roads tend to close in icy conditions, particularly the Crown Range Rd (between Queenstown and Wānaka) and Milford Sound Hwy.

KEA

Look out for kea (loveable mountain parrots) on alpine passes. But beware: they're enthusiastic thieves with a fondness for windscreen rubber.

SAFE SWIMMING

Safeswim *(safeswim.org.nz)* assesses water quality and lists the hours that lifeguards are on duty at popular beaches around the country.

SURF SAFETY

New Zealand's surf beaches can be treacherous. Where beaches are patrolled by surf lifesavers, always swim between the flags.

BEST COASTAL DRIVES

PEAK SEASON

January is the busiest beach month, so book well ahead if travelling to coastal hot spots, especially around New Year.

You're never far from the coast in this island nation, and New Zealand's 14,000km of coastline is just as spectacular and varied as its interior. Rugged, atmospheric, black-sand surf beaches are the hallmark of the west coast of both islands. The east coast of the North Island, especially its top half, has the country's prettiest white-sand swimming beaches.

① COROMANDEL PENINSULA

The nation's summertime playground, home to many of New Zealand's most beautiful beaches. p72

② PACIFIC COAST EXPLORER

Surf beaches galore, interesting regional cities and a wonderfully remote drive around the East Cape. p124

③ TASMAN & GOLDEN BAYS

Gorgeous golden beaches line the sun-kissed top of the South Island. p144

④ WEST COAST ROAD

A wild, elemental drive along bush-lined coastline at the base of the Southern Alps. p162

⑤ SOUTHERN SCENIC ROUTE

Sea lions and hardy surfers love this rugged stretch along the bottom of the South Island. p224

LEFT TO RIGHT: GREENS AND BLUES/SHUTTERSTOCK, TRAVELLIGHT/SHUTTERSTOCK

Left: Coromandel Peninsula (p72)
Far left: West Coast Road (p162)

CHRIS HOWEY/SHUTTERSTOCK

Māori carving, Rotorua

BEST HISTORY DRIVES

Humans only set foot here less than a millennium ago, but New Zealand's relatively short human history doesn't lack drama. There are plenty of places where you can engage with the richness of Māori culture and visit sites of historical and spiritual significance. Colonial history is brought to life in buildings dating to the earliest days of European settlement and in engaging museums devoted to local history and pioneering industries.

1 OTAGO HERITAGE TRAIL

Explore gold-rush settlements and old railway bridges, then return to the Victorian streetscapes of Dunedin. p232

STEP BACK IN TIME

If you like period dress-ups, visit Ōamaru during its Victorian Heritage Celebrations and Napier for its Art Deco Festival.

TE MATATINI

The biggest showcase of Māori performing arts is Te Matatini, a fiercely contested national competition held in odd-numbered years.

2 THERMAL DISCOVERER

Rotorua showcases Māori culture, and every city on this route has an excellent local-history museum. p34

3 EAST COAST EXPRESS

Ōamaru's well-preserved Victorian precinct is a suitably Dickensian setting for a spot of time travelling. p46

4 NORTHLAND & THE BAY OF ISLANDS

The birthplace of the nation, including NZ's oldest buildings and the most sacred site for Māori. p56

5 PACIFIC COAST EXPLORER

Around the East Cape, discover Māori artistry expressed in beautifully carved and decorated buildings. p124

BEST VOLCANIC DRIVES

WHAKAARI/ WHITE ISLANDS

As you tour the Bay of Plenty, keep an eye out for New Zealand's most active volcanic cone, 48km offshore.

There's a lot going on under New Zealand. The North Island in particular has numerous volcanoes and fascinating geothermal hot spots where steam rises, mud boils and minerals paint the ground in otherworldly colours. As a result, there are dozens of places to relax with a warm, mineral-enriched soak at the end of your day's explorations.

① THERMAL DISCOVERER

From Auckland (53 known volcanoes and counting), tour the geothermal sights of Rotorua and Taupō. p34

② COROMANDEL PENINSULA

Soak in hot springs at Whitianga, Hot Water Beach and Athenree (near Waihi Beach). p72

③ TARANAKI WANDERER

Circle and climb the most classically 'volcano' looking of all NZ's volcanic cones. p90

④ TONGARIRO NATIONAL PARK LOOP

Explore steamy Orakei Korako, soak in hot springs at Taupō, then circle three active volcanoes. p96

⑤ PACIFIC COAST EXPLORER

At Mt Maunganui, climb volcanic Mauao, then soak in the hot springs at its base. p124

Lake Taupō (p40)

GALYNA ANDRUSHKO/SHUTTERSTOCK

OUR PICKS

BEST CULINARY DRIVES

ROADSIDE STALLS

Roadside produce stalls with honesty boxes are a common sight on rural roads, so it pays to carry some cash.

New Zealand is well known internationally as an exporter of lamb, dairy products, mānuka honey and fine wine. Hit the road and you'll find all of that, as well as top-quality seafood (the oysters, scallops, mussels and crayfish are particularly good), game meats and a lively artisanal scene producing everything from fancy gin to truffle-infused olive oil.

1 KAIKŌURA COAST

Enjoy barbecued seafood at a beachside shack en route between Marlborough and Canterbury wine regions. p42

2 WAIHEKE ISLAND ESCAPE

Auckland's 'island of wine' also offers olive oil, oysters, gelato, and gin flavoured with local botanicals. p80

3 PACIFIC COAST EXPLORER

Notable wine regions Gisborne and Hawke's Bay also produce kiwifruit, berries and apples. p124

4 SUNSHINE & WINE

Visit Nelson and Marlborough wine regions, boutique breweries, farmers markets and 'mussel capital' Havelock. p136

5 CENTRAL OTAGO EXPLORER

Try Central Otago's stone fruits, Burgundy-style wine, and exemplary restaurants in Queenstown, Lake Hayes and Arrowtown. p218

Left: Seafood, Kaikōura Coast (p42)
Right: Vineyard, Waiheke Island (p80)

WINE TASTING

Many NZ wineries offer tastings, usually for a small fee, which is often reimbursed if you purchase a bottle.

PICK YOUR OWN

In summer, many roadside berry farms offer the opportunity to pick your own – a fun, family-friendly activity.

WHEN TO GO

Put simply, there's no bad time for a New Zealand road trip. Each season has merits of its own.

I LIVE HERE

I LOVE DRIVING HERE

Patrick Cole
Truck driver

I used to be a camera operator, but a solo camping road trip helped inspire me to become a full-time driver. It was late summer, when most people had already returned to work, and I set off zigzagging down the country. The most memorable drive for me was the Canterbury approach to Arthur's Pass. I'm a fan of winding roads – I think straight roads can be boring. At that time of year the days are still hot, but at Arthur's Pass the morning fog gave it an eerie beauty. I found myself constantly stopping to admire the views.

Aside from the queues escaping Auckland for the beaches between Christmas and New Year, driving in summertime is extremely pleasant. Autumn brings with it the added spectacle of changing leaves, especially in the south. In winter, some high-altitude roads are prone to temporary closures during heavy snowfall and icy conditions, but there's almost always an alternative route to take. Spring is a lovely time to drive through the reawakening countryside, with little fluffy lambs a common sight.

ACCOMMODATION

The places most affected by seasonal price variations are the beach towns during the Christmas/January school holidays, making this the peak season for family-friendly accommodation. If beaches are on your itinerary, consider booking for February or March instead. Similarly, prices shoot up during the ski season (roughly July to September) in places such as Queenstown, Wānaka and Ohakune. City prices are less variable, but rates will increase when there's a big event scheduled.

FOLLOW THE SUN

The most consistently sunny spots in New Zealand are the Bay of Plenty and Hawke's Bay (both in the east of the North Island), and Nelson and Marlborough (at the top of the South Island). Waiheke Island has its own dry, sunny microclimate.

WEATHER WATCH

JANUARY	FEBRUARY	MARCH	APRIL	MAY	JUNE
Avg. daytime max: **23°C**	Avg. daytime max: **24°C**	Avg. daytime max: **22°C**	Avg. daytime max: **20°C**	Avg. daytime max: **18°C**	Avg. daytime max: **16°C**
Days of rainfall: **8**	Days of rainfall: **7**	Days of rainfall: **8**	Days of rainfall: **11**	Days of rainfall: **12**	Days of rainfall: **15**

DMITRY PICHUGIN/SHUTTERSTOCK

Aoraki/Mt Cook (p33) in autumn

THE SUBTROPICAL NORTH

Northland and Auckland both have subtropical climates, resulting in mild, wet winters and sticky summers. Surrounded by water on all sides, Auckland is especially humid. A 25°C day in Auckland can feel much more sweaty than a 32°C day in much drier Christchurch.

STORMS & SLIPS

Climate change appears to be making NZ more prone to storms. Areas likely to be cut off during bad weather include Northland, the Coromandel Peninsula and the East Coast. If a storm is predicted, take it seriously.

SHINDIGS LARGE & SMALL

World Buskers Festival
All kinds of oddball performers take to the streets of Christchurch. **January**

Waitangi Day
New Zealand's national day on 6 February, with Māori food and culture. **February**

Marlborough Wine & Food Festival
Spend the day in the wine region world-famous for its sauvignon blanc. **February**

Hokitika Wildfoods Festival
Chow down on worms and hare's testicles at Hokitika's food fest. **March**

Matariki
Māori New Year is celebrated at the rising of the Matariki (or Pleiades) constellation. **June/July**

WOW – World of Wearable Art
Spectacular costumes take centre stage in Wellington. **September & October**

Ōamaru Victorian Heritage Celebrations
Hark back to the days when Queen Victoria sat on the throne. **November**

Rhythm & Vines
Around 23,000 young Kiwis head to Gisborne for this three-day music festival. **December**

JULY	AUGUST	SEPTEMBER	OCTOBER	NOVEMBER	DECEMBER
Avg. daytime max: **15°C**	Avg. daytime max: **15°C**	Avg. daytime max: **17°C**	Avg. daytime max: **18°C**	Avg. daytime max: **20°C**	Avg. daytime max: **22°C**
Days of rainfall: **16**	Days of rainfall: **15**	Days of rainfall: **13**	Days of rainfall: **12**	Days of rainfall: **10**	Days of rainfall: **10**

GET PREPARED FOR NEW ZEALAND

Useful things to load in your bag, your ears and your brain.

WATCH

- **Hunt for the Wilderpeople**
  (Taika Waititi; 2016)
  Comedy adventure featuring Sam Neill going on the run in the NZ bush with his foster child.

- **What We Do in the Shadows**
  (Jemaine Clement & Taika Waititi; 2014) Wellington is overrun by bickering vampires and polite werewolves in this mockumentary.

- **Whale Rider**
  (Niki Caro; 2002)
  Māori culture and family life on the East Coast, with a touch of the supernatural.

- **The Lord of the Rings trilogy**
  (Peter Jackson; 2001–03)
  NZ landscapes nearly steal the show in this adaptation of JRR Tolkien's classic fantasy novels.

- **The Piano**
  (Jane Campion; 1993)
  A piano and its owner arrive on a 19th-century NZ beach.

CLOTHING

Swimsuit (aka togs) Even if you're travelling in winter, pack something to wear in the water as there are hot springs and heated pools all around the country.

Walking shoes You'll get lots of mileage out of a comfortable pair of walking shoes in New Zealand. Most bushwalks can be tackled in sports shoes, although they may get muddy.

Hiking boots If you're contemplating a more substantial hike – particularly in the mountains, and especially in winter – a sturdy, comfortable pair of boots is a necessity.

Wool, fleece and waterproof layers Essential if you're hiking in the mountains. Temperatures can change suddenly, so it's good to be able to layer up and down as required.

Don't even think about hiking in jeans – as soon as it rains they'll be cold and heavy.

Jandals (aka flip-flops, thongs, slops) Kiwis are a casual lot, and you'll fit right in at a backyard barbecue in a pair of jandals in summer. (The NZ name is a contraction of 'Japanese sandals'.)

A 'good' set of clothes There are very few places where you would be turned away in a tidy T-shirt and jeans, but it's always good to have a dressy option for a fancy night out.

FROM LEFT TO RIGHT: LANDSCAPEMANIA/SHUTTERSTOCK, OLGAGI/SHUTTERSTOCK, NEW AFRICA/SHUTTERSTOCK, YEVGEN BELICH/SHUTTERSTOCK

Māori woman, Rotorua

WORDS

Many Māori words have made their way into New Zealand English and you're bound to encounter at least some in your travels. Common greetings include **kia ora** (hello), **mōrena** (good morning) and **tēnā koe** (greetings to you). You'll also hear words like **aroha** (love), **whanau** (family) and **kai** (food) used interchangeably with their English equivalents: 'I'm just going out for some **kai** with the **whanau**'.

In NZ, the word 'kiwi' is only ever used in relation to either the flightless native bird or to mean New Zealander. It's never used to refer to the green berry with the furry brown skin, which is a 'kiwifruit'. If you ask for a kiwi smoothie or say you want to buy some kiwis, expect to get a strange look.

The most treasured material for Māori carving is **pounamu**, which is also known as 'greenstone' in NZ English – although you will sometimes see it called 'jade' in tourist shops targeting an international market.

Other 'Kiwi-isms' include the aforementioned 'jandal' (flip-flop), 'tramp' (hike), 'jersey' (sweater, jumper or pullover) and 'bach' (pronounced 'batch' as it was originally short for 'bachelor pad'), which refers to a family holiday home that might be available to rent. In parts of the far south, 'baches' are known as 'cribs'.

Another peculiarity is the tendency to try to soften a negative response with a positive one; you may hear someone say 'yeah, nah' when they simply mean 'no'.

LISTEN

- **Leave Love out of This** *(Anthonie Tonnon; 2021)* Beautifully crafted songs by the sometime operator of Whanganui's Durie Hill Elevator.
- **Te Whare Tīwekaweka** *(Marlon Williams; 2025)* The fourth album from acclaimed Christchurch-based singer-songwriter is his first in te reo Māori.
- **Pure Heroine** *(Lorde; 2013)* Breakthrough debut for an international superstar featuring several songs about Auckland.
- **Crowded House** *(Crowded House; 1986)* Debut for Neil Finn's three-piece, with a mention of Te Awamutu in the very first song.

READ

- **The Luminaries** *(Eleanor Catton; 2013)* Man Booker Prize winner set on the West Coast.
- **The Bone People** *(Keri Hulme; 1984)* Magical and disturbing, this Booker winner is set on the West Coast too.
- **Rangatira** *(Paula Morris; 2011)* Historical novel based on a true story about a group of Māori chiefs travelling to London.
- **Bulibasha: King of the Gypsies** *(Witi Ihimaera; 1994)* Gripping saga about the rivalry between two Māori sheep-shearing families.

Lake Wakatipu (p33)
PRUCHAWAL / SHUTTERSTOCK

CONTENTS

01

EPIC TRIP: NEW ZEALAND ICONS

New Zealand may look tiny on a map, but there's a lot to explore on the two main islands. Starting in Auckland, head north to explore historic sites alongside subtropical beaches. Then turn south to glowworm caves, geothermal parks and wine country. Cross the ferry to the South Island and cruise along the Kaikōura coast, veering west over the Southern Alps and into the rugged West Coast. Native bush walks and alpine lakes abound in Otago and Southland, while Fiordland National Park's beauty provides a moment of quiet reflection. Stand below the mighty Aoraki/Mt Cook, the country's tallest mountain, before ending in a revitalised Christchurch.

BY ASHLYN OSWALT

Road to Aoraki/Mt Cook

MATT MUNRO/LONELY PLANET

EPIC TRIP

DURATION: 28-32 DAYS

DISTANCE: 4358KM / 2708 MILES

GREAT FOR: NATURE, HISTORY AND CULTURE

BEST TIME TO GO: ALL YEAR ROUND, BUT NOVEMBER TO MARCH FOR THE WARMEST WEATHER (NOTE JANUARY CROWDS)

01 Auckland

The nation's largest city and commercial hub sits inside **Waitematā Harbour**, overlooking the Hauraki Gulf. The landscape is dotted with the cones and craters of the Auckland Volcanic Field. It's a hilly place, so you can expect some inclines as you stroll the city

LINK YOUR TRIP

02 Thermal Discoverer
Link this journey from Auckland to discover the North Island's geothermal centre.

10 Tongariro National Park Loop
Continue through Taupō to explore Tongariro National Park's volcanic landscapes.

11 Waves & Caves to Whanganui
From Auckland, carry on to the surfing town of Raglan and artsy Whanganui.

16 Going West: From Picton to Westport
Head west from Picton for a scenic drive through Nelson Lakes National Park.

24 Central Otago Explorer
Explore Central Otago's gold-rush towns and wineries from Queenstown or Wānaka.

25 Southern Scenic Route
After Te Anau, discover the wild coast of the windswept Catlins.

MICHAEL HALL/GETTY IMAGES

Waipoua State Forest

streets. The **Auckland Museum** *(aucklandmuseum.com)*, situated atop the remains of ancient volcano Pukekawa, provides insight into New Zealand's nature and history – including a gallery on volcanoes and an entire floor dedicated to NZ's war involvement.

THE DRIVE: Follow SH1 north 211km until taking the roundabout to SH11 in Kawakawa. Turn right after Paihia and cross the one-way bridge into Waitangi. Pay tolls online at nzta.govt.nz. The journey takes just over three hours.

02 Waitangi

The **Waitangi Treaty Grounds** *(waitangi.org.nz)* are one of the most important cultural places in New Zealand. In 1840, the Treaty of Waitangi was signed by Māori chiefs and the British Crown here. Standard admission allows access to the grounds for two consecutive days – handy because there's a lot to take in. Start with a one-hour guided tour, included in admission, and make time to visit the two on-site museums. For an extra cost, book a *hāngī* dinner (cooked in a traditional Māori earthen oven) and a concert for an immersive cultural experience.

THE DRIVE: This leg is 213km. Drive back over the one-way bridge and rejoin SH11, following it west to Puketona, where you'll head north on SH10, hugging the coast at times. You'll rejoin SH1 in Awanui, the last leg of your journey, and drive 103km north to Cape Reinga Lighthouse.

03 Cape Reinga

Considered the symbolic top of the North Island, Cape Reinga is a special place in Māori culture. The **Cape Reinga Lighthouse** sits high above where the Tasman Sea and Pacific Ocean meet, creating a dramatic display of spray. Access inside the lighthouse isn't permitted, but there's an easy 800m stroll to its base. Enjoy the horizon views and try to spot the ancient **pōhutukawa** tree at the cape's northernmost point. This spot is where the spirits of deceased Māori are said to leap to return to their ancestral home.

THE DRIVE: This drive takes around 4½ hours. Retrace your path south on SH1 and continue past Awanui for 133km. Veer right onto Mangamuka Rd, then take the Twin Coast Discovery Hwy south at the fork. Take the Hokianga Vehicle Ferry, which runs hourly to Rawene, then continue 5.5km before turning right onto SH12. Turn right onto Waipoua River Rd, following signs to the Waipoua Campground.

04 Waipoua State Forest

The Waipoua State Forest is home to New Zealand's largest kauri tree, **Tāne Mahuta**, among other giants. Walk the short, accessible trail to this 2000-year-old tree between 9am and 5pm. Book a twilight tour with **Footprints Waipoua** *(footprintswaipoua.co.nz)* for an intimate and culturally enlightening experience. These magnificent trees can grow over 50m tall and are endemic to NZ. They're facing an extreme threat of kauri dieback, so take care during recreation in the area.

THE DRIVE: Return to SH12, heading south, for 131km. At Brynderwyn, turn right to rejoin SH1, making another right onto SH16 to follow the scenic route to Kaukapakapa. Turn left onto Peak Rd, left onto Old North Rd, and left again onto SH24. Finally, a sharp right onto Piha Rd. This leg is 263km.

TRABANTOS/SHUTTERSTOCK

Geyser, Te Puia, near Rotorua

LIVING ON THE ROAD

The best way to see New Zealand is in a campervan. This gives you the freedom to roam, explore hikes and viewpoints, and stop when you need to. NZ is best known for its outdoors, so sleeping among it allows you to soak in what the country has to offer. Hotels in major towns are often expensive, while small-town options are limited, filling up fast during peak season.

There are three major camping options for campervan travellers: holiday parks, DOC campsites and freedom camping. Note that it's illegal to pull over and camp wherever you like. Holiday parks are privately owned and range from flash (hot showers, rec rooms, hot tubs) to basic spots. More expensive than other options, they're lifesavers for laundry days or when you need a place to park up during bad weather.

DOC *(Department of Conservation; doc.govt.nz)* campsites are government-run and are more basic. It's becoming increasingly common to find flush toilets, but most simply have drop toilets and possibly a cooking shelter. These campsites tend to be much more affordable, due to the lack of amenities, and are usually set in idyllic spots.

Finally, freedom camping takes a bit of planning as it's highly regulated and rules are constantly changing. Some towns have designated freedom camping spots, either in paddocks or the centre of town, while other towns forbid freedom camping entirely. Check in with the local **i-SITE** *(isite.nz)* for freedom camping regulations, or save yourself the stress and book a campsite.

05 Piha

Under an hour from Auckland, this black-sand beach is popular among the city's day-trippers. Full of dramatic, rugged cliff vistas, it's a renowned surfing spot. Its strong current makes it dangerous to swim, so stay between the flags to keep within the watchful eye of lifeguards if you're keen for a dip. For views of the coast from above, walk the 2.2km **Mercer Bay Loop Track** *(aucklandcouncil.govt.nz)* and enjoy the shade from the regenerating forest.

THE DRIVE: This drive is 108km. Return to Piha Rd, which leads to Scenic Dr, continuing until veering right onto SH15. Follow the southern coast before catching SH20, linking up with SH1 and turning left onto SH2 before Pōkeno. Continue onto SH25, which will take you up through Thames and along the Coromandel coast.

06 Coromandel Town

Heritage streets and beaches make Coromandel Town a popular destination for artists and tourists alike. Check out the **Hauraki House Gallery** *(coromandeltown.nz)* showcasing local art. Head inland 15 minutes to experience **Waiau Falls** and **Kauri Grove Lookout Walk** *(doc.govt.nz)*. This short walk through kauri forest ends in a swimming hole below the majestic falls. Walk the **Kauri Block Track** *(doc.govt.nz)* from town for 1.6km to a Māori *pā* (fortified village) site with sweeping views of the Coromandel Range and islands.

THE DRIVE: Leave Coromandel Town and return to SH25, driving through the forested middle of the Coromandel Peninsula. After around 67km, turn left onto

Hot Water Beach Rd and follow signs for Cooks Beach Hahei. Park at the free Domain Road Carpark off Hot Water Beach Rd and walk a few hundred metres to the beach.

07 Hot Water Beach

Does a personal hot tub, dug from sand, with front-row views of the ocean sound like a good time? That's exactly what you'll find two hours either side of low tide at Hot Water Beach. Bring a spade, or rent one from **Hottie's** *(hottieseatery.co.nz)*, and start digging. Warm water will bubble up from the sand below, but only in front of the rocky outcrop in the middle of the beach. Hot tip: pack a bucket for dumping refreshing seawater into your hot tub.

THE DRIVE: Take Hot Water Beach Rd to SH25, veering right past Hikuai to get onto SH25A. It gets wiggly right before Kopu, where you'll rejoin SH25 with a roundabout. In Orongo, veer left onto Hauraki Rd, until turning right onto Awaiti Rd and right again onto Paeroa–Tahuna Rd to SH26 in Waihou. Turn left onto Tautiti Rd, right onto Bailey Rd, left onto Thomas Rd, and a right onto SH26 before a left onto Seddon Rd, right onto Waihekau Rd, and left onto Ngarua Rd. Turn left onto SH27 and follow it into town, about 20.6km. This leg is 144km.

08 Matamata

This sleepy little town quickly became a tourist destination once Peter Jackson used it as the set for *The Lord of the Rings* and *The Hobbit* trilogies. Explore **Hobbiton's** *(hobbitontours.com)* vast grounds on a 2½-hour guided walking tour, or book an evening banquet for a tour of the grounds, feast and lantern-lit evening walk. Bookings are essential and fill up fast.

THE DRIVE: This leg is 103km. Leave Matamata and rejoin SH27, before continuing onto Hopkins Rd and SH29. Follow SH29 and SH1 to Cambridge, then take the Thermal Explorer Hwy before a quick exit onto Shakespeare St, Cook St, then Pope Tce before continuing onto Cambridge Rd. Follow signs to Waitomo Caves before turning left onto SH3, and a right onto SH37 to the caves.

09 Waitomo Caves

These limestone caves and rivers are a perfect glowworm habitat, where they illuminate the dark caverns. For the most immersive experience, book a tour from one of the many operators in town. **Waitomo Glowworm Caves** *(waitomo.com)* offers a gentle 45-minute walk and boat ride through the caves, or opt for the adrenaline-fuelled three-hour Black Water Rafting tour, which includes waterfall jumps and floating down the river in an inner tube. Take a self-guided tour to **Piripiri Cave Walk** *(doc.govt.nz)*, 29km west of Waitomo, where a short walk affords the chance to spot glowworms for free.

THE DRIVE: Return to SH3 from SH37 and head north before turning right onto Allen Rd and right onto Arapuni Rd. Follow this winding road until Putāruru, where you briefly drive SH1 north until a right onto SH28. Join the Thermal Explorer Hwy for 42km until you reach Rotorua.

10 Rotorua

A geothermal hot spot, Rotorua is known for its natural and cultural assets. Shooting geysers and natural hot springs are the main attractions here, with hot-spring spas aplenty in town. **Polynesian Spa** *(polynesianspa.co.nz)* has thermal lakeside pools and spa treatments. Head to **Te Puia** *(tepuia.com)* for access to its geothermal valley and Māori cultural experiences like *haka* and *hāngī* meals.

THE DRIVE: From Rotorua, take the Thermal Explorer Hwy (SH5) to Taupō. You'll pass many geothermal areas along the 80km journey.

11 Taupō

Lake Taupō – NZ's largest lake – occupies a caldera formed by a supervolcanic eruption. The town sits on the northeast corner of the lake, with a swimming beach off the main drag. For fewer crowds, find a swimming hole off **Rangatira Point Track** *(lovetaupo.com)*, southwest of town. Check out the **Ngātoroirangi Mine Bay Māori Rock Carvings**, a 14m rock-carving portrait of Māori navigator Ngātoroirangi, with **Sail Barbary** *(sailbarbary.com)*.

THE DRIVE: SH5 leads east over farmland, climbing into some hilly areas for 137km before veering right onto SH2 before the coast. Head south and follow signs to Napier, then turn onto Meeanee Quay and east to Marine Pde.

12 Napier

Devastated by a 1931 earthquake, Napier was rebuilt in the art-deco style of the time. Take in the architecture with a visit to the **Art Deco Centre** *(artdeconapier.com)*. It hosts daily walking tours around the centre, pointing out the notable buildings. Don't miss the National Tobacco Company, built in 1933, and the Daily Telegraph Building, constructed in 1932. After a good walk, spend the afternoon at one of the area's 70-plus cellar doors. Rent a bike from **Tākaro Trails** *(takarotrails.co.nz)* to explore the region's established wineries.

THE DRIVE: This leg is 271km. Exit town to merge onto SH50 before taking SH2 south for 126km. Turn left onto Somerset Rd (signs for Parkvale), right onto Carters Line, and follow signs to Martinborough.

13 Martinborough

Martinborough oozes charm, though it hasn't always felt that way. The declining population in the 1970s led townspeople to plant grapes, hoping that a wine industry would revitalise the area. Their plan worked; Martinborough is now a destination for boutique wine with over 20 wineries. Explore with bikes from **Green Jersey** *(greenjersey.co.nz)*, and stop at **Poppies** *(poppiesmartinborough.co.nz)* for a lunch platter. Head to nearby **Margrain Vineyard** *(margrainvineyard.co.nz)* for a crisp chenin blanc on its patio overlooking the vines.

THE DRIVE: This 82km journey heads over the Remutaka Range, known for winding roads. Follow SH53 northwest to meet SH2 in Featherston, climb over the range, and drop down into the Upper Hutt before skirting Wellington Harbour into town.

14 Wellington

Take a stroll along the capital's art-filled waterfront for harbour views. Start at the colourful boat sheds of **Clyde Quay Boat Harbour** and end at **Taranaki Street Wharf**. Next, visit NZ's national museum **Te Papa** *(tepapa.govt.nz)* to explore the country's history through informative and interactive displays. Be sure to take the short outdoor walk with over 1400 native plants. Nearby **Cuba St** is popular for foodies. Enjoy authentic Ethiopian food at **Mother of Coffee** *(motherofcoffee.co.nz)*, at the end of Left Bank alleyway. Belly full, check out some of the city's best secondhand and vintage shops back on Cuba St.

THE DRIVE: The only way across with a car is by ferry, which takes about four hours. There are two options – Bluebridge or Interislander – and both run several crossings a day, seven days a week. Book a vehicle passage in advance to avoid long wait times. Expect delays in inclement weather.

15 Picton

Picton sits in one of the four sounds that make up Marlborough Sounds, an area known for hidden bays, walking tracks and great fishing. The 73.5km **Queen Charlotte Track** *(doc.govt.nz)* is a popular multiday track and will give you a real lay of the land. If you're short on time, walk a two-hour section from Anakiwa to Davies Bay, a beautiful swimming beach. Or check out the **Governors Bay Track** *(doc.govt.nz)*, an easy 10-minute walk to a quiet swimming bay.

THE DRIVE: Follow SH1 south for 156km, passing through Blenheim 28km out of Picton. You'll hug the coast from Wharanui on, with views of the sea.

16 Kaikōura

Kaikōura's mountain range tumbles dramatically into the sea, providing beautiful vistas at every turn. The real drama is below sea level, thanks to the Kaikōura Canyon, a 1200m-deep, nutrient-filled gorge that starts close to the shoreline. Spot whales, NZ fur seals and birds on a boat trip with **Whale Watch Kaikōura** *(whalewatch.co.nz)*. Look for dolphins and penguins on a sunset kayak with **Kaikōura Kayaks** *(kaikourakayaks.nz)*. The three-hour tour provides spectacular views of the Kaikōura Ranges.

THE DRIVE: Continue south on SH1 for 120km, before winery signs pop up in every direction. Greystone will be on your left.

17 Waipara Valley

One of New Zealand's best-kept wine secrets lies in the hills just north of Christchurch. The Waipara Valley is home to over 90 wineries producing a wide range of varieties. Plan a winery lunch on the patio at **Greystone** *(greystonewines.co.nz)*, and stop into **Pegasus Bay** *(pegasusbay.com)* to explore its notable gardens. Finish at the **Boneline** *(theboneline.co.nz)* for a tasting (bookings essential) and stroll through its vineyard walkway.

THE DRIVE: Follow SH1 south for 15km, turning right in Amberley onto Inland Scenic Rt 72. Pass Rangiora and Oxford before joining SH73 in Sheffield. Take this all the way to Castle Hill Dr, travelling a total of 133km.

18 Castle Hill/ Kura Tāwhiti

The rocky outcrops of Castle Hill/ Kura Tāwhiti will unfold as you drive along SH73. Framed by the Craigieburn and Torlesse Ranges, this scenery makes the perfect spot for a picnic. If you're lucky, you'll spot boulderers working their way over, under and around the limestone formations.

EPIC TRIP

Flaky Gold

In New Zealand, a road trip isn't measured in kilometres – it's measured in pie shops. The pies are the flaky pastry variety: hand pies that any Kiwi will wax poetic about if asked. Traditionally stuffed with meat and cheese, they're a meal eaten on the road, in the bakehouse or at a nearby viewpoint. Warming and hearty, they're perfect for New Zealand's unpredictable and changeable weather, offering a nourishing treat for trampers (hikers) and farmers alike who've been caught in the rain.

Disputed are the origins of the traditional meat pie: some trace it back to English settlers while others cite Greek and Roman culture. What's not disputed, however, is what a pie is, and what it can be. It's deliciously simple – flaky pastry filled with meat or vegetables (vegetarian options are becoming easier to find) to create a portable meal that feels home-cooked and special.

The classic flavours include mince, steak and cheese, butter chicken, bacon and egg, and potato top. Increasingly, bakeries are experimenting with new flavours and local ingredients.

A creamy paua (a shellfish) pie from Wild Grain Bakery Silverdale took gold in the 'Gourmet Meat' category from the Bakels Pie Awards in 2025. The same year, a brisket and cheese pie from Kells Kitchen won bronze in the 'Cafe Boutique' category. Lauded in the industry and among locals, these awards help denote who rises above the rest. Look for the window sticker at bakeries to find past winners.

What makes a bakery pie so good? For starters, it's all the other sensory cues that go with the bakery. They're normally tiny spots, either standalone or in a downtown strip, and lines often snake out the door, no matter the time. The glass cabinets that hold these little pastry jewels fog up from the heat, and the ding of the cash register is constant. If there's a seat inside, grab it to watch locals and tourists collide at the pie shop.

You can also enjoy a pie from the local petrol station. Some are surprisingly good, though they don't hold a candle to one from a local bakery. Try them side-by-side if you're really curious.

As a gluten-free vegetarian, I have limited pie experience. However, I never pass up the opportunity to stop at a pie shop – both for the enjoyment of my road-trip companions and the opportunity to soak in the buzz of a local favourite. It's the smell of yeast and simmering mince, plus the happy smiles of patrons, that make a stop at the bakery a true pleasure. The pie shop feels like the grand equaliser of Kiwi culture, and I relish the idea of taking part in such an iconic New Zealand experience.

Pork belly apple pie, Fairlie Bakehouse (p186)

FREEDOMKIM/SHUTTERSTOCK

THE DRIVE: Continue onto SH73 for 52km, passing another good picnic spot, Lake Pearson, along the way. You'll cross the Waimakariri River and follow a tributary north to the village.

19 Arthur's Pass

Tiny Arthur's Pass Village is the start of two easy hikes that showcase some of the national park's gems. The **Devils Punchbowl** *(doc.govt.nz)* is a one-hour return walk to the 131m waterfall, where the refreshing spray tumbles down over rocks to tickle the beech forest below. **Arthur's Pass Walking Track** *(doc.govt.nz)* is an easy 6.8km return walk through beech forest, wetlands and alpine shrublands. Stop at the **Otira Viaduct Lookout**, where impressive views of the bridge and mountains are almost eclipsed by the keas that hang out here.

THE DRIVE: This leg is 99km. You'll continue along SH73 north until it veers west to follow the Taramakau River. After 77km at Kumara Junction, head left onto SH6, following the rugged coast south to Hokitika.

20 Hokitika

Founded in 1864 after gold discovery, Hokitika was once one of the country's largest towns. While this is not the case today, it's a charming West Coast destination. Gold-mining relics are common on hikes here, with many meandering past ruins and sluice faces. Hike the 16km out-and-back **Goldsborough Track** *(doc.govt.nz)* or the 20-minute **Tunnel Trace Walk**, both of which wander through miners' tunnels. Be sure to grab a photo next to the driftwood sign spelling out 'Hokitika' on the main beach.

THE DRIVE: SH6 continues south through tiny settlements, hugging the coast for the majority. Franz Josef is 134km down the road, right before the Waiho River crossing.

21 Franz Josef Glacier

Up-close encounters with the Franz Josef Glacier require a guided tour, but you can take the **Franz Josef Glacier/Kā Roimata o Hine Hukatere Walk** *(doc.govt.nz)* to view the glacier from 2000m away. Book with **Franz Josef Glacier Guides** *(franzjosefglacier.com)* for a helicopter ride to the glacier plus ice time. Further south is the twin glacier **Fox Glacier**, seen from Peak Viewpoint on the roadside. Near Fox Glacier, 6km down Cook Flat Rd, famed **Lake Matheson** mirrors the Southern Alps in its reflection, with a 1½-hour accessible walk.

Franz Joseph Glacier

MATTHEW MICAH WRIGHT/GETTY IMAGES

THE DRIVE: Back on SH6, you'll wind through hilly, coastal territory. Stop in Ship Creek, 126km south of Franz Josef, for the views. Back on SH6, head south over the Haast Pass, following the river. Continue past the northern end of the lake, before taking SH84 west to Wānaka for 4km until you're in town.

22 Wānaka

Laid-back Wānaka has it all for outdoors lovers. The town's quaint main street overlooks the lake framed by mountains – the perfect backdrop for swimming, mountain biking and hiking. Amble around the lake on the shared bike and walking path, or hike up the challenging **Isthmus Peak Track**, a 16km steep walk up a rocky ascent for views of Lake Wānaka, Lake Hāwea and the Southern Alps. Reward your weary body with a brew and burger at **b.effect Brewing Co** *(beffect.nz)*.

THE DRIVE: This leg is 227km. Wind south on Cardrona Valley Rd, stopping at the iconic Cardrona Hotel for a meal. Continue on Crowne Range Rd to join SH6 for 146km before turning right onto SH97, following signs to Te Anau/Milford Sound. Turn right again at SH94, following the road 59km until you're in Te Anau.

23 Te Anau

The gateway to Fiordland National Park, Te Anau is a small but well-situated town on the southern end of **Lake Te Anau**. While walking along the lake is lovely, most visitors use Te Anau as a jumping-off point for tours and bus rides to Milford Sound/Piopiotahi. Transport to the **Milford Track Great Walk** *(doc.govt.nz)* starts

S WATSON/SHUTTERSTOCK

View of Lake Hāwea from Isthmus Peak Track, Wānaka

TAKING THINGS SLOW

Taking things slow is part of the culture in New Zealand, and it's imperative on the roads here. Distances may look short, but driving these roads, especially around mountain passes, can be exhausting. Most of the country's roads and highways are one-lane on either side, and you'll come across many one-way bridges.

While it can be tempting to plan long-distance drives to see more, we highly recommend seeing less but more thoroughly. Cramming too much into one day means missing out on the impromptu stops, lunches at beautiful viewpoints or a hike to stretch your legs. Plus, attempting to do long drives means you'll be too exhausted to enjoy all the goodness that you came to New Zealand to see. Stopping at all of the above is recommended to get the most out of NZ and remain alert.

Remaining alert is extremely important on NZ roads, especially during times of inclement weather. The country's beautiful, dramatic scenery can often lead to vulnerable infrastructure. Those stunning roads hugging cliff faces may become landslides in heavy rain, washing away the road. It's not uncommon for major highways to close due to damage from weather events. Check the **NZ Transport Agency** *(journeys.nzta.govt.nz)* journey planner to ensure your path is clear, especially during heavy rain or snow.

Allow yourself more time on your road trip to truly enjoy each step in the journey. We guarantee you'll get more out of your trip!

♥ WHY I LOVE THIS TRIP

ASHLYN OSWALT, WRITER

New Zealand's variety of landscapes crammed into a small landmass makes it one of the best countries to explore on a road trip. The best bits are not inhabited by people, only accessible by car or on foot. I'm originally from the United States, so I'm used to driving for hours – sometimes days! – for the scenery to change. Now, from my home in Christchurch, I can be on a different coast in three hours, driving through plains and over a mountain pass along the way. This trip is special because it gives you an immersive look into all that NZ has to offer, focusing on what the country does best – the outdoors. Aotearoa is a bucket-list destination for so many, and I believe that if you have the time, it's worth seeing both islands in all their splendour. I've travelled both islands in my campervan, and I love that the country offers different trips for different moods. If I need some warmth and sunshine, it's hard to beat Northland. If I want to feel the crisp alpine air and reinvigorate my body with glacial-fed lake dips, I head south to Otago. The towns along the way are part of the journey, too. From pubs full of friendly locals to the bustling city centres, you're never far from civilisation here – although it doesn't feel that way sometimes! It's hard to pick one kind of adventure in New Zealand, so my advice is: don't.

here, and the **Kepler Track Great Walk** trailhead is a few kilometres away. Stock up on supplies here if you plan on any multiday walks.

THE DRIVE: From Te Anau, return to SH94, north to Milford. Known as Milford Rd, it follows Lake Te Anau before skirting off to the postcard-worthy Eglinton Valley. Be prepared for delays at the one-way Homer Tunnel, which can take up to 20 minutes. Continue until you hit the sounds.

24 Milford Sound/ Piopiotahi

Fiordland National Park is part of **Te Wāhipounamu**, a UNESCO World Heritage Site. That'll be obvious as soon as you spot **Mitre Peak/ Rahotu** (if not before). Stare in awe as the cliffs tumble into inky waters below. The rainy climate is part of the appeal – it keeps Fiordland's many waterfalls gushing. To explore on the water, book a guided kayak tour with **Rosco's Milford Kayaks** *(roscosmilfordkayaks.com)*. Its unique 'Morning Glory' tour for experienced paddlers starts early in the morning, giving kayakers a chance to enjoy the fiord before the crowds. For less physical exertion, book a two-hour scenic cruise with **RealNZ** *(realnz.com)* for indoor and outdoor seating, guided wildlife talks and on-site coffee.

THE DRIVE: This leg is 288km. Retrace your drive south on SH94, turning left 57km later in Mossburn onto SH97. Follow signs for Queenstown, turning left onto SH6 and following that for 92km.

25 Queenstown

Known as the adventure capital of NZ, Queenstown has experiences for adrenaline-seekers and the laid-back alike. Get your heart racing with a bungy off the **Kawarau Bridge**, with **AJ Hackett Bungy** *(bungy.co.nz)*, the world's first commercial bungy. Or take in the views of **Lake Wakatipu** with a 1½-hour cruise on the historic **TSS Earnslaw steamship** *(realnz.com)*. Book a **Hop On Hop Off bus tour** *(hoponhopoffwinetours.com)* to explore the **Gibbston Valley** wineries, known for pinot noir production.

THE DRIVE: Exit Queenstown by following signs for SH6, turning right after 62km onto SH8 past Cromwell. Follow SH8 north through the Lindis Valley and through the golden tussocks and turquoise lakes of Mackenzie Country. Turn left onto SH80 towards Aoraki/Mt Cook just before Lake Pukaki and follow it 55km to the village.

26 Aoraki/Mt Cook National Park

New Zealand's tallest mountain, Aoraki/Mt Cook stands tall at 3724m. Spot the snowcapped peak on a clear day from the Lake Pukaki lookout on SH8, then head into the park. Many short walks leave from Mt Cook Village – easy, one-hour **Hooker Valley Track** *(doc.govt.nz)* is the most popular to see Aoraki on a fine day. Also easy, 30-minute **Tasman Glacier View Track** *(doc.govt.nz)* has views of NZ's longest glacier. Stop into the **Aoraki/ Mt Cook National Park Visitor Centre** for track and weather conditions, and to peruse the displays on the park's history.

THE DRIVE: Return to SH80 and drive south, turning left to get back onto SH8. Follow this for 48km, passing Lake Pukaki before turning into Lake Tekapo, on your left.

27 Lake Tekapo

The turquoise-coloured Lake Tekapo sparkles next to the lovely **Church of the Good Shepard** *(churchofthegoodshepherd.org.nz)*. Built in 1935, the stone church sits in the foreground of the lake and the Southern Alps. Volunteers open the church from 10am to 3pm Wednesday to Sunday, but this isn't guaranteed. For more sparkling views, book a tour with the **Dark Sky Project** *(darkskyproject.co.nz)* to enjoy the area's dark-sky reserve. Its guided experiences include high-powered telescope viewing.

THE DRIVE: This leg of the journey is 226km, riding over Burkes Pass and the foothills of the Southern Alps, to reach the flat farmland of Canterbury. Follow SH8 east until Fairlie, continuing east onto SH79 for 61km, before turning right in Rangitata. Follow SH1 for 120km to Christchurch.

28 Christchurch

Christchurch's coastal proximity isn't obvious when you're in the city centre, so take a short ride out of the city to enjoy its splendour. Harbour suburb **Lyttelton** hosts a popular Saturday morning farmers market. Hop on the **Coastal Path** *(ccc.govt.nz)* to Pony Point Reserve, a two-hour wander through pine forest, dropping into Lyttelton's swimming beaches. In beachy suburb **New Brighton**, enjoy ocean views while soaking at the **He Puna Taimoana Hot Pools** *(hepunataimoana.co.nz)*. You'll forget you're only 15 minutes from New Zealand's second-largest city.

Milford Sound/Piopiotahi fiord

WOOTTHISAK NIRONGBOOT/GETTY IMAGES

02

EPIC TRIPS

THERMAL DISCOVERER

DURATION: 5-6 DAYS

DISTANCE: 580KM / 360 MILES

GREAT FOR: HISTORY AND CULTURE

BEST TIME TO GO: FEBRUARY TO APRIL FOR WARM AND SETTLED WEATHER

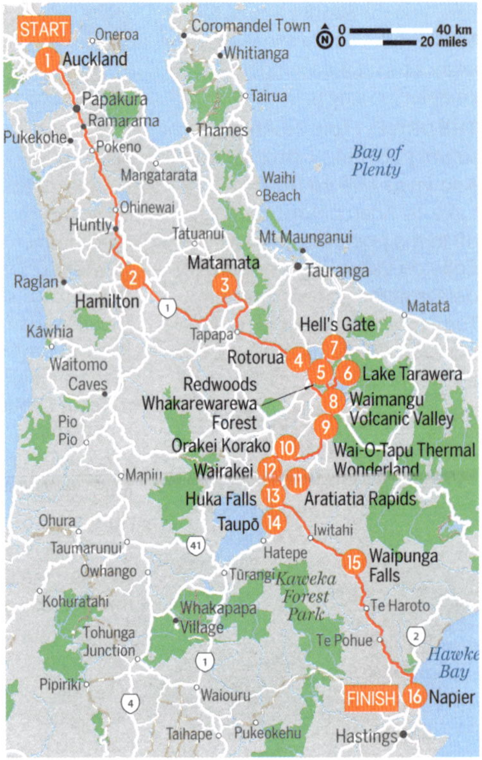

The central North Island, around Rotorua and Taupō, might easily be considered New Zealand's gurgling stomach. Here, the idiosyncratic landscape is punctuated by steaming, bubbling geothermal attractions – hot springs, mud pools and thermal terraces colourful enough to embarrass a rainbow – and destinations to the north and south include the fascinating Tolkien world of Hobbiton and the art-deco architectural heritage of Napier, itself a reaction to a devastating earthquake in 1931.

LINK YOUR TRIP

10 Tongariro National Park Loop
From Taupō, journey into the volcanic wonderland of the North Island's largest national park.

13 Pacific Coast Explorer
Napier is an interesting stop on this exploration of New Zealand's Pacific coastal fringes.

01 Auckland

Start as you mean to go on – further south, Rotorua and Taupō both have extreme activities on tap – by experiencing a more adventurous side of NZ's biggest city. With **Auckland Bridge Climb & Bungy** *(bungy.co.nz)* there's the option of negotiating the arches of this city landmark before taking a bungy leap of faith towards the waters of the **Waitematā Harbour**. The **Sky Tower** *(skycityauckland.co.nz)*, at 328m, is another Auckland icon, and riding the elevator to the observation decks is trumped by the spine-tingling thrills of the **SkyWalk** *(skywalk.co.nz)* or the **SkyJump** *(skyjump.co.nz)*. Alternatively, take a more sedate wander through the city exploring Auckland's interesting waterfront.

THE DRIVE: Depart Auckland on the Southern Motorway (SH1) and continue south for 125km to Hamilton. At times the road skirts the wide Waikato River.

WITR/SHUTTERSTOCK

★ BEST FOR

OUTDOORS

Mountain biking through the Redwoods Whakarewarewa Forest.

Redwoods Whakarewarewa Forest (p36)

02 Hamilton

One of NZ's most bustling provincial cities, Hamilton combines excellent cafes and restaurants with a compact riverside arts and culture precinct. The interesting **Waikato Museum** *(waikatomuseum.co.nz)* has four main areas: an art gallery; interactive science galleries; Tainui galleries housing Māori treasures, including the magnificently carved *waka taua* (war canoe), Te Winikawaka; and a Waikato River exhibition. Adjacent to the museum, **ArtsPost** *(wsa.org.nz)* is a contemporary gallery and gift shop housed in a grand former post office. It focuses on the best of local art.

THE DRIVE: Depart Hamilton south on Anglesea St and Cobham Dr, which becomes SH1. After 44km turn left onto SH29, then left onto SH27 after 14km, continuing a further 10km to Matamata. If you're joining a tour at the Hobbiton site, turn left at the signed turn-off 10km after the intersection of SH1 and SH29.

03 Matamata

Matamata was a pleasant country town people usually drove through until Peter Jackson's film trilogy *The Lord of the Rings* put it on the map. During filming, 300 locals got work as extras, and following the subsequent making of *The Hobbit*, the town has ardently embraced its Middle Earth credentials. There's a spooky statue of **Gollum** in the main street, and the **Matamata i-SITE** *(matamatanz.co.nz)* has been transformed into a wonderful Hobbit gatehouse. Tours to **Hobbiton** *(hobbitontours.com)* – including a very entertaining bus ride – leave from the i-SITE, and it's also possible to travel there with your own transport. Booking ahead is strongly recommended. The Evening Dinner Tours (Sunday to Wednesday) include a banquet dinner.

THE DRIVE: From Matamata, the drive beelines south again, paralleling the Kaimai Range along SH24 and SH28 to reach barely noticeable Tapapa after 24km. Turn left onto SH5 and continue for 43km through forest and farmland to Rotorua.

04 Rotorua

Home to spurting geysers, steaming hot springs and exploding mud pools, Rotorua is NZ's most dynamic thermal area and a sensory experience as much as a place. Māori revered this place, naming one of the most spectacular springs **Wai-O-Tapu** *(Sacred Waters)*. Today 37% of Rotorua's population is Māori, and the best places to experience their culture and the fascinating geothermal terrain are adjoining **Te Puia** *(tepuia.com)* and **Whakarewarewa** *(whakarewarewa.com)*. Experience the town's personal therapy with a dip in the lakeside pools at **Polynesian Spa** *(polynesianspa.co.nz)*.

THE DRIVE: Leave Rotorua on Hinemaru St, turn left onto SH30A, then right into Tarawera Rd and right again onto Long Mile Rd for the Redwoods Whakarewarewa Forest, 5km from town.

05 Redwoods Whakarewarewa Forest

This magical park of forest giants was originally home to more than 170 tree species, planted from 1899 to see which could be grown successfully for timber. Mighty Californian redwoods give the park its grandeur today. The spectacular **Redwoods Treewalk** *(treewalk.co.nz)* is a suspended walkway combining 28 wooden bridges between century-old trees. Walks range from a half-hour wander through the Redwood Memorial Grove to the all-day (34km) Whakarewarewa Track, which loops past the Blue and Green Lakes.

WORLD-CLASS MOUNTAIN BIKING

Edging Rotorua is the **Redwoods Whakarewarewa Forest**, home to some of NZ's best mountain-bike trails *(riderotorua.com)*, with 180km of tracks to keep riders of all skill levels happy for days. **Mountain Bike Rotorua** *(mtbrotorua.co.nz)* and **Planet Bike** *(planetbike.co.nz)* hire bikes from their outlets off Waipa State Mill Rd, and both also lead guided rides and can advise on trails.

Another essential destination for mountain bikers is the **Skyline MTB Gravity Park** *(skyline.co.nz)*, with 12km of tracks (mostly intermediate) accessed by the Skyline Rotorua gondola on Mt Ngongotahā.

THE DRIVE: Return to Tarawera Rd and turn right, climbing over low hills to round Lake Tikitapu (Blue Lake) and Lake Roto-kakahi (Green Lake) and finish at the shores of Lake Tarawera, 15km from Redwoods Whakarewarewa.

06 Lake Tarawera

Providing a mirror for the raw slopes of **Mt Tarawera** (1110m), pretty Lake Tarawera offers swimming, fishing and walks, and **Totally Tarawera** *(totallytarawera.com)* runs boat trips around the lake. Around 2km before the lake is **Te Wairoa**, the **Buried Village** *(buriedvillage.co.nz)*, which was the main staging post for Victorian-era travellers coming to see the famed Pink and White Terraces. When Mt Tarawera erupted in 1886, the entire village was covered in mud up to 2m thick and the terraces were destroyed.

Champagne Pool

JESPER BÜLOW/GETTY IMAGES

PHOTO OPPORTUNITY

The orange-rimmed Champagne Pool at Wai-O-Tapu Thermal Wonderland.

Today, Te Wairoa's excavated ruins tell a Pompeii-like story along a 40-minute walking track. A side trail descends steeply to the base of 30m-high Wairere Falls.

THE DRIVE: Return to SH30 and turn right, skirting Lake Rotorua to Hell's Gate (27km in total).

07 Hell's Gate

Known as Tikitere to Māori, **Hell's Gate** *(hellsgate.co.nz)* is a highly active geothermal reserve. It's not the most colourful of Rotorua's thermal areas but is noteworthy for having the southern hemisphere's only natural hot waterfall and a 2.4m-high mud volcano. Long regarded by Māori as a place of healing, it also has a small set of therapeutic outdoor sulphur pools.

THE DRIVE: Return to Rotorua on SH30. Just after the geothermal gasps of Pōhutu geyser, continue onto SH5 then turn left into Waimangu Rd, undulating through farmland for 6km to Waimangu Volcanic Valley (38km from Hell's Gate).

08 Waimangu Volcanic Valley

The most visible wound from Mt Tarawera's 1886 eruption, **Waimangu Volcanic Valley** *(waimangu.co.nz)* offers a downhill stroll past the powder-blue **Inferno Crater Lake**, which fills and empties every 38 days; **Frying Pan Lake**, the world's largest hot spring; and **Warbrick Terrace**, where the valley's colours are at their most intense. Buses return you back up the valley, but you can also take a 45-minute boat trip on **Lake Rotomahana** (Warm Lake) at the bottom of the walk.

THE DRIVE: Continue on Okaro Rd and turn right onto SH38

LEONARD ZHUKOVSKY/SHUTTERSTOCK

Kayakers on Lake Taupō (p27)

GETTING ACTIVE

On the spectacular central North Island, there are many exciting, fun and sometimes downright quirky opportunities to get active and energised.

Around Rotorua

Rotorua Canopy Tours *(canopytours.co.nz)* Explore high in the forest canopy on bridges, flying foxes, zip lines and platforms.

Paddle Board Rotorua *(paddleboardrotorua.com)* Glide through the evening on a stand-up paddle board to glowworm caves.

Zorb *(ogo.co.nz)* Sure, why not roll down a hillside in a giant inflatable ball filled with water?

Rotorua Rafting *(rotorua-rafting.co.nz)* Grade V rafting action, including over the 7m-high Tutea Falls, the world's highest commercially rafted waterfall.

Around Taupō

Hukafalls Jet *(hukafallsjet.com)* Get personal with Huka Falls on a 30-minute jetboat spin.

Taupō Bungy *(taupobungy.co.nz)* Plunge 47m towards – and even touching the waters of – Waikato River.

Taupo Kayaking Adventures *(tka.co.nz)* Paddle into Mine Bay to view the stunning Māori modern rock carvings.

Skydive Taupo *(skydivetaupo.co.nz)* Don't just enjoy the scenery; fall into it from 12,000ft, 15,000ft or a heady 18,500ft.

and then left back onto SH5. By the Waiotapu Tavern, turn left onto Waiotapu Loop Rd to reach Wai-O-Tapu Thermal Wonderland, 10km from Waimangu Volcanic Valley.

09 Wai-O-Tapu Thermal Wonderland

The most colourful of the region's geothermal attractions, **Wai-O-Tapu** *(waiotapu.co.nz)* has a variety of features packed into a small area. Highlights include the orange-rimmed, fizzing **Champagne Pool**, the unearthly lemon-lime-hued **Roto Kārikitea** and (situated separately but included in the entry fee) **Lady Knox Geyser**, which erupts (with prompting from an organic soap) punctually at 10.15am and gushes up to 20m – follow the park exodus just before 10am to witness it.

THE DRIVE: Return on the loop road to SH5 and turn left towards Taupō. Past Reporoa the landscape decidedly flattens, and just after the tiny hamlet of Mihi, turn right into Tutukau Rd then right again onto Orakei Korako Rd – the thermal area is 39km from Wai-O-Tapu.

10 Orakei Korako

Tucked away from other, more popular, thermal fields, **Orakei Korako** *(orakeikorako.co.nz)* is arguably NZ's most spectacular thermal area, with active geysers, stunning terraces and Ruatapu Cave, one of only two geothermal caves in the world. A 2.5km walking track (allow 1½ hours) follows stairs and boardwalks around the park's colourful silica terraces. Entry includes a boat ride across the lake from the visitor centre and cafe.

♥ WHY I LOVE THIS TRIP

ANDREW BAIN, WRITER

The world feels pliable and shape-shifting when you're on the central North Island, where the land steams as though it's still being cooked and there are places such as Waimangu Volcanic Valley that only materialised in 1886 when Mt Tarawera tore it open. Meanwhile the mountain biking is as good as anywhere in the world, Māori culture is at its strongest, and there are improbable geothermal spectacles pretty much anywhere you look.

THE DRIVE: Depart Orakei Korako and turn right onto Tutukau Rd. Continue left onto SH1 then take a left onto SH5, followed by a right into Aratiatia Rd, 32km from Orakei Korako.

11 Aratiatia Rapids

Two kilometres off SH5 is a gorge that was a spectacular part of the Waikato River until the government constructed a hydroelectric dam across the waterway, shutting off the flow. But the floodgates still open at 10am, noon, 2pm and 4pm from October to March and at 10am, noon and 2pm April to September, releasing 80,000L of water a second for 15 minutes. You can see the water surge through the dam from two good vantage points atop the cliffs. You can view them from below also, with a bit of extra punch, on a 35-minute jetboat spin with **Rapids Jet** *(rapidsjet.com)*.

THE DRIVE: Return to SH5 and continue over busy SH1 and the geothermal pipes to Wairakei Terraces & Thermal Health Spa, 5km from Aratiatia Rapids.

12 Wairakei

Wairakei is the site of NZ's only geothermal electricity-generation enterprise. The landscape features huge pipes and other infrastructure, and at **Wairakei Terraces & Thermal Health Spa**

MĀORI CONCERTS & HĀNGĪ

Entertainment celebrating Māori culture is big business in Rotorua and, though it's commercialised, it's a great opportunity to learn about the indigenous culture of NZ. The two big activities are concerts and *hāngī* feasts, often packaged together in an evening's entertainment featuring the famous *hongi* (Māori greeting; the pressing of foreheads and noses, and sharing of life breath) and *haka* and *poi* dances.

Tamaki Maori Village *(tamakimaorivillage.co.nz)* and family-run **Mitai Maori Village** *(mitai.co.nz)* are established favourites. Te Puia (p35) and Whakarewarewa (p35) also put on shows.

Orakei Korako thermal fields
DMITRY NAUMOV/SHUTTERSTOCK

TAUPIRI'S SACRED SLOPES

About 26km north of Hamilton on SH1 is Taupiri (287m), the sacred mountain of the Tainui people. You'll recognise it by the cemetery on its slopes and the honking of car horns – locals saying hi to their loved ones as they drive past. In August 2006 thousands gathered here as the much-loved Māori queen, Dame Te Atairangikaahu, was transported upriver by *waka* (canoe) to her final resting place, an unmarked grave on the summit.

(wairakeiterraces.co.nz), mineral-laden waters from the geothermal steamfield cascade over artificial silica terraces into pools (open to those 14 years and older) nestled in native gardens. There's also a short thermal walk with a geyser that churns out a thunderstorm of steam, but a far more interesting thermal walk can be found at the nearby **Craters of the Moon** *(cratersofthemoon.co.nz)*, a geothermal area that sprang to life when hydroelectric tinkering around the power station in 1958 caused water levels to fall.

THE DRIVE: Turn right from Wairakei Terraces & Thermal Health Spa back onto SH5, swinging left into Huka Falls Rd after 2km and following this road down past a lookout to the falls car park.

13 Huka Falls

At **Huka Falls**, the Waikato, NZ's longest river, squeezes through a narrow chasm, making a dramatic 11m drop into a surging crystal-blue pool at 220,000L per second. From the footbridge straddling the falls, you can see the full force of this torrent that the Māori called *Hukanui* (Great Body of Spray). Walkways run along both banks – upstream to Spa Thermal Park (3km) and downstream to Aratiatia Rapids (7km).

THE DRIVE: Continue on Huka Falls Rd with Waikato River on your left. After around 3km this route rejoins SH5 for a final 2km downhill push into Taupō, with views on a good day over the lake to the volcanoes of Tongariro National Park.

14 Taupō

Strung along the north-eastern shores of the lake, Taupō has a lot of adrenaline-pumping activities on offer, but for those with no appetite for white knuckles, there's plenty of enjoyment to be had simply meandering by the lake and enjoying the scenery. **Spa Thermal Park** *(County Ave)*, where a natural hot stream pours into the chilly Waikato River, can help you soak away the hours in a car, or you can get active by cycling the **Huka Trails** *(lovetaupo.com/en/operators/huka-trails)* or **Craters MTB Park** *(biketaupo.org.nz)*; **FourB** *(fourb.nz)*, at the base of the park, hires out bikes.

THE DRIVE: Departing Taupō south along the lakefront on Lake Tce, the drive turns away

Huka Falls

COCOPELLI/SHUTTERSTOCK

from the lake onto SH5, the Taupō–Napier road. The 53km from Taupō to Waipunga Falls takes you through striking alpine-like scenery and swathes of commercial forests.

15 Waipunga Falls

From the road, Waipunga Falls aren't signposted as such – look for a brown 'Scenic Lookout' sign. The lookout peers along the Waipunga River to the three parallel cascades of the 40m-high falls, framed with native scrub. To the left of the falls, you should be able to see the smaller but still spectacular Waiarua Falls, the pair just about meeting at their bases.

THE DRIVE: SH5 continues its winding and hilly way through spectacular country for 88km to Napier. Conditions on this road can often be misty, rainy...and atmospheric! The final stages meander through the vineyards and orchards around Eskdale (stop for a wine tasting?), before joining SH2 for the last 13km down the Pacific coast to Napier.

16 Napier

With a breezy ambience and a sparkling collection of art deco buildings, much of which was rebuilt in the architectural fashion of the day following a devastating earthquake in 1931. Book an architectural tour at the fab Art Deco Centre (p27). The encircling Hawke's Bay wine region is second only to the South Island's Marlborough region in volume of output, and showcases some of the country's oldest and most-established wineries. The restaurants, bars and cafes of the re-energised Ahuriri waterfront area, 2km northwest of town, are essential diversions after the long drive south.

TRISTANBNZ/GETTY IMAGES

Cycle trail, Hawkes Bay

CYCLING HAWKE'S BAY

Buoyed by the fun of mountain biking around Rotorua and Taupō, take the chance to explore the 200km network of **Hawke's Bay Trails** *(nzcycletrail.com/hawkes-bay-trails)* around Napier. Pick up the Hawke's Bay Trails brochure from the Napier i-SITE or online (napiernz.com).

Napier itself is very cycle friendly, particularly along Marine Pde, where you'll find **Tākaro Trails** *(takarotrails.co.nz)* renting comfortable bikes. **Napier City Bike Hire** *(bikehirenapier.co.nz)* is another option, and also runs self-guided coastal and winery tours, departing from the store with pick-up at the far end (16km to 27km; from $65 per person).

Mountain bikers head to **Pan Pac Mountain Bike Park** *(hawkesbaymtb.co.nz)* for a whole lot of fun in the forest; see the website or call for directions. You can hire mountain bikes from Tākaro Trails (takarotrails.co.nz) too.

Numerous companies run fully geared-up tours around Hawke's Bay, with winery visits near mandatory. Operators include:

Bike About Tours *(bikeabouttours.co.nz)*
Coastal Wine Cycles *(winecycles.co.nz)*
On Yer Bike Winery Tours *(onyerbikehb.co.nz)*

03

EPIC TRIPS

KAIKŌURA COAST

DURATION: 3-4 DAYS

DISTANCE: 352KM / 219 MILES

GREAT FOR: FAMILIES AND NATURE

BEST TIME TO GO: THE SCENERY, WINE AND WILDLIFE ARE GREAT YEAR-ROUND

This stretch of State Hwy 1 is a relatively quick and convenient route between the South Island's two major traveller gateways, Picton and Christchurch, but it also boasts several of the island's major highlights. The beautiful Marlborough Sounds, Blenheim's world-class wineries and Kaikōura's marine tours can hardly be missed, but hidden, low-key and up-and-coming attractions also abound.

LINK YOUR TRIP

12 North Island Southern Loop
Across Cook Strait, take in the nation's cosmopolitan capital, brilliant bird life, remote lighthouses and world-quality wine.

22 Southern Alps Circuit
Christchurch is a perfect departure point for a grand tour of the mountainous south.

01 Picton

The interisland ferry port town of Picton doubles as the departure point for adventures throughout the labyrinthine **Marlborough Sounds**. Often overlooked, however, are Picton's many enjoyable adventures for landlubbers, including some great walks. For an elevated perspective that makes the Sounds seem very much like the drowned valleys that they are, follow the **Snout Track** (7.8km return from the car park) along the headland flanking the harbour's east side. If the short, sharp climb to the ridge line isn't quite what you had in mind, indulge in Picton's simplest and most popular activity, namely lolling about in the pretty foreshore park for a picnic, ice cream or fish and chips, watching the comings and goings on both land and sea.

THE DRIVE: Following SH1, it's only 28km to Blenheim through the Tuamarina River valley

DOME NAPAT/SHUTTERSTOCK

★ BEST FOR

WILDLIFE

Kaikōura's ocean teems with dolphins, whales, seals and seabirds.

Vineyard, Blenheim

and Para Wetlands, then into the broad plains of the Wairau Valley.

02 Blenheim

Approaching the town of Blenheim, you'll be left in no doubt that you've entered wine country, and fortunately it's easy to dip a toe into Marlborough's wine barrels without straying too far from the highway. Just 3km off SH1, north of Blenheim, **Saint Clair Estate** *(saintclair.co.nz)* is a long-standing, family-owned operation crafting some of NZ's most interesting and well-regarded wines, including the Pioneer Block range showcasing Marlborough's varied terroir. The adjacent restaurant is an atmospheric spot for the obligatory vineyard lunch. The good news for wine lovers is that the bulk of Marlborough's 35 or so cellar doors are scattered through the valley within a 15-minute drive. Pick up the **Marlborough Wine Trail** map from **Blenheim i-SITE** *(marlboroughnz.com)*, or view it online at wine-marlborough.co.nz.

THE DRIVE: From Blenheim, SH1 cuts inland through Marlborough's second-largest grape-growing region, the Awatere Valley, before hitting the east coast just past Ward and crossing into the Canterbury region. Beyond the Clarence River, 88km from Blenheim, the peaks of the Seaward Kaikōura Range start to fill the picture. You may still strike roadworks on the remaining 41km to Kaikōura, a legacy of devastating earthquakes in 2016.

03 Kaikōura

Kaikōura is a pretty coastal town with a dramatic, snowy-peak backdrop. According to Māori legend, Kaikōura's handsome peninsula is the place where the demigod Māui placed his feet when he fished the North Island up from the depths. In 2016 the area was struck by a severe magnitude 7.8 earthquake. Following the reestablishment of badly damaged transport links, the town is once again easily reached (give or take the odd roadworks) and an essential destination for anyone with an interest in wildlife. Most people come here for marine tours, particularly whale-watching, but the town also sports a particularly good walk. Starting from town, the three- to four-hour **Peninsula Walkway** is a mighty fine way to soak up the scenery, and offers the chance to see seals, shearwaters and other seabirds while learning about the area via a series of insightful information panels. The walkway begins by following the town quay out to the peninsula's end, **Point Kean**, where seals laze around seemingly oblivious to their human admirers.

THE DRIVE: The SH1 hugs the coast, occasionally burrowing through odd tunnels in the rock, before climbing over the Hundalee Hills and heading down onto the bucolic Canterbury Plains. A 'Tourist Drive' signpost in the centre of Cheviot township directs you left down McQueen Rd to reach Gore Bay, 77km and a little over an hour from Kaikōura.

04 Gore Bay

This is old-school NZ: aged beachside baches (holiday cottages), some dating back to 1865, and a long beach good for swimming and surfing. Gore Bay's permanent population of around a dozen people balloons in the summer, mainly with Kiwi campers, but any time of the year you'll still have plenty of sand to yourself. Meander along the beach and the wetlands, taking in the serene views along with the peace and quiet. Once you've caught your breath, discover what Gore Bay is known for - **Cathedral Cliffs**, which can be reached by car or a brutally steep 10-minute walk at the southern end of the village. Sculpted by wind and rain – in the evocatively named process known as badlands erosion – the clay gully walls resemble cathedralesque organ pipes, also known as hoodoos.

THE DRIVE: Head south out of Gore Bay to complete the Gore Bay Tourist Drive, up and over the coastal hills to rejoin SH1. Shortly afterwards you'll cross the braided Hurunui River as you continue south to Waipara. Total distance to Waipara is 59km.

05 Waipara Valley

Conveniently stretched along SH1 near the Hanmer Springs turn-off, this resolutely rural area makes for a mouth-watering pit stop en route to Christchurch. The valley's warm, dry summers and cool autumn nights have proved a winning formula for growing grapes. While it accounts for less than 3% of NZ's wine production, it's responsible for some of the country's finest cool-climate wines including riesling and pinot noir. It's fitting that Waipara Valley's premier winery, **Pegasus Bay** *(pegasusbay.com)*, should also have the loveliest setting and one of Canterbury's best restaurants. The beautiful gardens and sun-drenched lawn encourage a very long linger over contemporary cuisine and luscious wines; try the Canterbury lamb matched with Prima Donna pinot noir. Yum. To fully indulge in the valley's bounty, check out the North Canterbury Wine Region map at

WHALE WORLD

Few places in the world are home to such a panoply of easily spottable marine wildlife as Kaikōura. Whales, dolphins, NZ fur seals, penguins, shearwaters, petrels and several species of albatross all live in the area or swing by. Marine animals converge here due to ocean-current and continental-shelf conditions: the seabed gradually slopes away from the land before plunging to depths of 1200m where the southerly current hits the continental shelf. This creates an upwelling of tasty nutrients from the ocean floor into the feeding zone.

Sperm whales congregate here all year-round, but depending on the time of year you may also spy humpbacks, southern rights, pilots, orcas and even behemoth blue whales, the heaviest animals ever to have graced this earth.

With knowledgeable guides and fascinating 'world of whales' on-board animation, the town's biggest operator, **Whale Watch Kaikōura** *(whalewatch.co.nz)*, heads out on boat trips (with admirable frequency) to introduce you to some of the big fellas. It'll refund 80% of your fare if no whales are sighted (success rate: 95%), but if this trip is a must for you, allow a few days' flexibility in case the weather turns to custard.

KONRAD MOSTERT/SHUTTERSTOCK

Humpback whale , Kaikōura

northcanterburywines.co.nz. Otherwise, you'll spot several of the main players from the highway.

THE DRIVE: Breaking out onto the Canterbury Plains south of Waipara, it's a flat and reasonably featureless 59km drive from Waipara to central Christchurch.

06 Christchurch

Christchurch remains a city in transition, rebuilding from the 2010 and 2011 earthquakes, and a new and modern architectural legacy is evident along the Avon River and in the emerging High St precinct. Many historic buildings were destroyed, but many of those remaining can be seen on walking tours. Stroll past the **Arts Centre** *(artscentre.org.nz)*, the 19th-century Gothic-styled buildings that housed the University of Canterbury. The stone clock tower was completed in 1877 and now hosts Rutherford's Den, a museum to honour New Zealand scientist Ernest Rutherford. Various shops and eateries are dotted about the heritage buildings. A short stroll leads to the **Christchurch Botanic Gardens** *(ccc.govt.nz)*, which offer a spectacular display of why Christchurch is called 'garden city'.

04

EPIC TRIPS

EAST COAST EXPRESS

DURATION: 5-7 DAYS

DISTANCE: 495KM / 308 MILES

GREAT FOR: FOOD AND DRINK

BEST TIME TO GO: SPRING AND AUTUMN FOR ABUNDANT WILDLIFE AND FEWER CROWDS

The West Coast Rd and Inland Scenic Route may hoover up most of the tourist traffic heading north and south, but the East Coast claims the crown of 'State Hwy 1'. Typical of New Zealand, though, it's mostly little more than a quiet country road, dotted with sweet-as towns and peppered with detours to surprising places such as Ōamaru's Victorian Precinct, and experiences such as swimming with dolphins in Akaroa.

LINK YOUR TRIP

03 Kaikōura Coast
Head up from Christchurch through wine country and New Zealand's marine-life mecca to the ferry port town of Picton.

25 Southern Scenic Route
Dunedin bookends this classic U-shaped coastal and countryside route through to Fiordland and Te Anau.

01 Dunedin

Dunedin is synonymous with the students who attend the country's oldest university. Swelling the city's population during term time, they inject an energy and edgy creativity that gives the city's Victorian streetscapes and cultural scene some zing. Settled by two shiploads of Scots in the mid-19th century, Dunedin is also defined by its Scottishness, and remains immensely proud of its heritage. Indeed, Dunedin's name is derived from the Gaelic name for Edinburgh: Dùn Èideann. The region's broader, multicultural backstory is present in conventional but

★ BEST FOR

DOLPHINS

Swim with the world's smallest and rarest dolphin in Akaroa Harbour.

MARTIN RUEGNER/GETTY IMAGES

Moeraki Boulders

satisfying style in **Otago Museum** *(otagomuseum.nz)*, the centrepiece of which is *Southern Land, Southern People*, showcasing Otago's past and present. The Tāngata Whenua Māori gallery houses an impressive *waka taua*, wonderfully worn old carvings, and some lovely *pounamu* weapons, tools and jewellery.

THE DRIVE: Drive north on SH1, over the Silverpeaks Range and back down to Blueskin Bay. SH1 then tracks mainly inland, passing through rural Palmerston before continuing along the coast. After 74km, turn right and drive 2km along Hillgrove-Moeraki Rd to Moeraki village.

02 Moeraki

The name Moeraki means 'a place to sleep by day', which should give you some clue as to the pace of life in this little fishing village – one of the first European settlements in NZ. The sleepy settlement once housed the famed Fleurs Place, a stunning example of sea-to-table gastronomy from celebrated NZ chef Fleur Sullivan. The town is still worth a wander, so stop in for fish and chips or to enjoy the charming tavern. Just north on SH1 is the turn-off to **Moeraki Boulders** (Te Kaihinaki), a collection of large spherical boulders scattered along a beautiful stretch of beach (best viewed at low tide; also accessible via a 45-minute beach walk from the village). Heading north along the beach, the **Kātiki Point Walking Track** leads to a cute wooden lighthouse, with the chance of spotting yellow-eyed penguins and fur seals.

THE DRIVE: Return to SH1 and head north for 40km to Ōamaru, driving through relatively flat pastoral land, a journey of just over 30 minutes.

03 Ōamaru

Ōamaru is quirky small-town New Zealand at its very best. Rattling around inside the enormous, ramshackle warehouses in its **Victorian Precinct** are oddballs, antiquarians and bohemians of all stripes who run offbeat galleries, make peculiar art and dress up at the drop of a top hat. Most visible are the steampunks, boldly celebrating the past and the future with an ethos of 'tomorrow as it used to be'. Inside **Steampunk HQ** *(steampunkoamaru.co.nz)*, imaginatively upcycled ancient machines wheeze and splutter. Bring a $2 coin to fire up the space-age locomotive out the front. Inside the **Grainstore Gallery** – a former Victorian grain store crammed with weird theatrical sculpture, papier-mâché masks and vintage curiosities – there's an ever-changing cornucopia of creativity. It also hosts occasional live music and other delightful distractions.

THE DRIVE: Drive northeast on SH1. Just before Waitaki Bridge, around 19km from Ōamaru, is a splurge-worthy restaurant, Riverstone Kitchen. Continue north through primarily agricultural land all the way to Timaru, 86km from Ōamaru.

04 Timaru

Highway travellers could be forgiven for thinking that this small port city is merely a handy stop for food and fuel. Not so. Straying into town reveals a remarkably intact Edwardian centre with some good dining and interesting shopping, not to mention a clutch of cultural attractions and lovely parks, all of which sustain at least a day's stopover. Fronting the town, expansive **Caroline Bay Park** ranges over an Edwardian-style garden under the Bay Hill cliff, then across broad lawns to low sand dunes and the beach itself. As well as a playground, skate park, sound shell and ice-cream kiosk, it boasts the triumphant **Trevor Griffiths Rose Garden** *(gardens.org.nz)*, particularly aromatic in the late afternoon sun. Eager aesthetes may wish to make the pilgrimage to the **Aigantighe Art Gallery** *(aigantighe.co.nz)*, one of the South

Steampunk HQ, Ōamaru

UWE ARANAS/SHUTTERSTOCK

PHOTO OPPORTUNITY

Upcycled industrial detritus at Ōamaru's Steampunk HQ.

Island's finest public galleries, with a notable collection of NZ and European art.

THE DRIVE: Stay on SH1 north to the Canterbury Plains, crossing NZ's longest bridge at Rakaia. At Burnham, 135km from Timaru, turn off SH1 and drive through Lincoln to Tai Tapu, turning right on to SH75 towards Akaroa on the Banks Peninsula via a winding drive. It'll take three hours to drive this 200km leg.

05 Akaroa

Charming Akaroa ('Long Harbour' in Māori) on the Banks Peninsula was the site of the country's first French settlement. It strives to recreate the feel of a sleepy, French provincial village, down to the names of its streets and houses, but its peacefulness is periodically shattered by hordes descending from gargantuan cruise ships. Seek refuge in the old churches, gardens and cemeteries that lend Akaroa its character. Hands down the most beautiful spot in Akaroa is the **Giant's House** *(thegiantshouse.co.nz)*, an 1880 residence once occupied by Akaroa's first bank manager but now the labour of love of artist Josie Martin. Her whimsical combination of sculpture and mosaics cascades down a hillside garden, echoing Gaudí and Miró in its intricate collages. It has to be seen to be believed.

THE DRIVE: Follow SH75 for 54km back around Akaroa Harbour and over to Little River. Turn right into Gebbies Pass Rd, and drive 9km to Teddington beside Lyttelton Harbour. Turn left to meander along the harbourside for 17km to Lyttelton town. Total distance is 80km.

IRYNA SHPULAK/SHUTTERSTOCK

Banks Peninsula

BANKS PENINSULA

Gorgeous Banks Peninsula (Horomaka) was formed by two giant volcanic eruptions about eight million years ago; the volcanoes are long extinct and have since been eroded by the elements. Harbours and bays radiate out from the peninsula's centre, giving it an unusual cogwheel shape. Akaroa – its main township – is popular with visitors, including many who now arrive on large cruise ships.

The must-do is the absurdly beautiful drive along **Summit Road**, around the edge of one of the original craters. It's also worth exploring the little bays that dot the peninsula's perimeter, accessible via steep and winding routes spidering off the Summit Rd – perfectly fine for driving, but take your time.

The waters around Banks Peninsula are home to one of the smallest and rarest dolphin species, the Hector's dolphin, found only in NZ waters. Tours (September to May) with **Black Cat Cruises** *(blackcat.co.nz)* provide good odds for striking the dolphin-swim off your bucket list: a 98% chance of spotting them and over 80% success rate of actually swimming with them. Other wildlife tours from Akaroa offer the chance to see white-flippered penguins, orcas, seals and other critters.

Note that while concerns over the impact of swimming tours on the bottlenose dolphins in the Bay of Islands have caused such tours to be banned there, they are still allowed here in Akaroa. All activities involving marine mammals such as dolphins are highly regulated and monitored by the Department of Conservation (DOC).

06 Lyttelton

Badly damaged during the 2010 and 2011 earthquakes, the port town of Lyttelton has re-emerged as one of Christchurch's most vibrant communities, one with an obsession with its stomach. For evidence, time your visit to coincide with the **Lyttelton Farmers Market** *(lytteltoninfocentre.nz)* on Saturday morning, a smorgasbord of local produce, artisan goodies and high-quality fast foods. The tiny town has a more than respectable selection of bars and restaurants, too, some of which have risen from the rubble in admirable fashion. One example is **Lyttelton Coffee Company** *(lytteltoncoffeeco.co.nz)*, a family-friendly cafe serving wholesome food in an atmospheric environment featuring edgy artwork, occasional music and harbour views from the back deck.

THE DRIVE: Drive through the 2km Lyttelton road tunnel, NZ's longest, and continue northwest on SH74 following signs for Christchurch city centre. Out of peak times, this 13km journey should take around 20 minutes.

07 Christchurch

Re-emerging amid a major rebuild, post-quake Christchurch emits a crazy, occasionally chaotic but undeniably exciting vibe. To see how far it has come, visit **Quake City** *(quakecity.co.nz)*. This compact museum retells stories through photography and various artefacts, including bits that have fallen off the cathedral, but most affecting is the film featuring locals recounting their own experiences. The suburb of Woolston, on the way between Lyttelton and the Christchurch CBD, is home to the **Tannery** *(thetannery.co.nz)*. A fine restoration job has seen this historic factory converted into a boutique but unpretentious shopping centre, complete with an art-house cinema and restaurants. The hub of the complex is the **Brewery** *(cassels brewery.co.nz)*, a notable gastropub featuring hand-pulled craft beers, wood-fired pizza, live music and a pleasant courtyard.

Tram on New Regent Street, Christchurch
TRAVELLIGHT/SHUTTERSTOCK

NOVOTEL
CITY TOUR
GROOVY GLASSES
www.groovy.co.nz
Sushi Sachi 21
NEXT STOP CASA PUBLICA
CASA PUBLICA
178

0 50 km
0 25 miles
Cape Reinga
Te Paki
Mokaikai Scenic Reserve
Te Kao
1F
Pukenui
Karikari Peninsula
Aupouri Forest
Mangōnui
10
Awanui
Kaitāia
Kaeo
Puketi Forest
Ahipara
Korikori
Herekino
05
Russell
1
Paihia
Kohukohu
Kaikohe
Russell Forest
Helena Bay
Opononi
Matapouri
Hikurangi
Tutukaka
Waipoua Kauri Forest
Maunganui Bluff
Kaihu
Whangārei
Hen & Chickens Islands
14
05
Dargaville
12
Brynderwyn
Matakohe
Kaiwaka
Mangawhai
Wellsford
Leigh
SOUTH PACIFIC OCEAN
Hauraki Gulf / Tīkapa Moana
Dome Forest
Warkworth
Tasman Sea
Puhoi
Port Charles
06
Waiwera
Mt Moehau
Coromandel Peninsula
Coromandel Town
Colville
Helensville
Waiheke Island
Kūaotunu
16
Oneroa
Whitianga
Muriwai Beach
Auckland
08
07
Hahei
Te Henga (Bethells Beach)
Piha
Clevedon
Coromandel Forest Park
Tapu
Waitākere Ranges Regional Park
Hunua Ranges Regional Park
Te Puru
Table Mountain
Drury
Kaiaua
Ramarama
Thames
Pukekohe
25
Maramarua
Koputai Wetland Management Reserve
Pukekawa
Waihi
Waihi Beach
Rangiriri
27
Tahuna
Mt Te Aroha
Huntly

DENNIS MACDONALD/SHUTTERSTOCK

Auckland harbour and skyline

AUCKLAND & THE NORTH

EXPLORE

AUCKLAND & THE NORTH

New Zealand's biggest city, Auckland provides a buzzy launching point for road trips to some of the country's most beautiful beaches. A circuit around North Auckland takes in black-sand surf beaches on the west coast and white-sand swimming beaches to the east, with wineries tucked in between. Further north, the unimaginatively named Northland offers still more extraordinary beaches, magnificent forests and the crucible of the nation's history. East from Auckland, the Hauraki Gulf is dotted with dozens of picturesque islands, sheltered by the protective arm of the Coromandel Peninsula – itself home to some of NZ's best beaches.

Auckland

Big-city bustle combines with impressive geology in NZ's only real metropolis, home to around a third of the country's entire population. Most of the houses are crammed onto a narrow isthmus squeezed between two harbours and dotted with the remnants of 53 small volcanoes, although the 'Supercity' also spreads out to encompass rainforest, farmland and a multitude of islands, only a handful of which are populated.

While the inner city has its appeal, parking is problematic and it doesn't really capture the essence of Auckland. To really get under the skin of the city you're better off basing yourself in one of its city-fringe suburbs full of elegant Victorian and Edwardian cottages. Good options include Ponsonby, Grey Lynn, Mt Eden, Parnell and Devonport. Dining and nightlife hot spots include the Britomart, Viaduct Harbour and Wynyard Quarter areas at the bottom of the city centre, uptown Karangahape Rd (ubiquitously known as 'K Rd') and nearby Ponsonby Rd. You'll have no problem picking up supplies in the city's many supermarkets and shopping centres.

Thames

A remnant of an 1860s gold rush, Thames is a charming heritage town that serves as the western gateway to the Coromandel Peninsula. Its

WHEN TO GO

Beaches are the big attraction here, and the best swimming months are from late December to early April. The peak time is Christmas to the end of January, when the beach towns are packed with summer holidaymakers and accommodation prices skyrocket. Conversely, Auckland empties out in the last week of December.

resident population of just under 8000 people is large enough to support a substantial supermarket, some good cafes, interesting shops and even an award-winning gin distillery. Pollen St is the main commercial strip, and you'll find a Pak'nSave supermarket and larger stores at the nearby Goldfields Shopping Centre. Cafe Melbourne on Pollen St is the best option for daytime dining, while Nakontong Thai across the road is a popular dinner spot. If you're travelling through on a Saturday morning, stock up on local produce from the market stalls lined up along the Grahamstown (northern) end of Pollen St.

Oneroa

Waiheke Island's main settlement is only a five-minute drive from the passenger ferry at Matiatia. Oneroa's lively shopping strip has plenty of cafes, bars and tourist-focused gift shops, a good butcher and deli, and a large grocery store, but for a proper supermarket you'll need to drive 4km to the Countdown in Ostend. The best dining options are Wai Kitchen (cafe breakfast and lunch), Oyster Inn (upmarket lunch and dinner), Dragonfired (a food truck at Little Oneroa Beach serving wood-fired fast food) and Island Gelato (indulgent ice cream).

TRANSPORT

Auckland is NZ's major travel hub, with the country's main international airport and extensive domestic connections. Buses depart for all of the major North Island cities, and there's a limited train service to Hamilton and Wellington. Ferries for Waiheke Island leave from central Auckland. Other domestic airports in the region include Whangārei, Bay of Islands (Kerikeri) and Kaitāia.

WHERE TO STAY

Auckland has a good spread of accommodation, ranging from hostels to fancy hotels. At the budget end, try Verandahs Parkside Lodge or LyLo. Mt Eden has some good midrange options, including Bavaria B&B and the Quest apartments. At the luxury end there are character-filled boutique properties such as Hotel Britomart, Hotel DeBrett, Franklin 38, The Convent and Eden Park B&B. In Thames, good choices include the well-kept Brookby Motel and the heritage Lady Bowen B&B, or, for something a little fancier, pretty Cotswold Cottage. On Waiheke Island, try Fossil Bay Lodge or Waiheke Waterfront Lodge.

RESOURCES

- **aucklandnz.com**
  Auckland's main visitor information centre, the SkyCity i-SITE, is located at the Sky Tower.
- **northlandnz.com**
  Operates i-SITEs in Whangārei, Paihia (Ipipiri Bay of Islands), Kaitāia and Opononi (Hokianga).
- **thecoromandel.nz**
  Whitianga and Waihi have i-SITEs.

WHAT'S ON

- **Auckland Lantern Festival**
  Celebrating lunar new year.
- **Waitangi Day**
  NZ's national day is celebrated on 6 February, but nowhere with more gusto and ceremony than at Waitangi in the Bay of Islands, where the 1840 treaty between Māori and the British Crown was first signed.
- **Pasifika Festival**
  In March, Auckland plays host to the world's largest annual event celebrating Pacific Islands culture.

05

AUCKLAND & THE NORTH

NORTHLAND & THE BAY OF ISLANDS

DURATION: 6-8 DAYS

DISTANCE: 1057KM / 657 MILES

GREAT FOR: NATURE, HISTORY AND CULTURE

BEST TIME TO GO: FEBRUARY TO APRIL OFFERS THE BEST WEATHER, BUT AVOID THE BUSY EASTER PERIOD

Known as the 'Winterless North', the traditionally milder weather of this area is but one reason to venture north of Auckland. The Bay of Islands combines Russell's heritage charm with boating adventures leaving from busy Paihia. Further north the attractions are more remote and even more spectacular, leading all the way to the very top of the North Island at spiritual Cape Reinga, where the Tasman Sea and the Pacific Ocean meet.

LINK YOUR TRIP

02 Thermal Discoverer
From Auckland, head south through the North Island's volcanic centre.

06 East & West Coast Explorer
Explore to the northeast and northwest of NZ's biggest city, Auckland.

01 Auckland

Framed by two harbours, NZ's most cosmopolitan city spreads vibrantly across a narrow coastal isthmus. Explore Auckland's ocean-going personality at the **New Zealand Maritime Museum** *(maritimemuseum.co.nz)*, or shoot the breeze on a sailing adventure on a genuine America's Cup yacht with **Explore** *(exploregroup.co.nz)*. Other waterborne options include a ferry across Waitematā Harbour to the heritage Edwardian and Victorian architecture of the seaside suburb of **Devonport**, or a sea-kayaking excursion to **Rangitoto Island**, a forested volcanic cone. Back on land, for the best view of Rangitoto, stroll along **Takapuna Beach** on Auckland's North Shore or ride a bike around the bays along **Tamaki Drive**.

★ BEST FOR

FAMILIES

Sandboarding down Northland's giant dunes

ADWO/SHUTTERSTOCK

Sandboarding on the dunes, Cape Regina (p61)

THE DRIVE: For the first leg of 104km, depart across the Auckland Harbour Bridge heading north on SH1. North of Warkworth, turn into Wayby Valley Rd continuing on to Mangawhai Heads. Pay tolls for the Northern Gateway Toll Road on SH1 online at nzta.govt.nz or take the last exit before the tolls.

02 Mangawhai Heads

Mangawhai village *(mangawhai-museum.org.nz)* lies on a horseshoe-shaped harbour, but it's Mangawhai Heads, 5km further on, that beach seekers love. A narrow sandspit stretches for kilometres to form the harbour's south head, sheltering a **seabird sanctuary**. There's an excellent surf beach, best viewed while traversing the **Mangawhai Cliffs Walkway**. Starting at Mangawhai Heads, this walking track (around two to three hours) offers extensive views of the ocean and the coast. Make sure you time it right to return down the beach at low tide. Other attractions around Mangawhai include **vineyards** and **olive groves**, and the **Mangawhai Museum** *(mangawhai-museum.org.nz)*. Check out the roof shaped like a stingray. Coffee at **Brewed As** *(brewedas.com)* is a must.

THE DRIVE: From Mangawhai Heads continue along Cove Rd to Waipu Cove (around 13km). This is a very pretty rural and coastal route away from the busier main roads. During summer, Langs Beach en route is enlivened with the scarlet blooms of the pōhutukawa, often dubbed 'NZ's Christmas tree'.

03 Waipu

The arcing beach at **Waipu Cove** looks out to Bream Bay. On the near horizon, islands include the **Hen and Chickens**. Waipu Cove is excellent for swimming – and body surfing if there are good waves – and there are shaded spots for a picnic. A further 8km along a coastal road, Waipu is a sleepy village with excellent cafes that comes to life on summer weekends. The area was originally colonised by Scottish settlers – via Nova Scotia in Canada – who arrived between 1853 and 1860. The **Waipu Museum** *(waipumuseum.com)* tells their story, and on 1 January, Waipu's annual **Highland Games** *(waipuhighlandgames.co.nz)* celebrate heather-infused events including caber tossing and Scottish dancing. Here's your chance to discover your inner Caledonian.

THE DRIVE: Rejoin SH1 from Waipu via Nova Scotia Dr, and continue north to Whangārei (39km). En route, Ruakākā and Uretiti offer excellent beaches, and the imposing profile of Marsden Point announces the entrance to Whangārei Harbour.

04 Whangārei

Northland's only city has a thriving local art scene, and an attractive riverside area for long walks and yacht envy. Explore **Claphams National Clock Museum** *(claphamsclocks.com)*, filled with more than 1600 ticking, gonging and cuckooing timepieces. Then while away a few hours in the Town Basin stores selling local arts and crafts. A revolving exhibitions schedule makes the adjacent (and free) **Whangārei Art Museum** *(whangareiartmuseum.co.nz)* a must-visit. The **Hundertwasser Art Centre** (hundertwasserartcentre.co.nz) opened here in 2022. Further afield, more contemporary art features at the **Quarry Arts Centre** *(quarryarts.org)*, a raffish village of artists' studios and cooperative galleries. Around 5km west of Whangārei, **Kiwi North** *(kiwinorth.co.nz)* combines a museum displaying Māori and colonial artefacts with a kiwi house.

THE DRIVE: Depart Whangārei via Bank St, Mill St and Ngunguru Rd to Tutukaka (30km).

> ♥ WHY I LOVE THIS TRIP
>
> ### TASMIN WABY, WRITER
>
> 
>
> The ever-present coastline is this journey's defining feature. When you're not glimpsing it from windy coastal roads, we recommend stopping for a beach stroll or swim in any number of beautiful bays and coves. Getting to Cape Reinga is an epic journey, but worth it. The stories of Māori and colonial settlers, brought to life in Northland through museums, Māori tours and self-guided heritage walks, are essential to understanding NZ history.

Stop for a stroll at Whangārei Falls, a spectacular 26m-high cascade 6km from Town Basin, and Ngunguru, a sleepy estuary settlement just before Tutukaka.

05 Tutukaka

Bursting with yachts, dive crews and game-fishing charter boats, the marina at Tutukaka presents opportunities to explore the stunning above- and below-water scenery in the surrounding area. Many travellers are here to go diving at the **Poor Knights Islands**, but the underwater thrills are also accessible for snorkelling fans. Surfing lessons are available nearby, and one of the best local walks is a blissful 20-minute coastal stroll from **Matapouri** to the compact cove at nearby **Whale Bay**.

THE DRIVE: Allow two hours for this 106km leg. Leaving Tutukaka and heading north, the coastal road veers inland before reaching the coast again at Matapouri. From Matapouri, continue west to SH1 at Hikurangi. Heading north on SH1 you have two options: continue to the ferry at Opua or turn right into Russell Rd just before Whakapara. It's a long winding road – take care – via Helena Bay to Russell.

06 Russell

Once known as 'the hellhole of the Pacific', Russell is a historic town with cafes, a few stylish shops and genteel B&Bs. Russell was originally **Kororareka**, a fortified Ngāpuhi village. In the early 19th century, visiting European and American ships began to trade with the local iwi. It quickly attracted roughnecks like fleeing convicts, whalers and drunken sailors, and in 1835 Charles Darwin described it as full of 'the refuse of society'. After the signing of the Treaty of Waitangi in 1840, nearby **Okiato** was the country's temporary capital before Auckland was made the new capital in 1841. Okiato, then known as Russell, was abandoned, and the name Russell eventually replaced Kororareka. Historical highlights now include **Pompallier Mission** *(visitheritage.co.nz/visit/northland/pompallier-mission-and-printery)*, an 1842 Catholic mission house, and **Christ Church** (1836), NZ's oldest church.

Hundertwasser Art Centre, Whangārei
HANDOKO KURNIAWAN/SHUTTERSTOCK

Kaitāia welcome sign

NGĀTI TARARA

As you're travelling around the north you might notice the preponderance of road names ending in '-ich'. As the sign leading into Kaitāia proclaims, 'haere mai, dobro došli and welcome' to one of the more peculiar ethnic conjunctions in the country.

From the end of the 19th century, men from the Dalmatian coast of what is now Croatia started arriving in NZ looking for work. Many ended up in Northland's gum fields. Pākehā society wasn't very welcoming to the new immigrants, particularly during WWI, as they were on Austrian passports. Not so the small Māori communities of the north. Here the Croatian men found an echo of Dalmatian village life, with its emphasis on extended family and hospitality, not to mention a shared history of injustice at the hands of colonial powers.

The Māori jokingly named them Tarara, as their rapid conversation in their native tongue sounded like 'ta-ra-ra-ra-ra' to Māori ears. Many Croatian men married local *wahine* (women), founding clans that have given several of today's famous Māori their Croatian surnames, like singer Margaret Urlich and former All Black Frano Botica. You'll find large Tarara communities in the Far North, Dargaville and West Auckland.

THE DRIVE: It's about 8km to Okiato. A car ferry – cash or card payment on board (car/motorcycle/passenger from $18/8.50/1) – crosses regularly from Okiato to Opua (5km from Paihia).

07 Paihia

Connected to Russell by passenger ferries across a narrow harbour, Paihia is more energetic than its sleepier sibling. Motels, hostels and restaurants are crammed during summer holidays, and Paihia's waterfront hosts maritime excursions including island sightseeing, dolphin-watching and sailing. A coastal road meanders 3km to the **Waitangi Treaty Grounds** (*waitangi.org.nz*). Occupying a headland draped in lawns and forest, this is NZ's most important historic site. On 6 February 1840, the first 43 of more than 500 Māori chiefs signed the Treaty of Waitangi with the British Crown. Admission to the Treaty Grounds includes a guided tour, Māori cultural performance and entry to the **Te Kōngahu Museum of Waitangi**, a showcase of the role of the treaty in NZ's past, present and future.

THE DRIVE: From Paihia, continue on SH11 (Black Bridge Rd) to Kerikeri, a meandering 24km route through citrus orchards. Around 4km from Paihia, the spectacular Haruru Falls can be reached by turning off Puketona Rd onto Haruru Falls Rd.

08 Kerikeri

Famous for its oranges, Kerikeri also produces kiwifruit, vegetables and wine. It's also increasingly popular with retirees and hosts some of Northland's best restaurants. A snapshot of early Māori and Pākehā (European New Zealander) interaction is offered by a cluster of historic sites centred on Kerikeri's picturesque river basin. Dating from 1836, the **Stone Store** *(stonestore.co.nz)* is NZ's oldest stone building, and tours depart from here for nearby Kemp House, NZ's oldest surviving building, dating from 1822. There's an ongoing campaign to have the Kerikeri Mission Stations area recognised as a Unesco World Heritage Site.

THE DRIVE: From Kerikeri, head north on SH10, turning east to Matauri Bay Rd to complete a stunning 41km loop back to SH10 just north of Kaeo. This coastal road takes in Matauri Bay, Tauranga Bay and the expansive Whangaroa Harbour. Back on SH10, continue 30km north to Mangōnui (90km from Kerikeri) and Doubtless Bay.

09 Mangōnui

Doubtless Bay gets its unusual name from an entry in Captain James Cook's logbook, where he wrote that the body of water was 'doubtless a bay'. The main centre, Mangōnui ('Big Shark'), retains a fishing-port ambience, and cafes and galleries fill its small historic waterfront. These timber buildings were constructed when Mangōnui was a centre of the whaling industry (1792 to 1850) and exported flax, kauri timber and gum. At Hihi, 15km northeast of Mangōnui, the **Butler Point Whaling Museum** *(whalingmuseumbutlerpoint.com)* showcases these earlier days. The nearby settlements of Coopers Beach, Cable Bay and Taipa are all pockets of beachside gentrification and well-tanned retirees.

THE DRIVE: his leg is 132km. From Mangōnui, drive west on SH10 to rejoin SH1 at Awanui. From Awanui head to NZ's northernmost point, Cape Reinga. An interesting stop is at the Nga-Tapuwae-o-te-Mangai Māori Ratana church at Te Kao, 58km north of Awanui. Look out for the two green-and-white domed towers.

DETOUR

Karikari Peninsula

Start: 09 Mangōnui

Around 9km west of Taipa on SH10, head north on Inland Rd to explore the Karikari Peninsula. The oddly shaped peninsula bends into a near-perfect right angle, resulting in beaches facing north, south, east and west in close proximity. This unique set-up makes Karikari Peninsula one of the world's best spots for kiteboarding, or at least that's the opinion of the experienced crew at **Airzone Kitesurfing School** *(kitesurfnz.com)*. Learners get to hone their skills on flat water before heading into the surf.

Despite its natural assets, the peninsula is blissfully undeveloped, with farmers well outnumbering tourist operators. Sun-kissed highlights include **Tokerau Beach**, a long, sandy stretch on the western edge of Doubtless Bay. Neighbouring **Whatuwhiwhi** is smaller and more built-up, facing back across the bay. **Matai Bay,** with its tiny twin coves, is the loveliest of them all, at the lonely end of the peninsula down an unsealed road. It's a great sheltered spot for swimming. **Rangiputa** faces west at the elbow of the peninsula; the pure white sand and crystal-clear sheltered waters come straight from a Pacific Island daydream. A turn-off on the road to Rangiputa takes you to remote **Puheke Beach**, a long, windswept stretch of snow-white sand dunes forming Karikari's northern edge.

Eating opportunities are limited, so stock up in Mangōnui for a beachside picnic.

Count on 80km for a return trip from Mangōnui to the Karikari Peninsula.

10 Cape Reinga

The waters off the windswept **Cape Reinga Lighthouse** (a rolling 1km walk from the car park) are where the Tasman Sea and Pacific Ocean meet, crashing in waves up to 10m high in stormy weather. Māori consider **Cape Reinga** *(Te Rerenga-Wairua)* the jumping-off point for souls as they depart on the journey to their spiritual homeland. Out of respect to the most sacred site of Māori people, refrain from eating or drinking anywhere in the area. Around 16km south of Cape Reinga on SH1, a road leads west for 4km to the **Te Paki Recreation Reserve**, where you can walk on giant sand dunes or rent sandboards nearby to toboggan down them.

THE DRIVE: It is possible to drive down Ninety Mile Beach, but every year several tourists – and their rental cars – get hopelessly stuck in the sand. To experience it risk-free, join a 4WD bus tour from Kaitāia (111km south of Cape Reinga on SH1). Continue 13km west of Kaitāia to Ahipara on the Ahipara Rd to reach the southern end of the beach.

> **PHOTO OPPORTUNITY**
>
> The iconic Cape Reinga Lighthouse.

11 Ahipara

All good things must come to an end, and Ninety Mile Beach does at this relaxed Far North beach town. A few holiday mansions have snuck in, but mostly it's just the locals keeping it real with visiting surfers. The area is known for its huge sand dunes and massive gum field where 2000 people once worked. Adventure activities are popular on the dunes above Ahipara and further around the **Tauroa Peninsula**. Ask locally for recommendations for surfing lessons.

THE DRIVE: From Ahipara, drive 64km through the verdant Herekino forest to the sleepy harbour settlement of Kohukohu. Around 4km past Kohukohu, a car ferry crosses the Hokianga Harbour to Rawene. The ferry leaves Kohukohu hourly to 8pm.

12 Rawene

During the height of the kauri industry **Kohukohu** was a busy town with a sawmill, shipyard, two newspapers and banks. These days it's a very quiet harbour backwater dotted with well-preserved heritage buildings. Have a coffee and one of NZ's best pies at the local streetside cafe, before catching the ferry across the harbour to Rawene. Founded as NZ's third European settlement, a number of historic buildings (including six churches) remain from a time when the harbour was considerably busier than it is now. Information boards outline a heritage trail of the main sights. Built in the bustling 1860s by a trader, stately **Clendon House** *(visitheritage.co.nz/visit/northland/clendon-house)* is now managed by Heritage New Zealand. A few browse-worthy art galleries fill other historic buildings.

THE DRIVE: Another winding and scenic road travels 20km to reach Opononi, near the entrance of the Hokianga Harbour.

13 Opononi & Omapere

The twin settlements of Opononi and Omapere lie on the south head of Hokianga Harbour. Views are dominated by mountainous sand dunes across the water at North Head. The **Arai te Uru Heritage Walk** (30 minutes return) starts at the car park at the

Omapere

JUDITH LIENERT/SHUTTERSTOCK

end of Signal Station Rd (right off SH12 at the top of the hill leaving Omapere), then follows the cliffs and passes through mānuka scrub before continuing to the Hokianga's southern headland. At the headland are the flagpole remains of an old signal station built to assist ships making the treacherous passage into the harbour.

THE DRIVE: Climbing south out of Omapere – don't miss the spectacular views back across the harbour – SH12 continues to the Waipoua State Forest – a meandering journey of around 20km.

14 Waipoua State Forest

This superb forest sanctuary – proclaimed in 1952 after public pressure – is the largest remnant of the once-extensive kauri forests of northern NZ. The forest road (SH12) stretches for 18km and passes huge trees. Near the northern end of the park stands mighty **Tāne Mahuta**, named after the Māori forest god. At 51.5m high with a 13.8m girth, it's the largest kauri alive, and has been growing for between 1200 and 2000 years. Other massive trees to discover include **Te Matua Ngahere** and the **Four Sisters**.

THE DRIVE: From the Waipoua Forest Visitor Centre, it's 107km on SH12 – via the riverine town of Dargaville – to Matakohe. Around 4km north of Dargaville, Baylys Coast Rd runs 9km west to Baylys Beach, a wild surf beach and small community.

15 Matakohe

Apart from the rural charms of this village, the key reason for visiting Matakohe is the superb **Kauri Museum** *(kau.nz)*. The giant cross-sections of trees are astounding, and the entire timber industry is brought to life through video kiosks, artefacts, fabulous furniture and marquetry, and reproductions of a pioneer sawmill, boarding house, gumdigger's hut and Victorian home. The Gum Room holds a weird and wonderful collection of kauri gum, an amber substance that can be carved, sculpted and polished to a jewel-like quality. The museum shop stocks mementos crafted from kauri wood and gum.

THE DRIVE: From Matakohe, travel east on SH12 to join SH1 again at Brynderwyn. Drive south to Wellsford and then take SH16 for the scenic route southwest back to Auckland (163km in total from Matakohe). From Wellsford to Auckland on SH16 is around 110km, taking in views of Kaipara Harbour and West Auckland's vineyards.

IV4NGRIGORYEV/SHUTTERSTOCK

Kauri tree, Waipoua State Forest

EXPLORING THE FOREST AFTER DARK

Led by Māori guides, the four-hour twilight tour into Waipoua Forest by **Footprints Waipoua** *(footprintswaipoua.co.nz)* is a fantastic introduction to both the culture and the forest giants. Tribal history and stories are shared, and mesmerising *karakia* (prayer, incantation) recited before the gargantuan trees. Daytime tours are also available, but the twilight tours amplify the sense of spirituality. Tours depart from the Copthorne Hotel & Resort on SH12 in Omapere.

STAY AWHILE

RUSSELL

BY ASHLYN OSWALT

Russell's lawless reputation earned it the nickname 'hellhole of the Pacific', but today the quaint town is an idyllic destination. Home to many of New Zealand's firsts – seaport, European settlement and licensed bar – it's full of history.

I always start my stay with a self-guided walking tour, stopping by the **Russell Museum** *(russell-museum.org.nz)* to contemplate the area's history before and after colonisation. It's small, but packed with local knowledge. Then, I check out the **Pompallier Mission and Printery** *(pompallier.co.nz)*, built in 1842, and **Christ Church** *(russellchurch.nz)*, the country's oldest church nearby.

Now that I'm warmed up, I walk up **Te Maiki/Flagstaff Hill** *(doc.govt.nz)* to take in the 360-degree views over the Bay of Islands. This is where Ngāpuhi leader Hōne Heke Pōkai cut down the Union Jack four times, to protest against the British undermining Māori chiefs following the Treaty of Waitangi. Rich history and views.

A trip to Russell isn't complete without a visit to the **Waitangi Treaty Grounds** *(waitangi.org.nz)*, a 40-minute drive away. This is where the Treaty of Waitangi was signed by Māori chiefs and the British Crown in 1840. Take the hour-long guided tour (included in the entry fee) to learn about Waitangi's history and explore the grounds' museums and historic buildings. Standard admission tickets are valid for two consecutive days, so plan wisely to avoid overwhelm.

The day is best topped with a wood-fired pizza and beer on tap at funky **Hōne's Garden** *(hones.co.nz)*, soaking in the sunshine on its tropical garden patio.

LINK YOUR TRIP

Russell is a great stop on the 05 **Northland & the Bay of Islands** road trip.

Left: Pompallier Mission and Printery
Right: View from Flagstaff Hill

LEFT: EOROY/SHUTTERSTOCK, RIGHT: HEAVENLYFLOWER/SHUTTERSTOCK

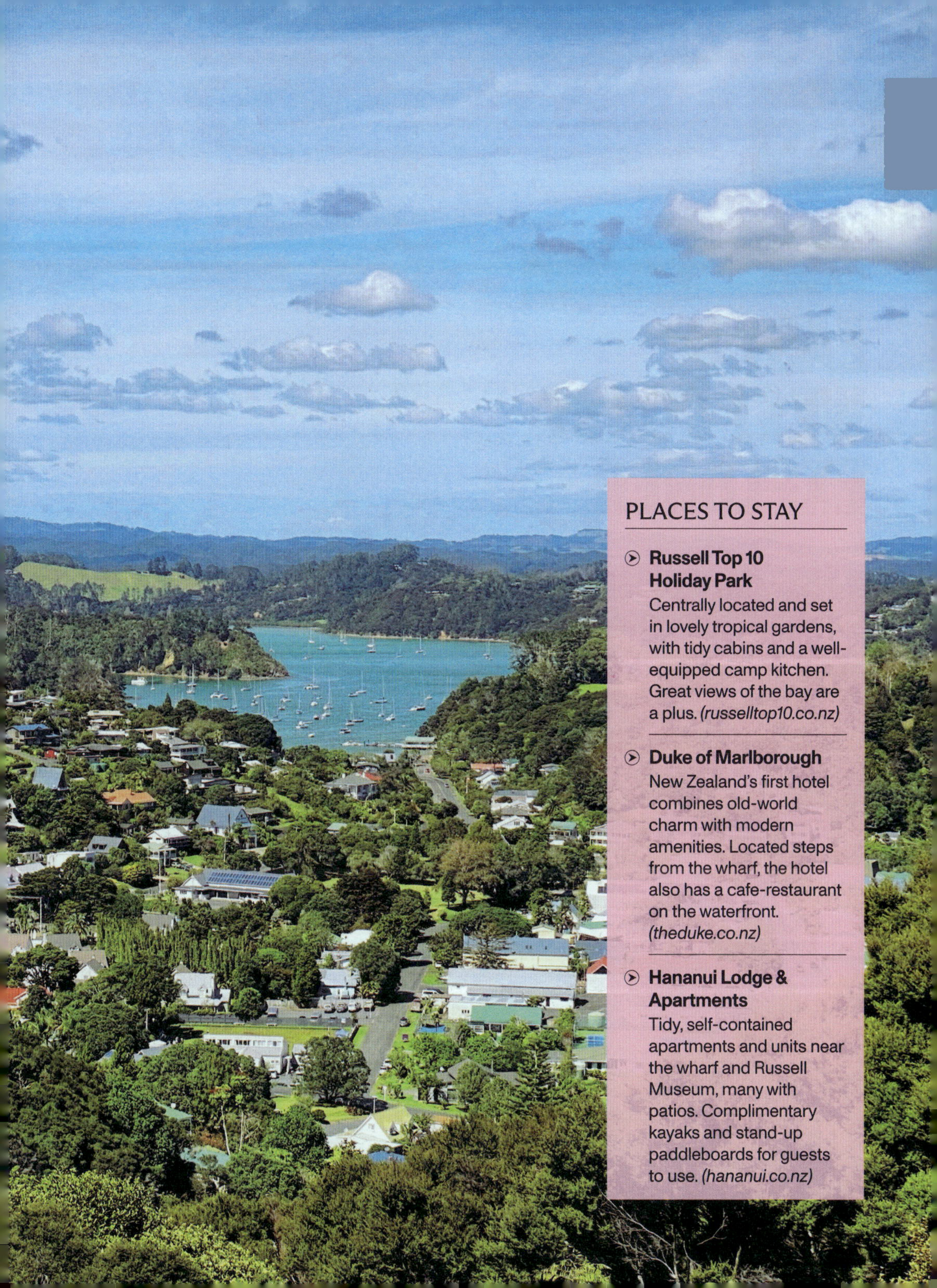

PLACES TO STAY

Russell Top 10 Holiday Park
Centrally located and set in lovely tropical gardens, with tidy cabins and a well-equipped camp kitchen. Great views of the bay are a plus. *(russelltop10.co.nz)*

Duke of Marlborough
New Zealand's first hotel combines old-world charm with modern amenities. Located steps from the wharf, the hotel also has a cafe-restaurant on the waterfront. *(theduke.co.nz)*

Hananui Lodge & Apartments
Tidy, self-contained apartments and units near the wharf and Russell Museum, many with patios. Complimentary kayaks and stand-up paddleboards for guests to use. *(hananui.co.nz)*

06

AUCKLAND & THE NORTH

EAST & WEST COAST EXPLORER

DURATION: 3 DAYS

DISTANCE: 317KM / 197 MILES

GREAT FOR: FAMILIES, NATURE AND WINE

BEST TIME TO GO: FEBRUARY TO APRIL FOR LEISURELY VINEYARD LUNCHES

The proud residents of Auckland are a lucky bunch, and this trip takes in some of their favourite day-escapes from the energy and bustle of the city. Plan your route to be slightly more leisurely, and enjoy a few days blending virtue and vice by combining fine wine, beer and local markets with coastal bush walks, beaches and active adventure.

LINK YOUR TRIP

05 Northland & the Bay of Islands
New Zealand's Māori and colonial history unfolds to the north along both coasts.

08 Waiheke Island Escape
Use Auckland as a base for more stellar beaches and vineyard restaurants.

01 Auckland

Before heading off on a journey where food, wine and markets are tasty features, explore the culinary scene of New Zealand's most diverse and cosmopolitan city. For a small-group city tour, including market visits, craft-beer pubs, artisan producers and loads of tastings, hook up with the crew at **Big Foody** *(thebigfoody.com)*.

THE DRIVE: Head north on SH1 and turn left to Puhoi after the spectacular Johnstone Hills tunnels. Pay tolls ($2.60) for the Northern Gateway Toll Road on SH1 online at nzta.govt.nz. The total distance of this leg is 43km.

02 Puhoi

Forget dingy cafes and earnest poets – this quaint riverside village is a slice of the real Bohemia. In 1863 around 200 German-speaking immigrants from the present-day Czech Republic settled in what

STARGRASS/SHUTTERSTOCK

★ BEST FOR

FAMILIES

Viewing the underwater spectacle at Goat Island.

Watersports, Puhoi

was then dense bush. The **Puhoi Heritage Museum** *(puhoiheritagemuseum.co.nz)* tells the story of the hardship and perseverance of these original pioneers. Raise a glass to their endeavour and endurance at the character-filled **Puhoi Pub** *(puhoipub.com)*. **Puhoi River Kayaks** *(puhoikayaks.co.nz)* rents kayaks and Canadian canoes, either by the hour, or for an excellent 8km downstream journey from the village to Wenderholm Regional Park. Bookings are essential.

THE DRIVE: Continue north on SH1 and turn right just after Warkworth to negotiate wine country and pretty coastal coves to Matakana, 25km from Puhoi.

03 Matakana

Around 15 years ago, Matakana was a rural village with a handful of heritage buildings and an old-fashioned country pub. Now its stylish wine bars and cafes are a weekend destination for day-tripping Aucklanders. An excellent Saturday-morning **farmers market** *(matakanavillage.co.nz)* is held in a shaded riverside location, and the area's boutique wineries are becoming renowned for pinot gris, merlot, syrah and a host of obscure varietals. Local vineyards are detailed in the free **Matakana Coast Wine Country** *(matakanacoast.com)* and **Matakana Wine Trail** *(matakanawine.co.nz)* brochures, available from the **Matakana Information Centre** *(matakanacoast.co.nz)*. Spend a few hours at the **Sculptureum** *(sculptureum.nz)* exploring local and international art in its galleries and gardens.

THE DRIVE: Leave Matakana on Leigh Rd and continue through the seaside village of Leigh before turning right into Goat Island Rd. Twelve kilometres north of Matakana, Mathesons Bay is a secluded cove with good swimming. The total distance to Goat Island is 16km.

DETOUR

Tawharanui Regional Park

Start: 03 Matakana

Around 1.5km northeast of Matakana en route to Leigh and Goat Island, turn right on Takatu Rd to follow a partly unsealed route for around 14km to **Tawharanui Regional Park** *(aucklandcouncil.govt.nz)*, a 588-hectare reserve at the end of a peninsula. This special place is an open sanctuary for native birds, protected by a pest-proof fence, while the northern coast is a marine park (bring a snorkel). There are plenty of walking tracks (1½ to four hours) but the main attraction is Anchor Bay, one of the region's finest white-sand beaches.

04 Goat Island

This 547-hectare aquatic area was established in 1975 as the country's first **marine reserve** *(doc.govt.nz)*, and has now developed into a giant outdoor aquarium. Wade knee-deep into the water to see snapper (the big fish with blue dots and fins), blue maomao and stripy parore swimming around. Excellent interpretive panels explain the area's Māori significance (it was the landing place of one of the ancestral canoes) and provide pictures of the fish species you're likely to encounter. Hire snorkels and wetsuits from **Goat Island Dive & Snorkel** *(goatislanddive.co.nz)* in Leigh or join a 45-minute boat trip with **Glass Bottom Boat Tours** *(glassbottomboat.co.nz)*.

THE DRIVE: Continue to Wellsford (34km) before taking SH16 to meander another 57km southwest through farmland and past Kaipara Harbour to Helensville

05 Helensville

Heritage buildings, antique shops and cafes make village-like Helensville a good whistle-stop for those negotiating SH16. Energetic and relaxing activities also combine for an interesting destination that's perfect for adventurous families. At the **Woodhill Mountain Bike Park** *(bikeparks.co.nz)*, 14km south of Helensville, challenging tracks (including jumps and beams) career through the Woodhill Forest, and at **Tree Adventures** *(treeadventures.co.nz)* high-ropes courses include swinging logs, climbing nets and a flying fox. Nearby **Parakai Springs** *(parakaisprings.co.nz)* has thermally heated swimming pools, private spas and a couple of hydroslides.

THE DRIVE: Continue south on SH16 to Waimauku (17km) and turn right for the 8km to Muriwai. Look forward to rolling pastures dotted with sheep, followed by a winding drive through the forest.

06 Muriwai

A black-sand surf beach, Muriwai features the Takapu Refuge **gannet colony**, which is spread over the southern headland and outlying rock stacks. Viewing platforms get you close enough to watch (and smell) these fascinating seabirds. Every August hundreds of adult birds return to this spot to hook up with their regular partners and get busy in spectacular (and noisy) displays of courting. The net result is a single chick per season; December and January are the best times to see them testing their wings before embarking on an impressive odyssey to Australia. Nearby, two short tracks wind through beautiful native bush to a **lookout** that offers views along the 60km length of the beach. Note this wild beach is only safe for swimming when patrolled. Always swim between the flags.

THE DRIVE: Return to SH16 and turn right to Kumeū. Orchards and vineyards feature along this 16km route, and it's a good area to buy fresh fruit.

07 Kumeū

West Auckland's main wine-producing area still has some vineyards owned by the original Croatian families who kick-started NZ's wine industry. The fancy restaurants that have mushroomed in recent years have done little to dint the relaxed farmland feel to the region, but everything to encourage an afternoon's indulgence on the way back from the beach or the hot pools. Most cellars offer free tastings. Top vineyards include **Coopers Creek** *(cooperscreek.co.nz)* and **Kumeu River** *(kumeuriver.co.nz)*. **Hallertau** *(hallertau.co.nz)*, at nearby **Riverhead**, is an excellent

Muriwai beach
MICHAEL SCHOLLUM/SHUTTERSTOCK

craft brewery with very good food. In nearby **Huapai**, the **Beer Spot** *(thebeerspot.co.nz)* is another hoppy haven in wine country.

THE DRIVE: Depart Kumeū on Waitākere Rd and turn right into Bethells Rd after 10km. It's 12km further to Te Henga (Bethells Beach).

08 Te Henga (Bethells Beach)

Breathtaking Bethells Beach is a raw, black-sand beach with surf, windswept dunes and walks, such as the popular one over giant sand dunes to **Lake Wainamu** (starting near the bridge on the approach to the beach). If you're keen to stay the night close to this rugged and beautiful spot, consider glamping at Wainamu Luxury Tents.

THE DRIVE: Leave Bethells Beach on Bethells Rd, which veers into Te Henga Rd. Around 11km from Bethells Beach, turn right into Scenic Dr and follow this winding bush-clad route, before turning back towards the coast onto Piha Rd. This leg is 37km in total.

09 Piha

This beautifully rugged, black-sand beach has long been an Aucklanders' favourite for day trips, teenage weekend roadies and family holidays. Although Piha is popular, it's also incredibly dangerous, with wild surf and strong undercurrents. Always swim between the flags, where lifeguards can help if you get into trouble. Near the centre of the beach is **Lion Rock** (101m), whose 'mane' glows golden in the evening light. It's actually the eroded core of an ancient volcano and a Māori *pa* (fortified village) site. A path at the southern end of the beach leads to great lookouts. At low tide you can walk south along the beach and watch the surf shooting through a ravine in another large rock known as the **Camel**.

THE DRIVE: Piha Rd leads back onto Scenic Dr, which continues through West Auckland suburbs to Titirangi, 25km from Piha.

10 Titirangi

This little village marks the end of Auckland's suburban sprawl and is a good place to meet relaxed and arty West Auckland locals over a coffee, wine or cold beer. Once home to NZ's greatest modern painter, Colin McCahon, there remains an artsy feel to the place. It's a mark of the esteem in which McCahon is held that the **house** *(facebook.com/mccahonhouse)* he lived and painted in during the 1950s has been opened to the public as a mini-museum. The swish pad next door is a temporary home to the artist lucky enough to win the McCahon Arts Residence. More art is on display at the **Te Uru Waitakere Contemporary Gallery** *(teuru.org.nz)*, an excellent modern gallery housed in the former Hotel Titirangi (1930) on the edge of the village. Titirangi means 'Fringe of Heaven' – an apt name given its proximity to the verdant Waitākere Ranges.

THE DRIVE: From Titirangi, continue through the West Auckland suburbs of New Lynn and Avondale to rejoin the motorway (SH16) back to central Auckland, 17km from Titirangi.

Lion Rock, Piha

JUSTIN FOULKES/LONELY PLANET

PHOTO OPPORTUNITY

Piha's Lion Rock from high above the beach.

07

AUCKLAND & THE NORTH

COROMANDEL PENINSULA

DURATION: 4-5 DAYS

DISTANCE: 299KM / 186 MILES

GREAT FOR: FOOD AND DRINK, OUTDOORS

BEST TIME TO GO: NOVEMBER TO APRIL, BUT TRY TO AVOID SCHOOL HOLIDAYS, CHRISTMAS AND EASTER

A favourite holiday spot for residents of nearby Auckland and Hamilton, the Coromandel Peninsula packs attractions aplenty into its beach-fringed coastline. The legacy of a gold-mining past lingers in the heritage streets of Thames, Coromandel Town and Waihi, and natural attractions like Cathedral Cove and Hot Water Beach combine with exciting and diverse opportunities to explore and get active around a stunning marine-scape.

LINK YOUR TRIP

02 Thermal Discoverer
Waihi Beach is 103km from Hamilton, linking to this journey through the North Island's volcanic centre.

13 Pacific Coast Explorer
Continue south from Waihi Beach to Tauranga (55km) and around the east coast.

01 Thames

Heritage wooden buildings from the 19th-century gold rush still dominate Thames – especially in the stately shopfronts along Pollen St – but grizzly prospectors have long been replaced by laid-back locals. Learn about the area's gold-flecked history at the **Goldmine Experience** *(goldmine-experience.co.nz)* – including watching a giant stamper battery effortlessly crush rock – and at the interesting **School of Mines & Mineralogical Museum** *(thamesschoolofmines.co.nz)*. The weekly Thames Market is packed with local arts and crafts, and Thames is also a good base for hiking or canyoning in the nearby **Kauaeranga Valley**.

THE DRIVE: Heading north up the Coromandel Peninsula's west coast, narrow SH25 meanders past pretty bays. At Tapu, 20km north of Thames, turn inland for 6km on a mainly sealed road to the Rapaura Water Gardens.

JAMESTHETHOMAS5/SHUTTERSTOCK

★ BEST FOR

BEACH LOVERS

The beautiful sandy arc of Opito.

Opito Beach (p74)

02 Rapaura Water Gardens

Beautifully located in a verdant stand of native forest, the **Rapaura Water Gardens** *(rapaurawatergardens.co.nz)* are a relaxing combination of water, greenery and art. Lily ponds, compact bridges and sculptures crafted from punga (a fern native to New Zealand) all blend at this soothing diversion from SH25, and there's also a very good cafe.

THE DRIVE: Rejoin SH25 at Tapu and continue north for 35km to Coromandel Town. Look forward to stunning coastal views, especially as you drop down off the winding hill road for the final drive into town.

03 Coromandel Town

Crammed with heritage buildings, Coromandel Town is a thoroughly quaint little place. Its natty cafes, interesting art stores, excellent sleeping options and delicious smoked mussels could keep you here longer than you expected. The **Driving Creek Railway** *(drivingcreek.nz)* was a lifelong labour of love for its conservationist owner, well-known potter, the late Barry Brickell. This unique train runs up steep grades, across four trestle bridges, along two spirals and a double switchback, and through two tunnels, finishing at the 'Eye-full Tower'. The one-hour trip passes artworks and regenerating native forest – more than 17,000 natives have been planted, including 9000 kauri trees. Booking ahead is recommended in summer. There's also a forest **zip line** *(drivingcreek.nz/activities/coromandel-zipline-tours)* here.

THE DRIVE: Leave Coromandel Town on Kapanga Rd, the settlement's sleepy main drag. Kapanga Rd leads into Rings Rd and then into Colville Rd. From Coromandel Town to Colville is around 27km, a stunning route negotiating beautiful beaches including Ōamaru Bay and Amodeo Bay.

04 Colville

The tiny settlement of Colville is a remote rural community

fringed by a muddy bay and framed by rolling green pastures. If you're continuing on the unsealed roads of Far North Coromandel, the Colville General Store is your last stop for both petrol and organic food. Wise travellers plan ahead for both. Around 1km south of Colville, the **Mahamudra Centre** *(mahamudra.org.nz)* is a serene Tibetan Buddhist retreat with a stupa, meditation hall and regular meditation courses. It offers simple accommodation in a park-like setting. Visiting is not possible if a retreat is scheduled, so phone ahead to check.

THE DRIVE: Return south from Colville and turn east onto SH25 around 500m south of Coromandel Town. En route to Kūaotunu (52km from Colville), a turn-off at Te Rerenga after 15km leads to Whangapoua (6km). From there is a walking track (one hour return) to New Chums Beach, regarded as one of NZ's finest beaches.

DETOUR

Far North Coromandel

Start: 04 Colville

The rugged northernmost tip of the Coromandel Peninsula is well worth the effort required to reach it. The best time to visit is summer (December to February), when the gravel roads are dry and the pōhutukawa trees are in their crimson glory. Northern Coromandel suffered storm damage from multiple events – check doc.govt.nz for track and campsite conditions.

Three kilometres north of Colville at Whangaahei, the sealed road turns to gravel and splits to straddle each side of the peninsula. Following the west coast, ancient pōhutukawa spread overhead as you pass turquoise waters and stony beaches. The small DOC-run **Fantail Bay campsite** *(doc.govt.nz)*, 23km north of Colville, has running water and a couple of long-drop toilets under the shade of puriri trees. Another 7km brings you to the **Port Jackson campsite** *(doc.govt.nz)*, a larger DOC site right on the beach. There's a spectacular lookout about 4km further on, where a metal dish identifies the various islands on the horizon. Great Barrier Island is only 20km away, looking every part the extension of the Coromandel Peninsula that it once was. The road stops at **Fletcher Bay** – a magical land's end. Although it's only 37km from Colville, allow an hour for the drive.

Note there is no road linking Fletcher Bay with the east coast of the peninsula, so you need to return to Whangaahei and turning left to return to Coromandel Town via a spectacular east-coast road taking in **Waikawau Bay** and **Kennedy Bay**. Sections of this road are unsealed gravel. For the entire journey north from Colville to Fletcher Bay, back south to Whangaahei, and then around the east coast back to Coromandel Town, allow around four to five hours of driving time.

05 Kūaotunu

Located at the end of a sweeping beach – with views of the Mercury Islands on the near horizon – Kūaotunu is an interesting holiday village with a fine **cafe and art gallery**, and access on scenic unsealed roads to the nearby beaches of Otama and Opito. Departing Kūaotunu by Blackjack Rd, Otama is 3.5km away and reached by a winding road over a spectacular headland. Dunes fringe the sandy arc of the beach, and a further 6km on lies **Opito**, more populated but arguably even more spectacular. Both beaches are good for a swim before you return to Kūaotunu.

THE DRIVE: From Kūaotunu it's an easy 15km drive on SH25 to Whitianga. The view coming down off the final hill towards Whitianga's Buffalo Beach is spectacular.

06 Whitianga

Whitianga's big attractions are the sandy beaches of **Mercury Bay**, and diving, boating and kayaking in the nearby **Te Whanganui-A-Hei Marine Reserve**. The pretty harbour is also a base for game fishing, especially marlin and tuna between January and March. North of the harbour, **Buffalo Beach** stretches along Mercury Bay, and the town is a magnet for holidaymakers throughout summer. The legendary Polynesian seafarer Kupe is believed to have landed near here around 950 CE, and the **Mercury Bay Museum** *(mercurybaymuseum.co.nz)* commemorates his visit and that of British maritime explorer Captain James Cook in 1769. Whitianga is a fast-growing town and has some of the peninsula's best restaurants. For a relaxing break from driving, book a spa session at the **Lost Spring** *(thelostspring.co.nz)*, a thermal complex comprising a series of hot pools in a lush jungle-like setting complete with an erupting volcano.

Fletcher Bay

DANITA DELIMONT/SHUTTERSTOCK

THE DRIVE: Depart south on SH25, skirting Whitianga Harbour to the east. Stay on SH25 to Whenuakite (26km), and turn left into Hot Water Beach Rd. After 5km, veer left onto Link Rd for 3km, and then turn right onto Hahei Beach Rd to Hahei (2km).

07 Hahei

A sleepy holiday town that explodes with visitors in summer – especially during school holidays – Hahei is located close to **Cathedral Cove**. The cove's gigantic stone arch and natural waterfall shower are best enjoyed early or late in the day to avoid the tourist buses and the worst of the hordes. From the start of the track 1km north of Hahei, it's a rolling walk of 30 to 40 minutes to the cove. On the way there's rocky **Gemstone Bay**, which has a snorkelling trail where you could see big snapper, crayfish and stingrays, and sandy **Stingray Bay**. Check doc.govt.nz for current conditions due to January 2026 storm damage. The **Cathedral Cove Water Taxi** *(cathedralcovewatertaxi.co.nz)* runs frequent waterborne transport from Hahei Beach to the cove. From October to April, a shuttle bus runs from Hahei to the beginning of the track to the cove. Leave your vehicle at the Hahei Visitor Car Park at the entrance to the village.

PHOTO OPPORTUNITY

The graceful and spectacular arch of Cathedral Cove.

THE DRIVE: From Hahei, depart on Hahei Beach Rd (2km) for Link Rd, turn left on Link Rd and continue for around 3km, then left onto Hot Water Beach Rd to Hot Water Beach (3km).

08 Hot Water Beach

Hot Water Beach is extraordinary. For two hours either side of low tide, you can access an area of sand in front of a rocky outcrop at the middle of the beach where hot water oozes up from beneath the surface. Bring a spade, dig a hole and you've got a personal spa pool. Spades can be hired from **Hotties** *(hottieseatery.co.nz)*, and local tourist information centres list tide schedules so you know when to rock up with scores of other fans of natural Jacuzzis. Note the car park

Gemstone Bay

FLASHGUN/SHUTTERSTOCK

outside the Hot Water Beach Store is pay and display, and it's enforced quite rigorously. Alternatively, park at the larger (free) car park before you get to the beach proper, and walk along the beach for a few hundred metres.

THE DRIVE: From Hot Water Beach, return by Hot Water Beach Rd to SH25 at Whenuakite, and continue south to Whangamatā, 59km from Hot Water Beach. En route at Tairua, a steep 15-minute walk to the summit of Paaku offers great harbour views across to Pauanui. At Opoutere, the Wharekawa Wildlife Refuge is a breeding ground for the endangered NZ dotterel.

09 Whangamatā

Outside of summer, 'Whanga' is a genteel seaside town (population 3560), but over Christmas, New Year and other key holiday periods, it can be a much more energetic spot, and the population swells to around 40,000 with holidaymakers from Auckland and Hamilton. It's an excellent surf beach, and a popular destination for kayaking and paddle boarding is **Whenuakura (Donut) Island**, around 1km from the beach. There's also good snorkelling at **Hauturu (Clarke) Island**. Note that in an effort to boost the islands' status as wildlife sanctuaries, landing on them is not permitted. Boating around the islands is allowed, however. The experienced team at **SurfSup** *(surfsup.nz)* offer paddle-boarding and surfing lessons, and also run daily kayaking and paddle-boarding tours to Whenuakura.

THE DRIVE: From Whangamatā, SH25 continues its meandering route south to Waihi (30km).

SHAUN JEFFERS/SHUTTERSTOCK

Catherdral Cove

EXPLORING THE TE WHANGANUI-A-HEI MARINE RESERVE

Departing from either Whitianga Harbour or from Hahei, local operators provide exciting and scenic access to the beautiful 840 hectares of the Te Whanganui-A-Hei Marine Reserve and around the surrounding coastline of Mercury Bay. The reserve was gazetted in 1992 and is centred on Cathedral Cove (Whanganui-A-Hei in Māori).

Hahei Explorer *(haheiexplorer.co.nz)* Hour-long jetboat rides touring the coast.

Cathedral Cove Sea Kayaking *(kayaktours.co.nz)* Guided kayaking trips around the rock arches, caves and islands in the Cathedral Cove and Mercury Bay area.

Banana Boat *(bananaboatwhitianga.weebly.com/rides)* Monkey around in Mercury Bay on the bright-yellow motorised Banana Boat – or split to Cathedral Cove.

Glass Bottom Boat *(glassbottomboatwhitianga.co.nz)* Two-hour bottom-gazing tours exploring the Te Whanganui-A-Hei Marine Reserve.

Cave Cruzer *(cavecruzer.co.nz)* Tours on a rigid-hull inflatable.

Ocean Leopard *(oceanleopardtours.co.nz)* Two-hour trips around coastal scenery, naturally including Cathedral Cove. The boat has a handy canopy for sun protection, and a one-hour 'Whirlwind Tour' is also on offer.

Sea Cave Adventures *(seacaveadventures.co.nz)* A two-hour sea cave adventure in an inflatable.

Windborne *(windborne.co.nz)* Day sails in a 19m schooner from 1928.

HAURAKI RAIL TRAIL

From Waihi township, an excellent day excursion is to combine a train ride on the heritage **Goldfields Railway** *(waihirail.co.nz)*, with a few hours' cycling along part of the popular Hauraki Rail Trail through the scenic Karangahake Gorge. Bikes can be rented at the railway's terminus in the gorge, the **Waikino Station Cafe** *(facebook.com/waikinostationcafe)* or at **Waihi Bicycle Hire** *(waihibicyclehire.co.nz)* in town and then carried on the train. This part of the Hauraki Rail Trail is spectacular as it winds on a gentle gradient through a beautiful river valley. Book ahead for lunch at **Bistro at the Falls Retreat** *(fallsretreat.co.nz)*, located in a cosy wooden cottage in the heart of a sun-dappled forest. Gourmet pizzas and rustic meat dishes emerge from the wood-fired oven on a regular basis, and there's a great little playground for children.

See haurakirailtrail.co.nz for detailed information, including trail maps and recommendations for other day rides on this popular cycle route linking Thames to the towns of Paeroa, Te Aroha and Waihi.

10 Waihi

Gold and silver have been dragged out of Waihi's Martha Mine (NZ's richest) since 1878, and Seddon St, the town's main street, has interesting sculptures and information panels about Waihi's golden legacy. The superb **Gold Discovery Centre** *(golddiscoverycentre.co.nz)* tells the area's gold-mining past, present and future through interactive displays, focusing on the personal and poignant to tell interesting stories. Holograms and short movies both feature, drawing visitors in and informing them through entertainment. Atmospherically lit at night, the skeleton of a derelict **Cornish Pumphouse** (1904) is the town's main landmark. From here the **Pit Rim Walkway** has fascinating views into the 250m-deep **Martha Mine**. To get down into the spectacular mine, join a 1½-hour excursion with **Waihi Gold Mine Tours** *(golddiscoverycentre.co.nz/tours)* departing from the Gold Discovery Centre.

THE DRIVE: Take SH2 south out of Waihi and turn left into Waihi Beach Rd after 3km.

11 Waihi Beach

Separated from Waihi township by 11km of prime Waikato farmland, this low sandy surf beach stretches 9km to **Bowentown** on the northern limits of Tauranga Harbour. As well as being a prime summertime destination for the good people of Hamilton, Waihi Beach is also a growing foodie hot spot with a number of fine little cafes; even the pub has had a makeover and attracts locals and weekenders alike. If you want to stretch your legs on more than the flat miles of golden beach, a good walk from the northern end of the beach leads to Orokawa Beach, 45 minutes away around the coastal headlands. In summer when the beachside pōhutukawa are flowering there is no finer Coromandel sight than scarlet trees, white sand and turquoise water.

BEX WALTON/FLICKR/CC BY 2.0

Coromandel Brewing Company at The Pour House, Hahei

COROMANDEL CRAFT BEER

Yes, the Kiwi craft-beer revolution has washed up on the pristine waters of Mercury Bay, and two excellent breweries are located near Hahei and Hot Water Beach. Good cafes and restaurants around the Coromandel Peninsula also stock beers from the Pour House and Hot Water Brewing Co.

Home base for the Coromandel Brewing Company, **Pour House** *(thepourhouse.co.nz)* in Hahei regularly features around five of its beers in a modern ambience. Mains of seafood and meat combine with decent pizzas in the beer garden. Our favourite brew is the Hahei Doctor American Pale Ale.

Located at the Sea Breeze Holiday Park in Whenuakite, **Hot Water Brewing Co** *(hotwaterbrewingco.com)* is a modern craft brewery with lots of outdoor seating. Bar snacks and pizzas make it easy to order another beer.

Karangahake Gorge

KAVRAM/SHUTTERSTOCK

08

★ BEST FOR

FOODIES

A leisurely lunch at a top vineyard restaurant.

The Shed at Te Mote (p82)

AUCKLAND & THE NORTH

WAIHEKE ISLAND ESCAPE

DURATION: 2 DAYS

DISTANCE: 62KM / 38 MILES

GREAT FOR: FAMILIES AND NATURE

BEST TIME TO GO: FEBRUARY TO APRIL BUT TRY AND AVOID BUSY WEEKENDS AND PUBLIC HOLIDAYS

Tantalisingly close to Auckland and blessed with its own warm, dry microclimate, blissful Waiheke Island has long been a favourite escape for both city dwellers and travellers. On the island's landward side, emerald waters lap at rocky bays, while its ocean flank has some of the region's best sandy beaches. Vineyards evoking a South Pacific spin on Tuscany or the south of France are other sybaritic diversions.

LINK YOUR TRIP

05 Northland & the Bay of Islands
More great beaches and discovering NZ's shared Māori and European heritage.

06 East & West Coast Explorer
More food- and wine-related fun amid Aucklanders' favourite day trips.

01 Auckland

One of the world's most beautiful harbour cities, Auckland is the gateway to the islands of the Hauraki Gulf. Regular ferries leave from downtown Auckland and other locations around the city to islands promising wine, art, walking and adventure.

THE DRIVE: From Auckland, Sealink (sealink.co.nz) runs car ferries to Kennedy Point on Waiheke Island. Most leave from Half Moon Bay in East Auckland (45 to 60 minutes), but some depart from Wynyard Wharf in the city (60 to 80 minutes). From Kennedy Point to Oneroa, Waiheke's main town, is 3km.

RORY DUNLEAVY/TE MOTU

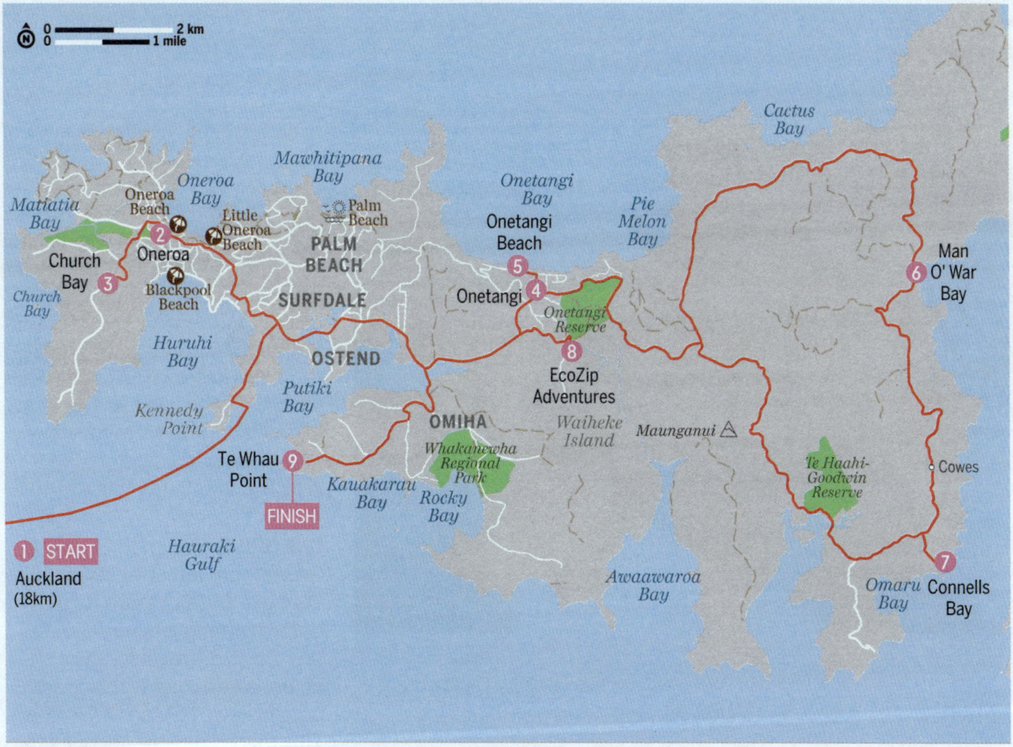

02 Oneroa

Waiheke's main settlement comprises a relaxed main street dotted with cafes, restaurants, gift shops and local stores. **Oneroa Beach** and the pretty cove of **Little Oneroa** nearby are both good for swimming. In town, attractions are conveniently centred on the **Waiheke Island Artworks** complex, and include the **Waiheke Community Art Gallery** *(waihekeartgallery.org.nz)* featuring local artists and an excellent gift shop. Drop in at the **Waiheke Wine Centre** *(waihekewinecentre.com)* featuring wine from all of Waiheke's 30-plus vineyards.

THE DRIVE: Leave Oneroa on Oceanview Rd – up the hill – and after 500m turn left into Church Bay Rd. Look for the small brown sign indicating 'Wineries'. Continue on Church Bay Rd for 2.5km to Mudbrick.

03 Church Bay

With spectacular views back to central Auckland – including the imposing profile of the Sky Tower – the two vineyards above pretty Church Bay are deservedly very popular. Auckland and the gulf are at their glistening best when viewed from the picturesque veranda at **Mudbrick** *(mudbrick.co.nz)*. The pretty, formal gardens make it popular with weddings, which periodically take over the restaurant (be sure to book ahead). The winery also offers tastings *(from $24; 10am to 5.30pm)*. One kilometre back down the hill towards Oneroa, **Cable Bay** *(cablebay.co.nz)* features contemporary architecture and more stunning vistas. There are two good restaurants and wine tasting *($20 for four wines, 11am to 5pm)* takes place in a stylish tasting room.

THE DRIVE: Return to Oceanview Rd via Church Bay Rd and continue for 2.7km before turning right into Surfdale Rd. Continue on this road for 5.5km until you see a sign for 'Wild on Waiheke' on your left.

04 Onetangi

Three Waiheke attractions are handily adjacent amid Onetangi's rural ambience. **Wild on Waiheke** *(wildonwaiheke.co.nz)* combines a winery and a microbrewery

Island Gelato

TIME FOR AN ICE CREAM...

Before school, after school, and on weekdays and weekends, Waiheke locals crowd the shipping-container garden at **Island Gelato** *(islandgelato.co.nz)* for delicious ice cream, coffee and bagels. Seasonal ice-cream flavours shine, including our favourite, the zingy kaffir-lime-and-coconut sorbet. You'll find all this irresistible goodness at the bottom end of Oneroa village.

with archery, laser clay shooting and a wooden castle playground. A secondary route leads to nearby **Stonyridge** *(stonyridge.com)*, Waiheke's most famous vineyard. It is home to world-beating reds, an atmospheric cafe and the occasional yoga session on the breezy decks. Combine a bottle with one of Stonyridge's deli platters and retreat to a garden cabana. Another nearby unsealed road meanders to **The Shed at Te Motu** *(temotu.co.nz/the-shed)*. Te Motu is most famous for stellar Bordeaux-style red wines, and sophisticated shared plates imbued with global culinary influences are served under umbrellas in the restaurant's rustic courtyard.

THE DRIVE: Continue east along Onetangi Rd for 2.5km to Onetangi Beach.

05 Onetangi Beach

Waiheke's best beach is a 1.9km sandy arc bookended by forested headlands. The humble baches (simple holiday homes) of earlier decades have now largely been replaced by million-dollar homes with ocean views, but the beach is still accessible to all. It's a wonderful spot for a leisurely stroll, and the gently rolling breakers coming in from the Hauraki Gulf are often perfect for bodysurfing. At the beach's eastern end, **Charlie's** *(charliefarleys.co.nz)* is the locals' favourite, and the pōhutukawa-tree-shaded deck is a top spot for a New Zealand craft beer or a leisurely lunch or dinner.

THE DRIVE: Return to Onetangi Rd and turn left after 300m into Waiheke Rd. Continue for 4.5km before turning left into Man O' War Bay Rd. Travel for 9km on an unsealed road with superb ocean views to Man O' War Bay. This road is narrow and winding in parts so take extra care.

06 Man O' War Bay

Yes, the drive to Man O' War Bay on unsealed roads can be bumpy, but it is definitely one of Waiheke's most beautiful spots. The beach is great for swimming, a slender wooden wharf stretches into the water, and there are great views of nearby **Pakatoa** and **Rotoroa Islands**. An essential island experience is to settle in with a tasting platter at the beachfront tasting room of the **Man O' War Vineyards** *(manowar.co.nz)*. The Valhalla chardonnay is an outstanding wine, and the rosé is highly recommended with tapas including charcuterie, cheeses and plump Waiheke olives.

Onetangi Beach

LEFT: ISLAND GELATO; RIGHT: IZANBAR/GETTY IMAGES

THE DRIVE: Leave Man O' War Bay on the unsealed road in front of the beach. Look for the heritage church that is used for summer weddings. Continue over the beach's southern headland for 6km before turning left down to Connells Bay.

07 Connells Bay

Reached by a road in the island's remote southeastern corner, the private sculpture park in beautiful **Connells Bay** *(connellsbay.co.nz)* features a stellar roster of NZ artists.

Around 30 different works punctuate the coastal terrain. Admission is by way of a two-hour guided tour. Note the park is only open from late October to mid-April and booking ahead is essential. Enquire about dates and book online.

THE DRIVE: Continue for 1.5km southwest on Cowes Bay Rd to the intersection with Orapiu Rd. Turn right into Orapiu Rd – this section is sealed again – and continue for 14km via Waiheke Rd to Onetangi Rd. Turn left on Onetangi Rd before turning left into Trig Hill Rd for 2km. Look for the sign to EcoZip Adventures.

08 EcoZip Adventures

Soar on a zip line above vineyards and native forest on Waiheke Island's most exciting experience. Three separate 200m-long stretches add up to a thrilling ride at **EcoZip Adventures** *(ecozipadventures.co.nz)*, but it's definitely a soft adventure suitable for most travellers. Look out to the skyline of Auckland's CBD as you're whizzing through the island air. Following the zip line, there is a pleasant 1.4km walk through the pristine forest. Just north of EcoZip, check out the 360-degree views from Trig Hill Lookout, where you can easily spot Auckland on a clear day.

THE DRIVE: Return via Trig Hill Rd to Onetangi Rd and continue left for 2.2km. Turn left into O'Brien Rd and then right onto Te Whau Dr for 4km out to the end of the Te Whau peninsula.

09 Te Whau Point

There are excellent views of the harbour and surroundings from the coastal peninsula at Te Whau Point, making for a spectacular conclusion to an island drive. On the peninsula you'll see well-kept olive groves flourishing in Waiheke's Mediterranean microclimate.

Ziplining, EcoZip Adventures
ECOZIP ADVENTURES

0
50 km
0
25 miles
Mt Moehau
Coromandel Town
Kūaotunu
Whitianga
Whenuakite
Coromandel Forest Park
Tapu
Table Mountain
Hikuai
Thames
Auckland
Maraetai
Waitākere Ranges Regional Park
Drury
Karaka East
Ramarama
Kaiaua
Pukekohe
Maramarua
Pukekawa
Glen Murray
Lake Waikare
Paeroa
Waihi
Bay of Plenty
Huntly
Mt Te Aroha
Morrinsville
Tatuanui
Ngāruawāhia
Mt Maunganui
Tauranga
Raglan
Hamilton
Kaimai Mamaku Forest Park
Matamata
Hinuera
Paengaroa
Matatā
Whatawhata
Mt Pirongia
Tapapa
Rotoehu Forest
Whakatāne
Tasman Sea
Kāwhia
Lake Rotoiti
Te Ngae
Lake Arapuni
Rotorua
Waitomo Caves
Ōtorohanga
Te Anga
Tokoroa
Mt Tarawera
Marokopa
Kinleith Forest
Tarawera Forest
Te Kuiti
Pureora Forest Park
Upper Atiamuri
Eight Mile Junction
Whakamaru
Kopaki
Wharerino Forest
Orakei Korako
Mihi
Te Urewera
North Taranaki Bight
Pureora
Mt Pureora
Te Whaiti
Awakino
Wairakei
Pureora Forest Park
Taupō
Mangatupoto
Whirinaki Te Pua-a-Tāne Conservation Park
Lake Taupō
Kuratau Junction
Ahititi
Ohura
Taumarunui
Iwitahi
Rangitaiki
New Plymouth
Tokirima
Brixton
Owhango
Tūrangi
Rangipo
Tarawera
Whangamomona
National Park Village
Tongariro National Park
Kaimanawa Forest Park
Te Haroto
Inglewood
Whakapapa Village
Kaweka Forest Park
Te Wara
Mt Taranaki
Mt Ruapehu
Dawson Falls
Stratford
Whanganui National Park
Lake Moawhango
Kuripapango
Opunake
Eltham
Raetihi
Ōhakune
Pipiriki
Waiouru
Otamauri
Rimunui State Forest
Erewhon
Napier
Hāwera
Kakatahi
Taihape
Hastings
Patea
Waitotara
Ruahine Forest Park
Whanganui
Hunterville
Waipawa
09
10
11
11
1
2
3
4
5
25
26
27
32
33
43
50

KLANARONG CHITMUNG/SHUTTERSTOCK

Hiker, Tongariro Alpine Crossing (p98)

ROTORUA & THE CENTRAL NORTH ISLAND

EXPLORE

ROTORUA & THE CENTRAL NORTH ISLAND

If there's a defining feature of the Central North Island, it's volcanic activity. Steam rises and mud bubbles at geothermal hot spots throughout the region, warning of the explosive potential of the many volcanic peaks. While towering Taranaki, Ruapehu, Ngauruhoe and Tongariro revel in their classically volcanic proportions, the most violent of them all has cloaked itself in placid respectability. The peaceful waters of vast Lake Taupō conceal the caldera of one of the world's most powerful supervolcanoes. It's a fascinating area to explore, with plenty of interesting highlights on its many scenic highways.

Raglan

The west-coast surfing hot spot of Raglan is a small town with an oversized buzz. Shopping is mainly limited to beach supplies, art shops and gift stores. There are a few small grocery stores, but you're better off saving your supermarket run for Hamilton. In the town centre, the best places to eat are The Shack and Orca, although our favourite is Cala, on the road to the surf beaches.

Hamilton

New Zealand's fourth-biggest city nestles within the loops of the broad Waikato River. You'll find any supplies you might need in the city centre, squeezed between Victoria and Anglesea Sts, and there are plenty of large supermarkets scattered around the periphery. There's memorable riverside dining on offer at Hayes Common cafe, hip Mr Pickles Bar & Eatery and upmarket Palate and Gothenburg. Other good cafes on the Victoria St strip include the River Kitchen and Scott's Epicurean.

Taupō

With several hot springs and an abundance of adrenaline-pumping activities, lakeside Taupō

WHEN TO GO

Warm summers and cold winters are the norm in these parts. Mt Ruapehu and Mt Taranaki are home to the North Island's ski fields, with the season generally running from June or July to October. Taranaki's many acclaimed gardens are at their very best in spring (September to November). January and February offer the best beach weather.

is a magnet for lovers of the outdoors. It's well set up for visitors, with plenty of places to stay and a compact town centre peppered with cafes and bars. Indian restaurants abound, the best of which is Master of India. For cafe fare, head to Replete, Storehouse or Victoria's. If you're after something a little more fancy, try the Bistro or Brantry Eatery.

New Plymouth

Sitting in the shadow of beautiful Mt Taranaki, New Plymouth is a prosperous midsize city with a breezy, outdoorsy vibe. Despite its relative isolation on North Island's left hip, the city has plenty of good cafes, restaurants, coffee roasteries, craft breweries and that newfound staple of 2020s life, a boutique distillery. For casual eating, try the food-truck alley on Liardet St or the White Hart complex, a heritage pub that's been hollowed out and converted into something akin to a swanky food hall. Other great options include Monica's Eatery and Social Kitchen.

Whanganui

This little river city has oodles of charm, in a large part due to its well-preserved heritage quarter where every other building seems to house a gallery. Grab a craft beer and burger from Porridge Watson, located in the historic Victoria House, a short walk from the acclaimed Sarjeant Gallery. Good cafes include Little Curious Bagels, the Yellow House and riverside Mud Ducks.

TRANSPORT

There are domestic airports in Hamilton, Taupō, New Plymouth and Whanganui. Buses connect the main towns and cities to Auckland and Wellington, and the Northern Explorer train linking Auckland and Wellington stops in Hamilton, Ōtorohanga, Taumarunui and National Park Village. SH1 barrels through the centre of the island, skirting Hamilton, Taupō, Tūrangi and Waiouru.

WHERE TO STAY

Excellent hostels include Raglan Backpackers, Finlay Jack's YHA in Taupō and Ducks & Drakes in New Plymouth. The Waitomo and Whanganui River Top 10 Holiday Parks both offer a combination of campsites and snazzy units. Noteworthy motels include Raglan Sunset Motel, Arena Court in Hamilton, Gables Lakefront and Lake Taupō Holiday Resort in Taupō, One Burgess Hill and The Dawson in New Plymouth, and 151 on London and Siena Motor Lodge in Whanganui. The region's best boutique hotel is King & Queen Hotel Suites in New Plymouth. Upmarket B&Bs near Taupō include Acacia Cliffs Lodge and Serenity on Wakeman.

RESOURCES

- **raglan.net.nz**
  The website of Raglan's iHub Information Centre, housed in the intriguing Raglan Museum.
- **visithamilton.co.nz**
  You'll find the Hamilton i-SITE Visitor Information Centre within the ArtsPost gallery.
- **lovetaupo.com**
  Taupō's official site, courtesy of the folks at the helpful Taupō Customer & Visitor Information Centre on Tongariro St.

WHAT'S ON

- **Festival of Lights**
  New Plymouth's Pukekura Park transforms into a fairy land from late December to the end of January.
- **Hamilton Arts Festival**
  Ten days of theatre, comedy and live shows in late February, taking place in the award-winning Hamilton Gardens.
- **Taupō Winter Festival**
  Celebrate winter with lights, an ice rink and family-friendly events in early July.
- **Taranaki Gardens Festival**
  Gardens open their gates right across Taranaki in October and November.
- **Lake Taupō Cycle Challenge**
  Two-wheeled warriors circle the lake in November.

09

ROTORUA & THE CENTRAL NORTH ISLAND

TARANAKI WANDERER

DURATION: 3 DAYS

DISTANCE: 343KM / 213 MILES

GREAT FOR: NATURE, CULTURE AND HISTORY

BEST TIME TO GO: FROM NOVEMBER TO MARCH, TARANAKI'S GARDENS ARE BLOOMIN' MARVELLOUS

★ BEST FOR

FAMILIES

New Plymouth's Festival of Lights is a colourful wonderland in late December and January.

Poet's Bridge, Pukekura Park

Taranaki is an interesting region that's still deliciously off the radar for many travellers. The seaside city of New Plymouth combines urban smarts with a laid-back, beachy vibe. Mt Taranaki – surely New Zealand's best-looking volcano – anchors an area with a proud history of dairy farming, while sleepy roads meander down to rugged surf beaches from the famed Surf Highway 45 (SH45).

LINK YOUR TRIP

10 Tongariro National Park Loop
Eyeball further amazing mountains via the short 42km hop south from Taumarunui to National Park Village.

11 Waves & Caves to Whanganui
Taumarunui is also a stop on this island-spanning route including the spectacular Waitomo Caves.

01 New Plymouth

Welcome to one of NZ's most engaging provincial cities. New Plymouth has a simmering arts scene and some excellent cafes, craft-beer bars and restaurants. The spectacular **Govett-Brewster Art Gallery/Len Lye Centre** *(govettbrewster.com)* is arguably the country's best regional art gallery, presenting contemporary, experimental and provocative works. The thrilling Len Lye Centre is an architectural homage to NZ artist Len Lye (1901–80). It's an interlocking facade of tall, mirror-clad concrete flutes, with internal galleries linked by ramps housing Lye's works – kinetic, noisy and surprising. **Pukekura Park** *(pukekura.org.nz)* is the pick of the city's green spaces, with 49 lush hectares of gardens, playgrounds, trails, streams and waterfalls.

THE DRIVE: From central New Plymouth, drive southwest on St Aubyn St, which merges into Breakwater Rd. Turn left into Ngamotu St and then right into Centennial Dr for Paritutu Centennial Park (around 5km from central New Plymouth).

DETOUR

Pukearuhe & Mokau

Start: 01 New Plymouth

About 35km north of New Plymouth on SH3 is the turn-off to Pukearuhe and White Cliffs, huge precipices resembling their Dover namesakes. From Pukearuhe boat ramp, you can tackle the **White Cliffs Walkway**, a three-hour loop walk with mesmerising views of the coast and mountains (Taranaki and Ruapehu). The tide can make things dicey along the beach: walk between two hours either side of low tide.

Back on SH3, continue 32km north towards Mokau. The **Three Sisters** rock formation is signposted just south of the Tongaporutu Bridge – you can traverse the shore at low tide. Two sisters stand somewhat forlornly off the coast: their other sister collapsed in a heap last decade, but a new sis is emerging from the eroding cliffs. Hanging out next to the sisters is **Elephant Rock** – you'll never guess what it looks like.

02 Paritutu

On the southwestern fringe of New Plymouth is the 156m-tall Paritutu – a craggy, steep-sided hill that's almost as tall as New Plymouth's old power-station chimney down at the port (198m). Paritutu translates as 'rising precipice'. 'Precipice' is right – it's a seriously knee-trembling, 15-minute scramble to the top, the upper reaches over bare rock with a chain to grip on to. If you can ignore your inner screams of common sense, you can see for miles around from the summit: out to the Sugar Loaf

Islands and down across the town to Mt Taranaki beyond.

THE DRIVE: Continue south on Centennial Dr with superb ocean views on your right. After 2.5km, Centennial Dr merges left into Beach Rd. At the end of Beach Rd, turn right onto SH45 and continue south towards Hāwera. Stop at Oākura, 12km from Paritutu.

03 Oākura

First stop on **Surf Highway 45** is laid-back little Oākura. For a town with not much more than a souvenir shop, petrol station and family medical centre, Oākura has a disproportionately high number of decent places to eat. **Oākura Beach** is a real beauty, but bring sandals – that black sand gets scorching hot! Drive about 4km down Weld Rd Lower to access its southern reaches, where the rusty, shipwrecked ribs of the SS **Gairlock** (wrecked 1903) arc upwards in the sand. From the shipwreck there are excellent views inland to the graceful profile of Mt Taranaki.

THE DRIVE: Backtrack to SH45, turn right and continue 23km south to Pungarehu. Turn right into Cape Rd towards the coast and the Cape Egmont Lighthouse, 32km from Oākura.

04 Cape Egmont Lighthouse

Poised on a gentle rise with superb coastal views, this photogenic, cast-iron **lighthouse** *(southtaranaki.com)* was prefabricated in London then moved here from Mana Island near Wellington in 1881. The Dutch explorer Abel Tasman sighted this cape in 1642 and called it 'Nieuw Zeeland'. You can't get inside the lighthouse, but it sure is a handsome devil. En route to the lighthouse is a distinctive rolling landscape of lahar mounds, caused by an explosive volcanic past. Some of these grassy hillocks show evidence of Māori fortifications from earlier centuries.

THE DRIVE: Return to SH45 along Cape Rd and turn right to continue south to Opunake, 25km from the lighthouse.

05 Opunake

A sleepy summer town and the surfing epicentre of the Taranaki region, Opunake has a sheltered family beach and plenty of challenging waves further out. If you feel like stretching your pins, the **Opunake Walkway** *(southtaranaki.com)* is a signposted 7km, three-hour ramble around the waterfront. In front of the town library is a **bronze statue** of legendary middle-distance runner and New Zealand's 'Sports Champion of the 20th Century' Peter Snell, born in Opunake in 1938. Snell won gold medals at the 1960 Rome and 1964 Tokyo Olympics.

THE DRIVE: Keep on trucking south on SH45 to Hāwera, a distance of 44km. It's the main town in South Taranaki.

06 Hāwera

South Taranaki's main agricultural service hub, Hāwera is a little low on urban virtues but has a few interesting sights. Don't miss **KD's Elvis Presley Museum** *(elvismuseum.co.nz)* – phone ahead to make an appointment – and the **Tawhiti Museum** *(tawhitimuseum.co.nz)*, which zeroes in on the traders, whalers and dairy farmers who developed the region.

Before you leave SH45 to travel inland to the north, bid farewell by admiring the 55m-tall **Hāwera Water Tower**. Although closed to the public, this historic tower built in 1914 is hard to miss and worthy of a gaze.

THE DRIVE: From Hāwera, drive north to Stratford on SH3. Look forward to brilliant clear-day vistas of Mt Taranaki on the left. Depart Stratford west on Celia St (which becomes Opunake Rd). Turn right into Manaia Rd and drive north to Dawson Falls on the slopes of Mt Taranaki, 52km from Hāwera.

07 Dawson Falls

Within Egmont National Park (the name of the mountain itself was changed back to Mt Taranaki from Mt Egmont in 1985), Dawson Falls is an excellent hiking base. Shorter options include the **Wilkies Pools Loop** (1¼ hours return) and the **Kapuni Loop Track** (one-hour loop), which runs to the impressive 18m **Dawson Falls** themselves. You can also see the falls from the visitor centre via a 10-minute walk to a viewpoint. More challenging is the hike to **Fanthams Peak** (five hours return), which is snowcapped during winter. Check in with the **Dawson Falls Visitor Centre** *(doc.govt.nz)* before you hit the trails.

THE DRIVE: Return 23km back to Stratford. After around 1km

Cape Egmont Lighthouse
HOT PIXELS PHOTOGRAPHY/SHUTTERSTOCK

heading north on SH3, turn right onto SH43 towards Taumarunui. The tiny forest hamlet of Whangamomona emerges after 62km. Note that there's no petrol along this route, so fill up in Stratford.

08 Whangamomona

Running 149km from Stratford northeast to Taumarunui, SH43 – aka the **Forgotten World Highway** – winds through hilly bush country, passing Māori *pā* (fortified villages) and abandoned coal mines en route. Excellent lookout spots include the **Whangamomona Saddle**, 6km before Whangamomona. This quirky village declared itself an independent republic in 1989 after disagreements with local councils, and the town celebrates **Republic Day** in January every odd-numbered year. Get your passport stamped at the grand old **Whangamomona Hotel** *(whangamomonahotel.co.nz)* as you're waiting for one of its big country meals. There's also simple accommodation with shared bathrooms and a separate self-contained cottage here.

THE DRIVE: From Whangamomona it is another 87km on winding and narrow roads to Taumarunui. Around 12km is unsealed gravel: take it slowly to avoid ending up in a ditch.

09 Taumarunui

On the edge of Taranaki and actually in the King Country region, Taumarunui is a good base for jetboating with **Forgotten World Jet** *(forgottenworldadventures.co.nz)* on the nearby Whanganui River, or mountain biking the 85km **Timber Trail** *(timbertrail.co.nz)* with **Epic Cycle Adventures** *(thetimbertrail.nz)*.

Forgotten World Highway (SH43)

ADWO/SHUTTERSTOCK

10

ROTORUA & THE CENTRAL NORTH ISLAND

TONGARIRO NATIONAL PARK LOOP

DURATION: 3-4 DAYS

DISTANCE: 311KM / 193 MILES

GREAT FOR: NATURE

BEST TIME TO GO: NOVEMBER TO APRIL FOR PRIME MOUNTAIN-BIKING WEATHER

★ BEST FOR

FAMILIES

Rafting on the Tongariro River near Tūrangi.

Rafting, Tūrangi

Tracing a circle around the volcanoes of the North Island's largest national park, this journey presents many energising opportunities to get active amid some of New Zealand's most inspiring landscapes. If mountain biking, rafting and hiking aren't on your agenda, trout fishing and boat trips around Lake Taupō offer more relaxing ways to be immersed in the spectacular scenery of the diverse Ruapehu region.

LINK YOUR TRIP

02 Thermal Discoverer
This journey through the North Island's geologically active heart also includes Taupō.

11 Waves & Caves to Whanganui
National Park Village is a stop on this island-spanning adventure.

01 Taupō

Sitting inside the caldera of one of the most violent volcanic eruptions on record, Taupō's existence should feel precarious and edgy. But when the lake wakes to a new day as flat as a windowpane, with the snowcapped peaks of Tongariro National Park rising from beyond its southern shores, it feels almost paradisiacal. The central **Taupō Museum** *(taupodc.govt.nz)* features an excellent Māori gallery and quirky displays, including a 1960s caravan set up as if the occupants have just popped down to the lake. The museum's centrepiece is an elaborately carved Māori meeting house, Te Aroha o Rongoheikume. A few steps away, boat operators run daily trips to the spectacular 10m-high **Māori Rock Carvings** etched into the cliffs of Mine Bay. They depict Ngatoro-i-rangi, the visionary Māori navigator who guided the Tuwharetoa and Te Arawa tribes

to the Taupō area a millennium ago. If you prefer to kayak there, seek out **Taupo Kayaking Adventures** (p37) in Acacia Bay.

THE DRIVE: Head out of Taupō north on SH5, turning onto SH1 just past the Wairakei Terraces. After 15km turn right onto Tutukau Rd and then left onto Orakei Korako Rd. The Orakei Korako thermal area is 5km ahead (36km from Taupō).

02 Orakei Korako

Strangely overshadowed by the likes of Wai-O-Tapu and Waimangu Volcanic Valley further north, Orakei Korako (p38) is a geothermal area par excellence. Colourful silica terraces step up a hillside above Lake Ohakuri, with adjoining **Ruatapu Cave** staking a claim as one of only two geothermal caves in the world. A 2.5km walking track (allow 1½ hours) follows stairs and boardwalks around the terraces. Entry includes a boat ride across the lake from the visitor centre and cafe.

THE DRIVE: Return to Taupō and continue south along the lake edge, past pretty Two Mile Bay, to rejoin SH1 by the airport. Enjoy the highway's wiggles and wriggles, with stunning lake views, to Tūrangi, 86km from Orakei Korako.

03 Tūrangi

Tūrangi is a fishing spot with a town thrown up around it. Once a service centre for the nearby hydroelectric power station, it backs onto the Tongariro River, one of the world's most famous trout fisheries. You can hire fishing gear and licences, and book a fishing guide locally, or simply view the legendary fish at the **Tongariro National Trout Centre** *(troutcentre.com)*, around 4km south of town. This centre has a hatchery, an underwater viewing chamber, a museum with polished educational displays, a collection of rods and reels dating as far back as the 1880s, and freshwater aquariums displaying river life. In summer, it operates a crèche for the endangered whio (blue duck), where ducklings are raised before being released. Tūrangi also offers superb white-water rafting. **Rafting New Zealand** *(raftingnewzealand.com)* runs a four-hour, Grade III trip through 60 rapids on the Tongariro River with an optional cliff jump, and a family-fun trip over more relaxed Grade II rapids.

THE DRIVE: Leave Tūrangi on SH41 before turning left onto SH47 and skirting the northern edge of Tongariro National Park, covered here in alpine tussocks. Turn left onto SH48 for the final push to Whakapapa Village, 48km from Tūrangi. In fine weather, there are views of the park's three volcanic peaks: Mts Ruapehu, Tongariro and Ngauruhoe. Enjoy the 'kiwi crossing' road signs!

04 Whakapapa Village

Located within the bounds of Tongariro National Park on the lower slopes of Mt Ruapehu, Whakapapa Village (pronounced 'fa-ka-pa-pa'; altitude 1140m) is the gateway to the national park. It's also home to the park **visitor centre** *(doc.govt.nz/tongarirovisitorcentre)* and one of the country's most evocative historic hotels (closed since

2023, but still a sight to behold), the Chateau Tongariro, built in the style of the original US national park hotels. During winter, the village is packed with skiers and snowboarders heading up to the slopes, but in summer hiking is the main attraction. The **Taranaki Falls Track** is a two-hour, 6km loop track from the village to the eponymous falls, which plunge 20m over an old lava flow into a boulder-fringed pool. If your legs still follow orders at this point, you can continue on to the **Tama Lakes**, a pair of bright and beautiful pools straddling a barren pass between Mts Ruapehu and Ngauruhoe (17km return). To go any higher, take the easy route, riding the new **Sky Waka** *(mtruapehu.com/sky-waka)* – NZ's longest gondola – to **Knoll Ridge Chalet** *(whakapapa.com/summer/knoll-ridge-chalet)* and the country's highest restaurants. The view is just as tasty as the food.

THE DRIVE: Return to SH47, where the volcanic views continue, with Mt Ruapehu filling the passenger-side windows as you head for National Park Village, 15km from Whakapapa.

05 National Park Village

The small sprawl of National Park Village lies at the junction of SH4 and SH47, 825m above sea level. In ski season the township is packed, and in summer the ski boots get replaced by boots. There's little to do in the village itself except watch the highway traffic pass (do check out the 3m-high driftwood kiwi sculpture out front of Schnapps, though), but it has great proximity to the national park's

TONGARIRO ALPINE CROSSING

You don't get to be routinely called the best day walk in New Zealand without being something pretty special. And the 19.4km **Tongariro Alpine Crossing** *(tongarirocrossing.org.nz)* is indeed that. This walk is like a mobile field guide to volcanoes, threading between Mt Tongariro and the conical perfection of Mt Ngauruhoe, passing neon-bright lakes that contrast with the black earth, while vents steam, hiss and fart in sulphurous clouds, and rocks spat from the volcanoes take on crazy shapes.

With big reputations come big crowds. In the early 1990s the Crossing would attract around 100,000 hikers. On the busiest days there can be more than 2000 people on the track. It's these sorts of numbers that have led to parking restrictions at the trailhead, making it all but compulsory to use the abundant shuttle services.

The crowds are the price of volcanic excellence, for the Alpine Crossing is truly something to behold. But don't let the big numbers fool you into thinking that it's a casual stroll. It's a long day – and fierce in bad weather – climbing 750m from its start to the top of Red Crater and then descending 700m to Ketetahi Rd. Be prepared for the fact that shuttle services typically don't run if the weather isn't cooperating.

Hiking, Tongariro Alpine Crossing

TOM JASTRAM/SHUTTERSTOCK

best hikes, including the Tongariro Alpine Crossing (p98), renowned as New Zealand's best day walk. Embark on this relatively challenging hike independently – regular shuttles run to the trailheads – or join a guided walk with **Adrift Tongariro** *(adriftnz.co.nz)* or **Adventure Outdoors** *(adventureoutdoors.co.nz)*. National Park Village is also a great hub for mountain biking on the nearby Fishers Track, 42 Traverse, Ōhakune Old Coach Road and multiday Mountains to Sea trail. Contact **Ski Biz** *(thealpinecentre.co.nz)* for bike rental and transport

THE DRIVE: Along the 36km on SH4 and SH49 to Ōhakune, verdant farmland and bush gradually takes over from more sparse alpine vegetation, especially around the Makatote River. The one constant is Mt Ruapehu – you've now swung around to its southern slopes. Stop at Horopito to see the quirky car graveyard known as 'Smash Palace'.

06 Ōhakune

Ōhakune is a true outdoors town. In winter it pumps with snow enthusiasts, who melt away into hikers and mountain bikers in summer. The vibe is best when snow drifts down on **Turoa Ski Area** *(whakapapa.com)* and people defrost together over a drink back in town. In summer, warmer adventures include the half-day Ōhakune Old Coach Road and exploring Whanganui River and the Great Walk that isn't really a walk – the Whanganui Journey canoe trip. Walking opportunities around Ōhakune include the 1½-hour (4km) **Waitonga Falls Walk** *(doc.govt.nz)*, which heads to Tongariro's highest waterfall (39m), and a remote one-hour stroll up to **Lake Rotokura**.

PHOTO OPPORTUNITY

The dazzling Emerald Lakes along the Tongariro Alpine Crossing (p98).

THE DRIVE: Stellar views of Mt Ruapehu and bucolic dairy farms feature on the 27km drive east on SH49 to Waiouru. About 9km before Waiouru sits

Emerald Lakes, Tongariro Alpine Crossing (p98)

DMITRY PICHUGIN/SHUTTERSTOCK

the memorial to the Tangiwai rail disaster. On Christmas Eve 1953, 151 people were killed here when an Auckland-bound train plunged into the river minutes after the rail bridge was swept away by volcanic mudflow when the rim of Mt Ruapehu's Crater Lake ruptured.

07 Waiouru

Waiouru (altitude 792m) is primarily an army base and a refuelling stop for SH1 motorists. Its main street is lined with greasy-spoon eateries and petrol stations, but housed in an almost-Stalinist concrete bunker at the south end of town is the **National Army Museum** *(armymuseum.co.nz)*. Proclaimed as 'history without the boring bits', it's actually a serious and fascinating journey through NZ's military history, including the New Zealand Wars. It houses an impressive collection of artillery, tanks, landing craft, uniforms and memorabilia in moving displays.

THE DRIVE: Back on SH1, it's 63km north through the moonlike landscape of the Desert Rd back to Tūrangi. The sparse landscape is the result of the massive Taupō eruption of 180 CE that coated the land with thick deposits of pumice and destroyed all vegetation.

BRIDGET_NZ/SHUTTERSTOCK

Ōhakune Old Coach Road

MOUNTAIN BIKING THE OLD COACH ROAD

The **Ōhakune Old Coach Road** *(doc.govt.nz/parks-and-recreation)* is a fantastic adventure for moderately fit cyclists. The walking and cycling track follows the original 15km coach track from Ōhakune to Horopito that was in use from 1886 until 1909, when SH49 opened. Largely forgotten and overgrown, the Old Coach Road was resurrected by locals and restored to glory.

One of NZ's most enjoyable half-day rides (three to four hours), the gently graded route passes unique engineering features, including the historic Hapuawhenua and Toanui viaducts, the only two remaining curved viaducts in the southern hemisphere. It also passes through ancient forests of giant rimu and totara that survived the Taupō blast of 180 CE as they were in the lee of Mt Ruapehu.

Starting at Horopito is recommended, with the trail descending around 150m to Ōhakune. A few uphill pushes are required, but sweeping downhill runs on historic cobblestones make it all worthwhile.

In Ōhakune, **Mountain Bike Station** *(mountainbikestation.co.nz)* has rental-and-shuttle packages, while **My Kiwi Adventure** *(info@mykiwiadventure.co.nz)* in National Park Village can also get you on the trail.

11

★ BEST FOR

WATER SPORTS

Paddle boarding on Lake Otamangakau in Tongariro National Park.

ROTORUA & THE CENTRAL NORTH ISLAND

WAVES & CAVES TO WHANGANUI

DURATION: 5 DAYS

DISTANCE: 560KM / 348 MILES

GREAT FOR: NATURE

BEST TIME TO GO: NOVEMBER TO APRIL FOR A SPRING OR SUMMER TONGARIRO ALPINE CROSSING

Waitomo Caves (p106)

On this journey traversing the western side of the North Island, the urban attractions of Auckland and Hamilton give way to a rugged surf-fringed coastline, viewing New Zealand's national bird at Ōtorohanga, and experiencing the flickering glowworms at Waitomo. Further south there's spectacle and adventure amid the Tongariro and Whanganui National Parks, before reaching the historic and arty riverside city of Whanganui.

LINK YOUR TRIP

10 Tongariro National Park Loop
Around National Park Village, explore the North Island's biggest national park in detail.

02 Thermal Discoverer
Combine Hobbiton and Rotorua's geothermal activity on this trip, which also incorporates Hamilton.

01 Auckland

Before heading south, explore the historical side of NZ's biggest and most cosmopolitan city. In the **Auckland Museum** *(aucklandmuseum.com)*, the displays of Pacific Island and Māori artefacts on the ground floor are essential viewing. Highlights include a 25m war canoe and an extant carved meeting house (remove your shoes before entering). Dominating the Auckland Domain, the museum is housed in an imposing neoclassical temple (1929), capped with an impressive copper-and-glass dome (2007). The grand building is a prominent part of the Auckland skyline, especially when viewed from the harbour. Admission packages can be purchased incorporating a highlights tour and a Māori cultural performance. Or take a stroll along the harbour.

ROMANSLAVIK.COM/SHUTTERSTOCK

THE DRIVE: Leave Auckland on the Southern Motorway and continue south on SH1 to Ngāruawāhia. Turn right on SH39 to Whatawhata before turning right on SH23 and continuing to Raglan. Look out for the 28 wind turbines of the Te Uku Wind Farm on the hills above Raglan, 161km from Auckland.

02 Raglan

Laid-back Raglan may well be NZ's perfect surfing town. It's small enough to have escaped mass development, but big enough to have great restaurants and a couple of pubs that attract big-name bands in summer. Along with famous surf spots to the south, the harbour just begs to be explored. **Raglan Kayak & Paddleboard** *(raglankayak.co.nz)* offer paddle-boarding and kayaking tours. There's also an excellent arts scene – check out **Jet Collective** *(facebook.com/jetcollective)* for local crafts and **Toi Hauāuru Studio** *(toihauauru.com)* for contemporary Māori design – and at the Raglan Wharf, **Soul Shoes** *(soulshoes.co.nz)* and **Tony Sly Pottery** *(tonyslypottery.com)* both offer unique styles handmade in Raglan.

THE DRIVE: Leave Raglan on Wainui Rd and after 4km turn right into Ngarunui Rd down to the car park above the beach.

03 Ngarunui Beach

Welcome to the wild west of NZ's North Island, a rugged series of black-sand surf beaches stretching all the way down the coast to Taranaki. Ngarunui's broad expanse is packed during summer – it is the area's best ocean beach for swimming – and is protected by lifeguards from October to April. Around 2.5km south of Ngarunui Beach, **Manu Bay** is a legendary surf spot said to have the longest left-hand break in the world. The elongated uniform waves are created by the angle at which the Tasman Sea swell meets the coastline. The Manu Bay car park is a great spot to watch local surfers taking on the waves. Accessed by Calvert Rd, **Whale Bay** is another world-renowned surf spot around 1km west of Manu Bay.

THE DRIVE: Return from Whale Bay to Raglan (8km), leave Raglan on SH23 and continue a further 46km to Hamilton.

04 Hamilton

Hamilton is the Waikato region's biggest city, and university students contribute a dynamism to the more conservative vibe of the surrounding agricultural hinterland. Vibrant restaurants, cafes and bars punctuate Hood and Victoria Sts, and southeast of the city centre, the glorious **Hamilton Gardens** *(hamiltongardens.co.nz)* incorporate Italian Renaissance, Chinese, Japanese, English, American and Indian gardens complete with colonnade and pagodas. There's also a garden inspired by a short story by NZ author Katherine Mansfield. It's a wonderful area to have a picnic or stretch your legs. Look for the impressive Nga Uri O Hinetuparimaunga (Earth Blanket) Māori sculpture at the main gates.

THE DRIVE: Depart central Hamilton south via Anglesea St and Cobham Dr, and turn right after 2km into SH3. Continue on SH3 south to Te Awamutu, 30km from Hamilton.

05 Te Awamutu

Deep into dairy-farming country, Te Awamutu (which means 'the river cut short'; the Waikato beyond this point was unsuitable for large canoes) is a pleasant rural service centre. With a blossom tree-lined main street and good cafes, TA (aka Rose Town) is an appealing stop. The town's **Rose Garden** has around 2500 colourful bushes, and from November to May there's always a blooming good display. The **Te Awamutu Museum** *(tamuseum.org.nz)* showcases a superb collection of Māori *taonga* (treasures) - the highlight is the revered **Te Uenuku** (The Rainbow), an ancient Māori carving estimated to be up to 600 years old. The museum also features an interesting display on the Waikato War between Māori and British colonial forces in the 1860s.

THE DRIVE: From Te Awamutu to Ōtorohanga on SH3, it's a pleasant 30km journey through bucolic farmland dotted with black-and-white Friesian cows. Yes, it does look like a Far Side cartoon waiting to happen.

DETOUR

Sanctuary Mountain Maungatautari
Start: 05 Te Awamutu

Can a landlocked volcano become an island paradise? Inspired by the success of pest eradication and native species reintroduction in the Hauraki Gulf, a community trust has erected 47km of pest-proof fencing around the triple peaks of Maungatautari (797m) to create the impressive **Sanctuary Mountain Maungatautari** *(sanctuarymountain.co.nz)*. This atoll of rainforest dominates the skyline between Te Awamutu and Karapiro and is now home to its first kiwi chicks in 100 years. There is also a 'tuatarium', where NZ's iconic reptile the tuatara can be seen.

The main entrance is at the visitor centre at the sanctuary's southern side, 30km east of Te Awamutu and reached by SH3 and Arapuni Rd. There is a handy map on the sanctuary's website. Guided tours leaving from the visitor centre from Tuesday to Sunday include an afternoon wetlands tour, and morning and afternoon departures exploring the bird and insect life of the sanctuary's Southern Enclosure. Online or phone bookings for guided tours must be made at least 24 hours in advance. Guided night walks are also available.

06 Ōtorohanga

Before heading underground at the nearby Waitomo Caves, visit the **Otorohanga Kiwi House & Native Bird Park** *(kiwihouse.org.nz)* to see NZ's national

SECRET LIFE OF A GLOWWORM

Glowworms are the larvae of the fungus gnat. The larva glowworm has luminescent organs that produce a soft, greenish light. Living in a sort of hammock suspended from an overhang, it weaves sticky threads that trail down and catch unwary insects attracted by its light. When an insect flies towards the light it gets stuck in the threads – the glowworm just has to reel it in for a feed.

The larval stage lasts from six to nine months, depending on how much food the glowworm gets. When it has grown to about the size of a matchstick, it goes into a pupa stage, much like a cocoon. The adult fungus gnat emerges about two weeks later. The adult insect doesn't live very long because it doesn't have a mouth. It emerges, mates, lays eggs and dies, all within about two or three days. The sticky eggs, laid in groups of 40 or 50, hatch in about three weeks to become larval glowworms. Glowworms thrive in moist, dark caves but they can survive anywhere if they have the requisites of moisture, an overhang to suspend from and insects to eat. Waitomo is famous for its glowworms but you can see them in other places around NZ, in caves and outdoors. When you come upon glowworms, don't touch their hammocks or hanging threads, try not to make loud noises and don't shine a light right on them. All of these things will cause them to dim their lights. It takes them a few hours to become bright again.

Tuatara, Sanctuary Mountain Maungatautari
EL PACO 33/SHUTTERSTOCK

bird, the kiwi, scurrying around a nocturnal enclosure searching for food with its long beak. This is one of the only places where you can see a great spotted kiwi, the biggest of the three kiwi species. The bird park is at the northern end of town. In Ōtorohanga's main street, the **Ed Hillary Walkway** – named after the NZ mountaineer who was one of the first two people to conquer Mt Everest, in 1953 – presents cherished icons of Kiwiana including sheep, jandals, the All Blacks and NZ's beloved pavlova dessert.

THE DRIVE: Depart Ōtorohanga south on SH3 for 8km and turn right at the large roundabout into Waitomo Caves Rd (SH37). From the intersection it is around 7.5km to the centre of Waitomo Caves village.

07 Waitomo Caves

The labyrinth of limestone caves, caverns and underground rivers under the Waitomo region is one of the North Island's top attractions, and experiencing the subterranean wonders can either be gentle and reflective, or crammed with action and adventure. The name Waitomo comes from *wai* (water) and *tomo* (hole or shaft): dotted across this region are numerous shafts dropping into underground cave systems and streams. Bookings to visit the big-three Waitomo Caves – Glowworm, Ruakuri and Aranui – can be made online or at the **Waitomo Caves Visitor Centre** (*waitomo.com*). For cave tours, try to avoid the large tour groups, most of which arrive between 10.30am and 2.30pm. Other Waitomo operators provide more thrilling ways to experience the underworld including abseiling, climbing and negotiating underground rivers on inflatable inner tubes.

PHOTO OPPORTUNITY

Emerging back into the daylight after a Waitomo Caves adventure.

THE DRIVE: Return to the intersection of SH37 and SH3. Turn right and head south on SH3 to Eight Mile Junction, then turn left onto SH4 to Taumarunui, 100km from Waitomo Caves.

Kiwis, Otorohanga Kiwi House & Native Bird Park (p104)

HOLGER LEUE/GETTY IMAGES

08 Taumarunui

Once a bustling stop on the main trunk railway line from Auckland to Wellington, Taumarunui is now a sleepy combination of provincial service town and base for exciting outdoor adventures. Go jetboating with Forgotten World Jet (p94) on the nearby Whanganui River, or tackle the 85km Timber Trail on a mountain bike with Epic Cycle Adventures (p94). Also based in Taumarunui, **Forgotten World Adventures** *(forgottenworldadventures.co.nz)* runs trips on converted golf carts along an abandoned railway line to the tiny hamlet of Whangamomona in the Taranaki region. The most spectacular trip takes in 20 tunnels. Overnight stays in the heritage Whangamomona Hotel (p94) are also available.

THE DRIVE: From Taumarunui, continue south on SH4 for 43km to National Park Village. The vegetation becomes alpine scrub and Tongariro's mountains rise above the near horizon.

09 National Park Village

On the western fringe of Mt Ruapehu in Tongariro National Park, this tiny settlement is packed with skiers and snowboarders in winter, and hikers undertaking the Tongariro Alpine Crossing (p98) in summer. Combining a kaleidoscope of volcanic colours, steaming hot springs, hissing fumaroles and crazy rock formations, this 19.4km hike is almost universally regarded as the finest day walk in NZ, and can be tackled independently (if you're properly equipped) or with local

CHARLENE MANET/SHUTTERSTOCK

Glowworms, Waitomo Caves

GOING UNDERGROUND

Waitomo excels with a range of exciting, challenging and unique ways to explore the area's subterranean wonders. Note that most operators offer a discount for prebooking online, and during summer this strategy is also recommended to avoid disappointment.

Legendary Black Water Rafting Company *(waitomo.com)* Don a wetsuit and float down an underground river in an inner tube. Other options incorporate a flying fox and negotiating high wires.

CaveWorld *(caveworld.co.nz)* Black-water rafting on inner tubes through glowworm-filled Te Anaroa. The Footwhistle Glowworm Cave Tour incorporates a forest stop for a mug of restorative kawakawa bush tea.

Waitomo Adventures *(waitomo.co.nz)* A variety of intrepid excursions incorporating rock climbing, abseiling, swimming, caving and a subterranean flying fox.

Spellbound *(glowworm.co.nz)* Small-group tours access the heavily glowworm-dappled Mangawhitiakau cave system in a raft. Still an exciting experience, and you get to stay dry.

operators Adrift Tongariro (p100) or Adventure Outdoors (p100). For something more serene, check out nearby Lake Otamangakau for a (very cold) dip or renowned trout fishing.

THE DRIVE: Continuing south on SH4 via Raetihi (35km) before travelling a further 87km to Whanganui is the recommended route.

DETOUR

Whanganui River Road

Start: 01 Detour Starting Point

The direct route on SH4 south from National Park Village to Whanganui is definitely no slouch visually, but this alternative route following the Whanganui River to the coast is a real stunner. It's a winding route on narrow but sealed roads that is around one hour longer than the 70 minutes it takes on SH4.

Instead of continuing on SH4 south of Raetihi, turn west to travel 27km to tiny **Pipiriki**, a sleepy river town that was once a humming holiday hotspot serviced by river steamers and paddle boats.

South on the Whanganui River Rd, the graceful spire of **St Joseph's Church** *(compassion.org.nz)* stands tall on a spur of land above a deep river bend near Hiruhārama (aka Jerusalem), around 15km south of Pipiriki. A French Catholic mission led by Suzanne Aubert established the Daughters of Our Lady of Compassion here in 1892, and esteemed NZ poet James K Baxter (1926–72) founded a commune here in the late 1960s. He's buried in Hiruhārama.

Moutoa Island, the site of a historic 1864 battle, is just downriver, followed by the remote Māori villages of Ranana, Matahiwi, Koriniti and Atene as you continue south. Near Matahiwi, the 1854 **Kawana Flour Mill** *(nzhistory.govt.nz/media/photo/kawana-flourmill)* is a curious remnant from days when the river was a trade route. There are several Māori marae (meeting houses) hereabouts – you can look around **Koriniti Marae** *(wrmtb.co.nz)* if there's not a function happening. At Atene, about 22km north of the junction with SH4, the Atene Viewpoint Walk is a one-hour ascent offering great views of the Whanganui National Park. The Whanganui River Rd rejoins SH4 just north of Upokongaro and continues 15km south to Whanganui.

10 Whanganui

With rafts of riverside charm, this historic town lies on the banks of the wide brown Whanganui River. Despite the occasional flood (the city centre has at times been subaquatic) the old town has been rejuvenated, the local arts community is thriving and former port buildings are being turned into glass-art studios. At **New Zealand Glassworks** *(nzglassworks.com)* visitors can watch glass-blowers in action, check out the gallery, or take a one-hour 'Make a Paperweight' lesson. Across City Bridge from downtown Whanganui, the **Durie Hill Elevator** *(visitwhanganui.nz/durie-hill-underground-elevator)* was built with grand visions for the city's residential future. A tunnel burrows 213m into the hillside, from where an elevator rattles to the top. You can then climb the 176 steps of the **War Memorial Tower** and scan the horizon for Mt Taranaki and Mt Ruapehu.

Whanganui River
PK289/SHUTTERSTOCK

STAY AWHILE

RAGLAN

BY ASHLYN OSWALT

The road to Raglan offers glimpses of surf over the hills and an ever-sunny horizon. As a budding surfer, I was drawn to Raglan's reputation for great surfing, making it a must-visit. My own amateur skills led me to the beginner-friendly **Ngarunui Beach**, home of **Raglan Surf School** *(raglansurfschool.co.nz)*, for board rentals and beginner group lessons.

To watch the pros (or if you're a pro yourself), head to nearby **Manu Bay**. World-renowned, the bay was featured in the classic 1966 surf movie *The Endless Summer* and hosts international surfing competitions each year. Its rough terrain makes this a spot for intermediate or expert surfers only. Further beyond, **Whale Bay** is another great spot to watch surfers glide on the water.

After my surf, I grab a coffee at Raglan Roast (raglanroast.co.nz) and stroll the town's artsy shops, finding a vintage piece (or five) at **ULO's Vintage** *(instagram.com/ulosvintage)*. Adding another piece of **Tony Sly Pottery** *(tonyslypottery.com)* to my collection is non-negotiable.

If I'm keen to explore out of town, I'll drive to **Waireinga/Bridal Veil Falls** *(doc.govt.nz)*, an impressive 55m waterfall with a 20-minute walk to the base of the falls. The falls are only a 20-minute drive away, but if you prefer to stay close to Raglan, take a guided kayak tour around Raglan's Pancake Rocks with **Raglan Kayak** *(raglankayak.co.nz)*.

The town's vibrant atmosphere comes alive at night, especially at **ULO's Kitchen** *(instagram.com/uloskitchen)*. This Japanese spot serves great cocktails and ramen, often to the tune of a live DJ.

LINK YOUR TRIP

Raglan is a great coastal detour on the **11 Waves & Caves to Whanganui** road trip.

Left: Ngarunui Beach
Right: Surfer, Manu Bay

LEFT: JORDAN TAN/SHUTTERSTOCK; RIGHT: RODCOFFEE/SHUTTERSTOCK

PLACES TO STAY

- **Barralled Wines**
  Staying at a winery of the same name, you'll look out onto the vines and beyond to the waves. Choose between a self-contained guesthouse with a hot tub or a self-contained studio with a sauna. *(barrelledwinesraglan.co.nz)*

- **Raglan Backpackers**
  A social hostel with private and shared rooms, located right in town. Surf lessons and board hire are also available. *(raglanbackpackers.co.nz)*

- **Te Whaanga Retreat & Spa**
  Luxury spa and lodge in an intimate setting. Grounds include a pool, deck overlooking the surf, and firepit for cosy evenings. There's also a full-service restaurant on-site. *(tewhaangaretreat.com)*

Bay of Plenty
Cape Runaway
Hicks Bay
Waihau Bay
Te Araroa
East Cape
Te Kaha
Mt Hikurangi
Raukumara Forest Park
Ruatoria
Tokomaru Bay
Tolaga Bay
Gisborne
Ōpōtiki
Ōhope
Whakatāne
Matatā
Te Puke
Mt Maunganui
Tauranga
Kaimai Mamaku Forest Park
Rotoehu Forest
Lake Rotoiti
Rotorua
Tarawera Forest
Te Urewera
Maungapohatu
Te Whaiti
Minginui
Whirinaki Te Pua-a-Tāne Conservation Park
Matawai
Huntly
Hamilton
Raglan
Matamata
Kāwhia
Putāruru
Waitomo Caves
Ōtorohanga
Te Kuiti
Whareorino Forest
Aratoro
Whakamaru
Mangatupoto
Pureora Forest Park
Taupō
Lake Taupō
Ohura
Taumarunui
Tūrangi
Kaimanawa Forest Park
Mt Tongariro
Whakapapa Village
Whanganui National Park
Tongariro National Park
Kaweka Forest Park
Kuripapango
Ōhakune
Tarere State Forest
Whanganui River
Otamauri
Fraserstown
Wairoa
Nuhaka
Putorino
Hawke Bay
Mahia Peninsula
Napier
Cape Kidnappers/ Te Kauwae-a-Māui
Hastings
Havelock North
Waimarama
Ruahine Forest Park
Waipawa
Waipukurau
Whanganui
Hunterville
Dannevirke
Sanson
Palmerston North
Woodville
Levin
Eketahuna
Kāpiti Island
Mitre
Tararua Forest Park
Masterton
Castlepoint
Tauweru
Upper Hutt
Porirua
Petone
Martinborough
WELLINGTON
Palliser Bay
Ngawi
Cape Palliser
SOUTH PACIFIC OCEAN
12
13
1
2
3
5
30
35
38
50
0
50 km
0
25 miles

Mahia Peninsula (p128)

WELLINGTON & THE EAST COAST

12 North Island Southern Loop

Circle from Wellington up the Kāpiti Coast and back through the Manawatū and Wairarapa regions, with key detours along the way. **p116**

13 Pacific Coast Explorer

Trace the North Island's eastern extremities along the Bay of Plenty, around the East Cape and through Gisborne to Hawke's Bay. **p124**

EXPLORE

WELLINGTON & THE EAST COAST

Arrayed around a harbour and hemmed in by craggy hills, Wellington's compact centre offers more big-city buzz than you'd expect for a population of around 212,000. The Wellington Region stretches north to include the long, sandy beaches of the Kāpiti Coast, and east over the ranges to the rural Wairarapa District. The wild Wairarapa coastline stands in stark contrast to the sunny surf beaches of the Bay of Plenty and Gisborne, and the genteel vineyards, orchards and art-deco architecture of Hawke's Bay. Between the two, the Manawatū is a farming district punctuated by the student-filled city of Palmerston North.

Wellington

Wellington sits on a hook-shaped harbour ringed with ranges that wear a snowy cloak in winter. Being the capital, it's well endowed with museums, galleries and arts organisations, and it turns on the charm with a sophisticated dining and raffish drinking scene. Wellingtonians are rightly proud of their coffee and craft-beer culture, but the city is infamous for two things: its frequent tremors and the umbrella-shredding gales that regularly barrel through.

The city offers a full range of accommodation options, including the complete set of pricey hotels, with plenty of choice close to the centre. The inner city is studded with restaurants, cafes and bars, with high concentrations around raucous Courtenay Pl, bohemian Cuba St and along the waterfront. A particular hot spot is Hannah's Laneway, a converted factory near Cuba St, where you'll find Leeds Street Bakery, Garage Project Leeds Street (craft beer), Pizza Pomodoro, Goldings Free Dive (more craft beer) and Hanging Ditch (cocktails). The most convenient place to stock up on supplies is the big New World supermarket on Cable St.

Napier

New Zealand's art-deco city spreads along a pebbly coastline at the centre of Hawke's Bay. Accommodation includes hostels, B&Bs, motels and

WHEN TO GO

Summer is the peak time along the East Coast, with accommodation in short supply during Gisborne's Rhythm & Vines music festival. The busiest time to visit Napier is during February's Art Deco Festival, when accommodation needs to be booked well in advance. Wellington is worth a trip any time of the year.

hotels, the best of which inhabit elegant 1930s buildings. Within a few blocks of Emmerson St, the main drag, you'll find all the shops you'll need, including a large Countdown supermarket. Culinary highlights include Mister D (breakfast, lunch, and dinner on weekends) and top-end Bistronomy, serving Modern NZ cuisine (dinner and weekend lunches).

Gisborne

The sunny, surfy city of Gisborne is a great place to put your feet up for a few days and sit on a deckchair sipping local chardonnay. It has a similar array of accommodation as Napier, and some excellent cafes and bistros. Highlights include Crawford Road Kitchen, Muirs Bookshop Cafe and Neighbourhood Pizzeria.

Tauranga

Incorporating Mt Maunganui, Papamoa Beach and Tauranga proper, the city of Tauranga is NZ's fifth-largest metropolis and growing fast. If you're stocking up on supplies, you'll find most of the shops in Tauranga's centre. However, beachy Mt Maunganui is a nicer place to stay, with plenty of motels and holiday parks, and an appealing strip of cafes, bars and surf shops. On the Tauranga side, the best places to eat are Grindz Cafe and Macau. At the Mount, try Eightyeight, Eddies & Elspeth and Three One One Six.

TRANSPORT

Wellington is a major transport hub, with an international airport, ferries departing for the South Island, a train service to Auckland (stopping along the Kāpiti Coast and in Palmerston North) and buses to all major towns and cities. There are also domestic airports in Kāpiti Coast (Paraparaumu), Palmerston North, Hawke's Bay (Napier), Gisborne, Whakatāne and Tauranga.

RESOURCES

- **wellingtonnz.com**
  The capital's i-SITE Visitor Information Centre can be found in the Michael Fowler Centre on Wakefield St.
- **napiernz.com**
  Napier's i-SITE is next to the Soundshell on Marine Pde.
- **tairawhitigisborne.co.nz**
  Gisborne i-SITE is on Grey St, at the edge of Alfred Cox Park.

WHAT'S ON

- **Art Deco Festival**
  Napier returns to the 1930s in the third weekend in February.
- **Aotearoa New Zealand Festival of the Arts**
  Month-long festival in Wellington from late February in even-numbered years.
- **World of WeearableArt**
  Spectacular creations take to the stage over three weeks from mid-September in Wellington.
- **Rhythm & Vines**
  Around 30,000 young Kiwis see in the New Year at this three-day music festival in Gisborne.

WHERE TO STAY

Wellington has the region's best hostels (such as Marion and Worldwide Backpackers) and hotels (especially QT, Ohtel and Intrepid), and atmospheric self-contained units at City Cottages. Campgrounds are spread along the coasts; good options include Wellington Top 10 Holiday Park, Cosy Corner Holiday Park in Mt Maunganui and Ohiwa Beach Holiday Park near Ōpotiki. Good motels are also plentiful, such as Asure Harbour View in Tauranga, Mission Belle Motel in Mt Maunganui, AhiKaa in Gisborne and Greyfriars in Greytown. For a luxurious stay in Hawke's Bay, try Kiwiesque near Napier or Millar Road near Havelock North.

12

WELLINGTON & THE EAST COAST

NORTH ISLAND SOUTHERN LOOP

★ BEST FOR

WINE BUFFS

Taste testing some world-renowned pinot noir around Martinborough.

Vineyard in winter, Martinborough (p121)

DURATION: 3-4 DAYS

DISTANCE: 523KM / 325 MILES

GREAT FOR: FOOD AND DRINK, NATURE

BEST TIME TO GO: EXPECT MORE BLUE SKIES BETWEEN NOVEMBER AND APRIL

This rambling sojourn covers the agricultural and wine-making heartland north of Wellington. The island sanctuary of Kāpiti offers excellent walking and birdlife, while a visit to studenty city Palmerston North goes some of the way towards explaining NZ's fascination with rugby. In nearby Masterton you can meet some of NZ's unique wildlife – including the beloved kiwi – with East Coast diversions to remote rockscapes and lighthouses.

LINK YOUR TRIP

11 Waves & Caves to Whanganui
From Palmerston North it's a short hop to the river city of Whanganui, at the end of this adventurous North Island tour.

14 Sunshine & Wine
Catch the interisland ferry to Picton, the starting point for this luscious loop around the top of the South Island.

01 Wellington

Wellington is NZ's constitutional and cultural capital, its compact CBD thrumming with museums, theatres, galleries and boutiques. Tasty diversions include great cafes and restaurants, plus an excellent **craft-beer scene** *(craftbeercapital.com)*. With a spectacular harbourside location, **Te Papa** *(tepapa.govt.nz)* is NZ's national museum, crammed with interactive, fun and informative displays telling the nation's story. Introductory and Māori Highlights tours depart from the information desk on level two; book ahead. Film buffs will dig the **Wētā Workshop** *(wetaworkshop.com)*, a mind-blowing mini-museum of the Academy Award–winning

NASKA RASPOPINA/SHUTTERSTOCK

special-effects company that brought *The Lord of the Rings, King Kong* and *The Hobbit* to life. It's 9km from town in Miramar.

THE DRIVE: Track north to Paraparaumu Beach (53km) on SH1 with west-coast views of Kāpiti Island on the near horizon.

02 Kāpiti Island

Paraparaumu Beach is the departure point for ferries to Kāpiti Island, a 10km by 2km predator-free sanctuary that's home to bird species now rare or extinct on the mainland. The island is open to limited numbers of day walkers at Rangatira – where you can hike up to the 521m high point, **Tuteremoana** – and at the island's northern end, which has gentle walks to viewpoints and around a lagoon. To visit the island, book in advance with a licensed operator. Reconfirm arrangements on the morning of departure, as sailings are weather dependent. Contact **Kāpiti Island Nature Tours** *(kapitiislandnaturetours.com).*

THE DRIVE: From Paraparaumu Beach to Waikanae is around 12km along busy SH1 (Kāpiti Expressway).

03 Waikanae

Around 60km north of Wellington, Waikanae is a seaside suburban enclave, good for some salt-tinged R&R and natural-realm experiences. The **Ngā Manu Nature Reserve** *(ngamanu.co.nz)* is a 15-hectare bird sanctuary dotted with picnic areas, bush walks, aviaries and a nocturnal house with kiwi, owls and tuatara. The reserve's endangered long-fin eels get a feed at 2pm daily; guided bird-feeding tours run at 11am daily.

THE DRIVE: From Waikanae, follow SH1 north through dairy-farming country to Sanson. The west-coast beaches of Foxton (14km return) and Himatangi (16km return) are broad and shallow. At Sanson, turn east on SH3 to Palmerston North, 108km from Waikanae.

04 Palmerston North

On the banks of the Manawatū River, rurally bookish Palmerston North lies at the heart of the prosperous Manawatu region. Massey University, NZ's largest, informs the town's cultural and social structures. Find out all about NZ's national game at the **New Zealand Rugby Museum** *(rugbymuseum.co.nz),* an amazing space overflowing with rugby paraphernalia and history. New Zealand won back-to-back Rugby World Cups in 2011 and 2015, but bombed out in 2019. Ask the staff about the All Blacks performance at the 2023 World Cup. Adjacent **Te Manawa** *(temanawa.co.nz)* merges a museum and art gallery into one experience, with vast collections joining the dots between art, science and history. The city's heart and soul is **The Square** *(pncc.govt.nz),* with 6.5 spacious hectares featuring a clock tower, Māori carvings and sculptures. A little further out, the spectacular **He Ara Kotahi Bridge** *(pncc.govt.nz)* links 9km of lush walkways between the city and Massey.

THE DRIVE: Exit Palmerston North south on Fitzherbert Ave, veer left onto SH57 then right onto Pahiatua Aokautere Rd, 8km from central Palmy. After 30 wiggly kilometres you'll hit SH2: turn right and drive 54km to Masterton (92km from Palmerston North) past fields dotted with sheep.

05 Masterton

The hub of the agriculturally rich Wairarapa region, Masterton is home to the **Wool Shed** *(thewoolshednz.com)*, a great little museum dedicated to NZ's sheep-shearing and wool-production industries. It's a good spot to pick up a home-knitted hat. About 30km north of Masterton, the 1000-hectare **Pūkaha National Wildlife Centre** *(pukaha.org.nz)* is one of NZ's most successful wildlife breeding centres. The scenic two-hour Te Arapiki o Tawhiki loop walk gives a good overview; there's also a kiwi house here, featuring Manukura the white kiwi. Guided walks kick off at 10am and 2pm daily; book in advance.

THE DRIVE: From Masterton east to Castlepoint is 68km through increasingly remote farming country. Give yourself an hour each way – it's definitely worth it.

06 Castlepoint

On a remote reach of coast, Castlepoint is a truly awesome, end-of-the-world place, with a reef, the lofty 162m-high **Castle Rock**, some safe swimming beaches and walking tracks. There's an easy (but sometimes ludicrously windy) 30-minute return walk that goes across the reef to the **lighthouse**, where 70-plus shell species are fossilised in the cliffs. A one-hour return walk runs to a huge limestone cave (take a torch), or take the 1½-hour return track from **Deliverance Cove** to Castle Rock. It's a bit of a no-brainer, but keep away from the lower reef when there are heavy seas (fairly often!).

THE DRIVE: Returning 68km to Masterton from Castlepoint, it's a further 42km journey on SH2 to Martinborough via Carterton and historic Greytown, with its boutique sleeps, restaurants and high-street pubs. In Greytown, turn left off SH2 onto Bidwills Cutting Rd, and continue to Martinborough.

Castlepoint Lighthouse

SALOMENAEF/SHUTTERSTOCK

PHOTO OPPORTUNITY

A wild and windswept selfie at Castlepoint Lighthouse.

07 Martinborough

Laid out in the shape of a Union Jack with a leafy square at its heart, Martinborough (Wharekaka) is a photogenic town with endearing old buildings. It's famed for its wineries, which lure visitors to swill some pinot noir, pair it with fine food, and then snooze it off at boutique accommodation. An excellent spot to buy local wine and taste a few is **Martinborough Wine Merchants** *(martinboroughwinemerchants.com)*. It also runs **walking tours** *(martinboroughwinewalks.com)* and rents out bikes for cellar-door adventures, or you can join a tour with **Green Jersey Cycle Tours** *(greenjersey.co.nz)*. Pick up the **Wairarapa Visitor Guide** from the local **i-SITE** *(wairarapanz.com)* for vineyard info. **Ata Rangi** *(atarangi.co.nz)*, **Coney Wines** *(coneywines.co.nz)* and **Martinborough Vineyard** *(martinborough-vineyard.co.nz)* are just a few of our favourites.

THE DRIVE: Head for Featherston northwest on SH53, then pick up SH2 to travel across the hilly Remutaka Range back to Wellington, 80km from Martinborough.

DETOUR

Cape Palliser

Start: 07 Martinborough

From Martinborough, the road winds through picturesque farmland before hitting the coast along Cape Palliser Rd. Impossibly scenic, this route hugs the coast between wild ocean and black-sand beaches on one side and sheer cliffs on the other. The shadows of the South Island are sometimes visible on a clear day.

Further south in the wind-worn fishing village of **Ngawi**, rusty beach-bound bulldozers are used to drag fishing boats ashore. Next stop is a malodorous seal colony, the North Island's largest breeding area for these fellas. Hot tip: don't get between the territorial seals and their escape route to the sea.

Just beyond stands the candy-striped **Cape Palliser Lighthouse** *(wairarapanz.com/cape-palliser)*. Get a few puffs into your lungs on the 250-step climb to its base – a great place to linger if the wind isn't blowing your eyeballs into the back of your head.

On the way there or back, take a short detour to the crusty waterside settlement of **Lake Ferry**, overlooking Lake Onoke. There's the characterful old **Lake Ferry Hotel** *(lakeferryhotel.co.nz)* here, plus ranks of grey, shingled dunes at the river mouth. This is a classic coastal corner of NZ where nothing ever happens but there's plenty to see.

From Martinborough to the lighthouse is 67km, but allow 1¼ hours' drive-time to get there.

Cape Palliser

NAZAR_AB/GETTY IMAGES

STAY AWHILE

MARTINBOROUGH

BY ASHLYN OSWALT

Martinborough's charm is palpable from the moment you set foot in the town square. Set in the shape of the Union Jack, it's framed by the many wineries that have made this little town a destination. Only an hour from bustling Wellington, its laid-back vibe makes it feel worlds away.

Boutique wineries are the draw-card here, so rent a bike through **Green Jersey** *(greenjersey.co.nz)* or book a shuttle bus from **Martinborough Wine Tours** *(martinboroughwinetours.co.nz)* to get around. With over 20 wineries around town, it may feel hard to pick a route. My advice? Stop at **Cambridge Road** *(cambridgeroad.co.nz)* for an intimate setting and biodynamic wines and pick up a bottle of pinot noir at the small but impressive **Nga Waka** *(ngawaka.co.nz)*.

It's not all about wine here, though – for me, exploring the rural townships of Castle Point and Ngawi by car is always on the cards. The rugged shoreline is dotted with bulldozers at the ready to pull in fishing boats, showcasing the coastline's intensity.

Stretch your legs on the **Pinnacles Ridge Track** *(doc.govt.nz)*, a 45-minute climb among ancient rock formations overlooking the sea. If you still have some strength in your legs, climb the 250 steps to **Cape Palliser Lighthouse** and enjoy views out onto the Cook Strait.

End the evening with a 90-minute stargazing tour with **Star Safari** *(star-safari.nz)*, led by an astrobiologist and astrophysicist. Wairarapa became an internationally recognised Dark Sky Reserve in 2023, so a memorable evening of stargazing is almost guaranteed. Good night, indeed.

LINK YOUR TRIP

At the end of the 12 **North Island Southern Loop**, Martinborough ia 80km from Wellington.

Left and right: Vineyards

LEFT: WALTER BIBIKOW/GETTY IMAGES; RIGHT: WESTEND61/GETTY IMAGES

PLACES TO STAY

POPPIES
A vineyard stay is the best way to experience Martinborough, and it's hard to pass up the beloved Poppies. The self-contained studio apartment is hidden among the vines, a perfect getaway for two. *(poppiesmartinborough.co.nz)*

Martinborough Hotel
Located in the heart of town, this historic hotel has tidy, elegant rooms. The bistro and bar serve breakfast, lunch and dinner with a French flair. *(martinboroughhotel.co.nz)*

Swan House
A short walk from town lie three cosy units tucked into a private backyard. The friendly owners offer complimentary bikes for guest use – handy for touring the nearby wineries. *(swanhouse.co.nz)*

13

WELLINGTON & THE EAST COAST

PACIFIC COAST EXPLORER

★ BEST FOR

FOODIES

Hawke's Bay Farmers Market in Hastings serves up brilliant local edibles.

Hawke's Bay Farmers' Market (p130)

DURATION: 5-7 DAYS

DISTANCE: 802KM / 498 MILES

GREAT FOR: FOOD AND DRINK, CULTURE

BEST TIME TO GO: JANUARY TO MARCH FOR LONG BEACHY EVENINGS AND (RELATIVELY) WARM SEAS

Describing a languid arc around New Zealand's Pacific Ocean coastline, this epic journey combines sandy beaches, spectacular scenery and day excursions to rugged and idiosyncratic islands. Māori culture is thriving in Whakatāne, Ōpōtiki and around the remote East Cape, while the bountiful foodie scenes of Hastings and Gisborne are complemented by sun-kissed vineyards. In Napier, classy art-deco architecture echoes from a tragic past.

LINK YOUR TRIP

07 Coromandel Peninsula
From Tauranga, drive 55km north to hit the sand at Waihi Beach.

02 Thermal Discoverer
Art-deco Napier is the end of the line on this journey from Auckland to Hawke's Bay, via the North Island's volcanic heartland.

01 Tauranga

Tauranga (pronounced 'toe-rung-ah') has been booming since the 1990s, and is now the fifth-largest city in the country. Restaurants and bars line the waterfront, and an easy-going vibe prevails. The **Tauranga Art Gallery** *(artgallery.org.nz)*, inside a former bank, pushes well beyond provincial notions with exhibitions of thought-provoking contemporary work. For a diverse day on the ocean, **Bay Explorer** *(bayexplorer.co.nz)* offers a day cruise incorporating wildlife spotting – potentially whales, dolphins, orcas and birdlife – with the opportunity to go paddle boarding, kayaking and swimming.

THE DRIVE: Depart Tauranga northeast across Tauranga Harbour on SH2. Beyond the harbour, turn left onto Totara St and drive through the port area before merging left onto Maunganui Rd into Mt Maunganui, 8km from Tauranga.

02 Mt Maunganui

Rather grandiosely named after the 232m hill punctuating the sandy peninsula occupied by the township, Mt Maunganui is often just called 'the Mount'. To Māori it's Mauao, which translates as 'caught by the light of day'. Down at sea level, the town's hip bars, fab beaches, cafes and restaurants far exceed the expectations you might have of a small seaside enclave. Sunseekers and surfers can't get enough. The steep summit walk takes about an hour return – it's a morning ritual for many locals. If you don't have the climb in your legs, the **Mauao Base Track** (3.4km, 45 minutes) is a pleasant stroll circumnavigating Mauao's forest-clad lower slopes. Mt Maunganui suffered a devastating landslide in January 2026 and walks in the area may be affected. Check the local i-SITE or bayofplentynz.com for up-to-date information.

THE DRIVE: Depart Mt Maunganui along Maunganui Rd onto SH2. After 13km, the Tauranga Eastern Link Toll Road begins, but stay on SH2 to take the more scenic route via Te Puke and on to Whakatāne, 86km from Mt Maunganui. Moutohorā (Whale Island) sits off to your left as you approach Whakatāne. Due to the extreme rainfall event in January 2026, you may encounter roadworks and delays.

03 Whakatāne

Pinched between a bush-smothered ridge and the mouth of the Whakatāne River, Whakatāne (pronounced 'fokka-tar-nay') is one of NZ's sunniest cities, and looks across to the volcanic **Whakaari/White Island** on the horizon, the scene of a disastrous eruption in 2019 that killed 22 tourists who were visiting the island at the time. **Te Kōputu a te whanga a Toi** *(Whakatāne Library & Exhibition Centre; whakatanemuseum.org.nz)* is a museum with excellent displays on early Māori and European settlement, while **Mataatua** *(mataatua.com)* is a *marae* (traditional meeting place) that features a beautifully carved 1875 *wharenui* (Māori meeting house). In 1879 it was dismantled and shipped overseas before spending 71 years in the Otago Museum in Dunedin. It only came home to Whakatāne in 2011.

THE DRIVE: Depart Whakatāne south on Commerce St, turning left into Gorge Rd and climbing over the headland that separates Whakatāne and Ōhope, 7km away. En route, detour left onto Otarawairere Rd to Kohi Point Lookout for views over Whakatāne and the coast.

04 Ōhope

Signs proclaim Ōhope as NZ's most loved beach, and it's hard not to become infatuated with this 11km-long stretch of sand that's custom-made for lazing or surfing. The beach is backed by sleepy Ohiwa Harbour. If you want to stretch your legs, a 15-minute walk from West End around the headland ends on **Otarawairere Bay** (check signposting for alternative routes as a major slip has caused damage to the track)– a beach that may be even more beautiful than Ōhope itself. **Salt Spray Surf School** *(saltspraysurfschool.co.nz)* can have you trying to ride the waves, while **KG Kayaks** *(kgkayaks.co.nz)* sets up on Port Ōhope Wharf during summer if you fancy hiring a kayak or taking a guided paddle in the harbour or in the waters around Moutohorā.

THE DRIVE: Leave Ōhope Beach on Wainui Rd and skirt Ohiwa Harbour – covered in water or mud, depending on the tide – before turning left to rejoin SH2. It soon becomes a gorgeous coast-hugging drive into Ōpōtiki, 37km from Ōhope. Check journeys.nzta.govt.nz before heading out to confirm the road is open – SH2 was damaged in the severe rainfall event of January 2026.

05 Ōpōtiki

The Ōpōtiki area was settled from at least 1150, some 200 years before the larger 14th-century Māori migration. It's a worn-around-the-edges kind of town with a scattering of historic buildings and top beaches at nearby Ohiwa and Waiotahi. The **Ōpōtiki Museum** *(ohas.wordpress.com)* has interesting heritage displays, including Māori *taonga* (treasures), militaria and recreated shopfronts. The **Mōtū Trails** *(motutrails.co.nz)* have helped put Ōpōtiki on the Great Rides cycle map – the Dunes Trail is one part of the Mōtū Trails, and offers a 19km-long, one-day mountain-biking diversion. **Motu Trails** *(bushaven.co.nz)* hires out bikes and runs an on-demand shuttle.

THE DRIVE: Leaving Ōpōtiki on SH35, after 42km this super-scenic coastal road crosses the broad and pebble-strewn Mōtū River, before continuing via the fishing town of Te Kaha and Hicks Bay to Te Araroa and the East Cape Lighthouse. Allow 2½ hours for the winding 179km journey from Ōpōtiki. Fill up with petrol before you head off, and bring snacks: shops and petrol stations are scarce out here.

06 Te Araroa

Around 10km east of Hicks Bay is **Te Araroa**, a lone-dog village with a few shops, a petrol station and a beautifully carved marae. The geology changes here from igneous outcrops to sandstone cliffs, all blanketed by dense native bush. Dominating the Te Araroa schoolyard, **Te-Waha-O-Rerekohu** is allegedly NZ's largest pōhutukawa tree – more than 350 years old, 20m high and 40m wide. From Te Araroa, drive out to see the East Cape Lighthouse, the easterly tip of mainland NZ. It's 21km (30 minutes) east of Te Araroa with a 25-minute climb up 750 steps to the lighthouse.

THE DRIVE: Returning 21km from the lighthouse to SH35, travel south through rough-hewn farmland to Tokomaru Bay (79km from Te Araroa), stopping to check out the fascinating Māori-style interior at St Mary's Church in Tikitiki (24km from Te Araroa). Dominating the inland horizon is Mt Hikurangi (1752m), the first spot on Earth to see the sun each day.

07 Tokomaru Bay

With a broad beach framed by sweeping cliffs, sleepy Tokomaru Bay is perhaps East Cape's most interesting spot. The town has weathered hard times since the freezing works closed in the 1950s, but it still offers good beginners' surf, safe swimming, a great pub and a few crumbling surprises at the far end of the bay. Heading south from Tokomaru Bay it's a bucolic 22km to the turn-off to **Anaura Bay**, 6km away. It's a definite 'wow' moment when the beautiful bay springs into view far below. The **Anaura Bay Walkway** *(doc.govt.nz; off*

DAY TRIP TO MOUTOHORĀ

Nine kilometres offshore from Whakatāne is Moutohorā (Whale Island – no prizes for guessing what it looks like). This island is another of the volcanoes along the Taupō Volcanic Zone but it's much less active than Whakaari/White Island, though there are hot springs along its shore. The island's high point is 353m above the sea, and the island has several historic sites, including an ancient *pā* (fortified village) site.

Moutohorā was once home to a Māori settlement. In 1829 Māori massacred sailors from the trading vessel Haweis while it was anchored at Sulphur Bay. In 1867 the island passed into European ownership and remains privately owned, but since 1965 it has been a DOC-protected wildlife refuge for seabirds and shorebirds. New Zealand fur seals are also frequently spotted.

Operators heading to Moutohorā from Whakatāne include **Diveworks** *(diveworks-charters.com)*.

Ōhope Beach (p125)

MEHDI33300/SHUTTERSTOCK

Anaura Bay Rd) was designed as a loop track but is only open to the pines lookout due to storm damage. Start the track from the northern entrance.

THE DRIVE: Back on SH35 from Anaura Bay, it's a further 14km south to Tolaga Bay, the largest community on East Cape (population 830).

08 Tolaga Bay

Workaday Tolaga Bay is defined by its amazing historic wharf. Built in 1929 and commercially functional until 1968, it's one of the longest in the southern hemisphere at 660m, and is now largely restored after dedicated (and expensive) preservation efforts. Nearby is **Cooks Cove Walkway** *(doc.govt.nz)*, an easy 5.8km, 2½-hour loop through farmland and native bush to a cove where the captain landed. Around 40km south of Tolaga Bay, the **Te Tapuwae o Rongokako Marine Reserve** is a 2450-hectare haven for fur seals, dolphins, rays and whales. Get out amongst it with **Dive Tatapouri** *(divetatapouri.com)*.

THE DRIVE: From Tolaga Bay, SH35 meanders 55km south to Gisborne.

09 Gisborne

Squeezed between surf beaches and a sea of chardonnay, Gisborne proudly claims to be the first city on Earth to see the sun. It's a good spot to hit the beach: there's safe swimming between the flags at **Waikanae Beach**, or sign up for some surf lessons with **Surfing with Sarah** *(surfingwithsarah.co.nz)*. Recuperate with a few Gisborne Gold lagers at **Sunshine Brewery** *(sunshinebrewery.co.nz)*. Focusing on east coast Māori and colonial history, the **Tairāwhiti Museum** *(tairawhitimuseum.org.nz)* has rotating exhibits and excellent historic photographic displays. And indeed, history runs deep in Gisborne: the moving **Puhi Kai Iti Cook Landing Site** *(gdc.govt.nz; Kaiti Beach Rd)* is where Captain James Cook first landed in NZ in 1769, and where nine Māori were killed by his crew.

THE DRIVE: From Gisborne south, SH2 combines rural vistas and occasional views of the sea on its 214km run to Napier.

DETOUR

Mahia Peninsula

Start: 09 Gisborne

Between Gisborne and Napier, the Mahia Peninsula's eroded hills, sandy beaches and vivid

Te Mata Peak (p130), Havelock North

JANICE CHEN/SHUTTERSTOCK

blue sea make it a mini ringer for the Coromandel Peninsula, minus the crowds. Spend a day or two exploring the scenic reserve and the bird-filled **Maungawhio Lagoon**, hanging out at the beach (**Mahia Beach** at sunset can be spectacular), or teeing off with some golf. Mahia has several small settlements offering between them a few guesthouses, a holiday park, a bar-bistro and a couple of stores. From Gisborne, drive south on SH2 to Nuhaka (66km), and then turn left (east) for 17km to Mahia Beach.

10 Napier

The Napier of today – a charismatic, sunny, composed city with the air of an affluent English seaside resort – is the silver lining of the dark cloud that was the deadly 1931 earthquake. Rebuilt in the prevailing architectural style of the time, the city retains a unique concentration of art-deco buildings. A one-stop shop for all things deco, the **Art Deco Centre** *(artdeconapier.com)* runs daily tours to see the architectural highlights, including the **Daily Telegraph Building** *(heritage.org.nz/places)* and the **National Tobacco Company Building** *(heritage.org.nz/places)*. Also worth a look is the non-deco **MTG Hawke's Bay** *(Museum Theatre Gallery; mtghawkesbay.com)*, a gleaming-white museum-theatre-gallery space by the water.

THE DRIVE: Napier along Marine Pde (SH2), and just after Clive (10km) turn left into Mill Rd for 6km before turning left into East Rd. Turn right into Clifton Rd and continue another 450m to the Clifton waterfront, 21km from Napier.

BOYLOSO/SHUTTERSTOCK

Art-deco T&G Building, Napier

ART-DECO NAPIER

At 10.46am on 3 February 1931, the city of Napier was levelled by a catastrophic earthquake (7.9 on the Richter scale). Fatalities in Napier and nearby Hastings numbered 258. Napier suddenly found itself 40 sq km larger, as the earthquake heaved sections of what was once a lagoon 2m above sea level (Napier airport was once more 'port', less 'air').

A fevered rebuilding program ensued, resulting in one of the world's most uniformly art-deco cities. Don't expect the Chrysler Building – Napier is resolutely low-rise – but you will find amazingly intact 1930s facades and streetscapes, which can provoke a Great Gatsby–esque swagger in the least romantic soul. If you haven't got time for an art-deco walking tour, just take to the streets – particularly Tennyson and Emerson. Remember to look up! And if you're here in February, plan ahead for some good times at the annual **Art Deco Festival** *(artdeconapier.com)*.

11 Cape Kidnappers/ Te Kauwae-a-Māui

From mid-September to late April, Cape Kidnappers/Te Kauwae-a-Māui erupts with squawking Australasian gannets. These big ocean birds usually nest on remote islands but here they settle for the mainland, completely unfazed by human spectators. It's the world's biggest gannet colony. The birds nest as soon as they arrive, and eggs take about six weeks to hatch, with the chicks arriving in early November. Take a guided tour (November to February is the best time) through farmland in a 4WD with **Gannet Safaris** *(gannetsafaris.co.nz)*.

THE DRIVE: Return to Clifton Rd and turn left into East Rd, which becomes Parkhill Rd. Turn left onto Lawn Rd and right onto Pilcher, heading toward SH51, about 28km from Cape Kidnappers/Te Kauwae-a-Māui.

12 Hastings

Like Napier, Hastings was devastated by the 1931 earthquake and also boasts some fine art-deco and Spanish Mission buildings built in the aftermath. Main-street highlights include the **Spanish Mission Westerman's Building** *(heritage.org.nz/places)*, home to the **Hastings i-SITE** *(hawkesbaynz.com)*. Pick up the Art Deco Hastings brochure ($1) inside. The compact but interesting **Hastings City Art Gallery** *(hastingscityartgallery.co.nz)* presents contemporary NZ (including Māori) and international art. On the lawns out the front is Ngā Pou o Heretaunga – 19 fantastic Māori totems. Also in Hastings is Sunday morning's **Hawke's Bay Farmers' Market** *(hawkesbayfarmersmarket.co.nz)*, one of NZ's best.

THE DRIVE: From central Hastings, Heretaunga St runs southeast to lead into Havelock St, then on to Havelock North after 5km.

13 Havelock North

A few kilometres of orchards still separate Hastings from Havelock North, with its prosperous village atmosphere, great cafes and bars, and the towering backdrop of **Te Mata Peak** *(tematapark.co.nz)*, around 16km to the south. The road to the 399m summit passes sheep trails, rickety fences and vertigo-inducing stone escarpments, cowled in a bleak, lunar-landscape-meets-Scottish-Highlands atmosphere. On a clear day, views stretch to the Mahia Peninsula and distant Mt Ruapehu. The park's 30km of walking trails range from 30 minutes to two hours: ask for a map at the local **i-SITE** *(havelocknorthnz.com)*.

THE BEST OF NEW ZEALAND'S PACIFIC-COAST WINERIES

Hawke's Bay Wine Region

Once upon a time, in a wine-free era long, long ago, this district was famous for its orchards. Today it's vines that have top billing, with Hawke's Bay now New Zealand's second-largest wine-producing region (behind Marlborough). Expect excellent bordeaux-style reds, shiraz and chardonnay. Pick up the *Hawke's Bay Winery Guide* map or the *Hawke's Bay Trails* cycling map from Hastings or Napier *(napiernz.com)* i-SITEs, or download them from hawkesbaywine.co.nz. A few of our faves:

- **Black Barn Vineyards** *(blackbarn.com)*
- **Elephant Hill** *(elephanthill.co.nz)*
- **Mission Estate Winery** *(missionestate.co.nz)*

Gisborne Wine Region

With hot summers and fertile loamy soils, the Waipaoa River valley to the northwest of Gisborne is one of New Zealand's foremost grape-growing areas. The region is traditionally famous for its chardonnay, and is increasingly noted for gewürztraminer and pinot gris. Check out gisbornewine.co.nz for a cellar-door map, or pick one up from the visitor centre *(tairawhitigisborne.co.nz)*. Three of the best:

- **Bushmere Estate** *(bushmere.com)*
- **Matawhero** *(matawhero.co.nz)*
- **Millton Vineyards & Winery** *(millton.co.nz)*

Tolago Bay (p128)
DAVID KERR/SHUTTERSTOCK

PHOTO OPPORTUNITY

The impressively long Tolaga Bay wharf, jutting 660m out into the sea.

Cape Farewell
Puponga
Farewell Spit
Wharariki Beach
Pakawau
Collingwood
Ōnekakā
Pōhara
Tōtaranui
Tākaka
Abel Tasman National Park
Devil River Peak
TASMAN SEA
15
Mārahau
Upper Tākaka
Kaiteriteri
Marlborough Sounds
Riwaka
Kōhaihai
Kahurangi National Park
Motueka
60
Māpua
14
Mt Arthur
Karamea
Havelock
Waikawa
Nelson
Picton
Little Wanganui
Brightwater
Richmond
Pelorus River
Tapawera
1
Karamea Bight
67
Wakefield
Mt Owen
Mt Richmond Forest Park
Blenheim
6
Wairau River
Seddonville
Renwick
Granity
Hector
Seddon
Kawatiri
Westport
Grassmere
Lyell
16
Lake Rotoroa
63
Cape Campbell
St Arnaud
6
Murchison
Lake Rotoiti
Ward
Inangahua
Charleston
Mt Travers
Molesworth Station Homestead
Tapuae-o-Uenuku
Severn
69
Mt Uriah
Victoria Forest Park
Nelson Lakes National Park
Kekerengu
65
Paparoa National Park
Reefton
Mt Una
Clarence River
Clarence
Dillon Cone
Mt Haast
Ikamatua
Springs Junction
Kaikōura
Stillwater
7
Hanmer Springs Forest Park
Mt Lyford
Goose Bay
Oaro
Lake Sumner Forest Park
70
Mt Ajax
Hanmer Springs
Moana
1
Waiau
Lake Brunner (Moana)
Lake Sumner
Jacksons
Parnassus
Arthur's Pass National Park
Culverden
Otira
Hurunui River
Cheviot
7
Arthur's Pass
Hurunui
Bealey
Cass
Waipara
SOUTH PACIFIC OCEAN
73
Amberley
Castle Hill
Oxford
Lake Coleridge
Springfield
Woodend
Kaiapoi
Pegasus Bay
Sheffield
Belfast
Windwhistle
Darfield
Mt Hutt
Christchurch
Rolleston
0
50 km
0
25 miles

DMITRY NAUMOV/SHUTTERSTOCK

Queen Charlotte Sound

MARLBOROUGH & NELSON

EXPLORE

MARLBOROUGH & NELSON

Welcome to warm and sunny Marlborough and Nelson, the first port of call for travellers crossing Cook Strait from windy Wellington to the mainland (as South Islanders like to call it). The neighbouring regions have more in common than an amenable climate. Both boast a combination of coastal holiday hot spots backed by an abundance of mountains. They're also known for their delicious food and drink, from game meats, green-lipped mussels and summer fruits to craft beer and world-class wines. Combined, the Top of the South makes for splendid road-trip country, with an emphasis on sunshine and good times.

Blenheim

Primarily a service town for the Marlborough Wine Region, Blenheim has plenty of supermarkets and outdoor stores, and a decent food scene. For breakfast or lunch, head to Herb + Olive or Hakuna Matata Cafe. Little Amigos and Noodle Corner both open for lunch, while the best dinner options are Scotch Wine Bar and Gramado's (Brazilian).

Picton

Half asleep in winter but hyperactive in summer (with multiple fully laden ferry arrivals per day), Picton clusters round a deep and beautiful gulch at the head of Queen Charlotte Sound. The little town has plenty of cafes and bars, a good supermarket and an excellent Dutch-style bakery, Picton Village Bakkerij. Gusto is the best of the cafes, while cosy Seumus' Irish Bar is good for a Guinness and a pub meal.

Nelson

In summer the sunny city of Nelson fills with local and international visitors, all there to take advantage of its proximity to beaches and hiking trails. Nelson has everything you'd expect of a city of around 50,000 people, including multiple supermarkets, bakeries and breweries, and an oversized range of outdoor stores. The best restaurants (Hawker House, Hopgood's & Co) congregate at the cathedral end

WHEN TO GO

This area is one of New Zealand's sunniest, with January and February the warmest months. From around Christmas until the end of January the whole region teems with Kiwi holidaymakers, so plan ahead during this time. However, winters here can also be wonderful, with frosty mornings often giving way to clear skies and T-shirt temperatures.

of Trafalgar St, with another strip overlooking the water on Wakefield Quay (Nahm, Boat Shed Cafe). Other good options scattered around the city include Urban Oyster Bar & Eatery, Nicola's Cantina, DeVille, The Indian Cafe, Little Dove Cafe and Melrose House Cafe. For delectable baked goods, head to The Swiss Bakery.

Motueka

Home to around 8000 people, Motueka is the closest decent-size town to Abel Tasman National Park. A large supermarket, roadside fruit stalls and a popular Sunday-morning market make it a good place to stock up on supplies on your way north. Good places to eat include TOAD Hall (cafe), Smoking Barrel (barbecue) and Sprig + Fern (pub grub).

Tākaka

With a population of little over 1300, there's not a lot to Tākaka, but it's still the biggest settlement on Golden Bay. The main street has cafes, some interesting shops selling homespun art, a pub and a boutique gin distillery. There's also a supermarket at the southern end of the strip. The best cafes are only a couple of doors apart: Wholemeal Cafe and Dangerous Kitchen. In the evening, grab a burger at Roots Bar or head to O'Sha for authentic Thai, including vegan meals.

TRANSPORT

Picton is the South Island's interisland ferry port, with multiple daily car-ferry sailings to and from Wellington. Nelson has the busiest domestic airport, followed by Blenheim and Picton. Buses link the region to Canterbury and the West Coast. From October to April, KiwiRail's Coastal Pacific train makes the scenic journey between Picton and Christchurch.

RESOURCES

★ **marlboroughwinenz.com**
Portal for NZ's biggest-producing wine region, including a digital version of the indispensable *Marlborough Wine Trail* map.

★ **marlboroughnz.com**
Regional information, with details of i-SITE visitor information centres in Blenheim and Picton.

★ **nelsontasman.nz**
Nelson, Motueka and Tākaka (Golden Bay) all have i-SITEs.

WHAT'S ON

★ **Marlborough Food & Wine Festival**
Regional showcase held in Renwick on the second Saturday in February.

★ **Havelock Mussel & Seafood Festival**
Celebrating the tiny Marlborough Sounds town's main claim to fame in mid-March.

★ **Classic Fighters Omaka Airshow**
Fighter planes from both World Wars spread their wings over Blenheim on Easter weekend.

★ **Nelson Arts Festival**
Eleven days of arts experiences in October.

WHERE TO STAY

There are plenty of good holiday parks along the coast, including Tahuna Beach in Nelson and Pōhara Beach Top 10 in Golden Bay. There are also some exceptional hostels, such as Picton's Tombstone Backpackers and Nelson's Tasman Bay Backpackers. For midrange options, try Eden's Edge Lodge in Riwaka, Kaiteri Motels & Apartments in Kaiteriteri and Zatori in Collingwood. There's also plenty of choice at the luxury end, including Pihopa Retreat and Grand Arden Monaco (swanky suites in Nelson), Shady Rest (top-end B&B in Tākaka) and Adrift in Golden Bay (upmarket cottages right on the beach).

14

★ BEST FOR

WINE TOURS

Marlborough's world-class wines and unstuffy cellar doors.

MARLBOROUGH & NELSON

SUNSHINE & WINE

DURATION: 5-7 DAYS

DISTANCE: 425KM / 264 MILES

GREAT FOR: FOOD AND DRINK, OUTDOORS

BEST TIME TO GO: NOVEMBER TO MARCH WHEN THE WEATHER'S BEST, BUT EXPECT CROWDS IN JANUARY

Vineyard, Marlborough (p141)

Blenheim and Nelson vie annually for the crown of New Zealand's sunniest centre, so odds are on for blue skies on this trip around the Top of the South. A high concentration of attractions and short driving times allow you to maximise enjoyment of outdoor adventures in hot spots such as Queen Charlotte Sound and Nelson Lakes National Park, as well as meander around wineries and restaurants.

LINK YOUR TRIP

15 Tasman & Golden Bays
Nelson is the starting point for this trip around two of NZ's sunniest bays.

03 Kaikōura Coast
From Picton you can head down the east coast to Christchurch, taking in more wineries and the odd whale along the way.

01 Picton

Spread around two pretty bays secreted deep within Queen Charlotte Sound, Picton is much more than just the interisland ferry port and departure point for trips throughout the Marlborough Sounds. The town and its environs can be surveyed from the popular **Snout Track** (7.8km return from car park), sidling along the Victoria Domain headland flanking the harbour's east side. A side track makes for a shorter walk to **Bob's Bay** (1.5km from the marina), a good spot for a swim. One of Picton's lesser-known but worthy attractions is the **Tirohanga Track**, a 5.5km leg-stretching loop around a hill just behind the town. Taking you much higher than the Snout Track, it affords dress-circle views of the town and the endless ridges of the Sounds beyond.

THE DRIVE: Follow signs for Queen Charlotte Drive, which

TRAVELLIGHTR/SHUTTERSTOCK

winds around bay after bay for 34km to Havelock, providing a panoramic Marlborough Sounds' snapshot.

02 Havelock

The western bookend of Queen Charlotte Drive, the little town of Havelock is the hopping-off point for forays into Kenepuru and Pelorus Sounds. It is also the self-proclaimed 'Greenshell Mussel Capital of the World'. You can familiarise yourself with this ubiquitous bivalve at cheap-and-cheerful **Mills Bay Mussels** *(millsbaymussels.co.nz)*, where you can try them steamed with white wine and garlic, grilled in garlic butter, beer battered, crumbed, or in a chowder, fritter or Dutch-style croquette. If you can't decide, try a tasting platter. Haven't had enough? Head to **Slip Inn** *(slipinnhavelock.com)*, grab a table on the deck jutting over the marina, and tuck into a delicious bowl of *oka* – a Samoan dish of raw fish and mussels cured in a lime, coconut cream and green-chilli broth.

THE DRIVE: Follow SH6 west along the Pelorus River past the old gold-mining settlement of Canvastown and on to Pelorus Bridge, 20km away.

03 Pelorus Bridge

A pocket of deep, green forest tucked between paddocks and plantation forests, the **Pelorus Bridge Scenic Reserve** *(doc.govt.nz)* contains one of the last stands of river-flat forest in Marlborough. It survived only because a town planned in 1865 didn't get off the ground by 1912, by which time loggers' obliteration of surrounding forest made this little remnant look precious.

Explore the reserve's many tracks, admire the historic bridge, take a dip in the clear **Pelorus River** (alluring enough to star in Peter Jackson's *The Hobbit*), and then partake in some home-baked goods at the cafe. Come sundown, keep an eye out for long-tailed bats, known to Māori as pekapeka – the reserve is home to one of the last remaining populations in Marlborough. If you're travelling in a campervan or with a tent, consider overnighting here in DOC's small but perfectly formed **Pelorus Bridge**

(Kahikatea Flat) Campground *(doc.govt.nz)*, with its snazzy facilities building, lush lawns and riverside setting.

THE DRIVE: Turn left onto SH6, continuing on for 54km. At the roundabout, take the second exit to stay on SH6, heading towards Tāhunanui/Richmond, until you're in town.

04 Nelson

Dishing up a winning combination of beautiful surroundings, sophisticated art and culinary scenes, and lashings of sunshine, Nelson is hailed as one of New Zealand's most liveable cities. Redeveloped in 2016, the excellent **Suter Art Gallery** *(thesuter.org.nz)* presents ever-changing exhibitions within light-filled exhibition spaces. A particularly vibrant side of the city's creative scene is on show at the **World of WearableArt** and **Classic Cars Museum** *(nelsonclassiccarmuseum.nz)*, where you can ogle a selection of past entries in NZ's most zany fashion pageant. You name it, they've made a garment out of it: wood, metal, shells, cable ties, dried leaves, even ping-pong balls. Revel in sensory overload as you wander around the museum's galleries, including a 'Bizarre Bras' room. More interested in cars than bras? Under the same roof are more than 100 mint-condition classic vehicles.

THE DRIVE: Take the scenic route out of town via Tahunanui and Stoke, and alongside Waimea Inlet to Richmond. Turn right onto SH60 and then left onto the Moutere Hwy, which hooks right and climbs into the Moutere Hills.

05 Moutere

Upper Moutere village was established by German immigrants, who originally named it Sarau. Today it's a sleepy hamlet set among farms, orchards and lifestyle blocks, with a pretty church, a couple of interesting shops and one of NZ's oldest pubs. Built c 1850 (although the extensions and questionable decor don't make this obvious), the **Moutere Inn** *(moutereinn.co.nz)* is a welcoming establishment serving honest meals and predominantly local craft beer, including its own Moutere Brewing Co range. Sit in the sunshine with a burger and brew, or settle down inside on folk-flavoured music nights. Four kilometres from Upper Moutere, just off the highway to Motueka, bijou **Neudorf Vineyards** *(neudorf.co.nz)* is one of the Nelson region's most celebrated wineries. Signature tipples include pinot noir and some of NZ's finest chardonnay, available to taste at the agriculturally chic cellar door.

THE DRIVE: Turn off the Moutere Hwy onto Gardner Valley Rd, and then turn right for a brief (1.6km) spin on SH60. You'll hardly reach the speed limit before you need to turn left onto Māpua Dr and follow the signs to Māpua Wharf.

06 Māpua

Positioned at the start of the Ruby Coast, little Māpua is an unlikely locale for a hip wharf precinct. Once used mainly for the transportation of apples, it's now home to chic cafes, artsy shops, a brewery, a wine bar and a coffee roastery. Stock up on wood-smoked fish and pâté at the **Smokehouse** *(smokehouse.co.nz)*, and order a serve of fish and chips to devour on the wharf under the beady eyes of recklessly opportunistic gulls. During daylight hours, ferries run to **Moturoa/Rabbit Island**, a low-lying expanse with a gorgeous sandy

MARLBOROUGH SOUNDS

The Marlborough Sounds are a scenic labyrinth of peaks, bays, beaches and watery reaches, formed when the sea flooded deep river valleys after the last ice age. They are very convoluted, accounting for almost one-fifth of NZ's total coastline.

Exploring the Sounds is invariably quicker by boat, with driving times up to three times longer. Accordingly, an armada of vessels offers scheduled and on-demand boat services, with the bulk operating out of Picton for the Queen Charlotte Sound, and some from Havelock for Kenepuru and Pelorus Sounds.

Indulgence combined with gentle recreation is a Queen Charlotte Sound speciality, with lunch cruises de rigueur. A fine choice is schmick **Bay of Many Coves Resort** *(bayofmanycoves.co.nz)*. Nestled into a secluded bay, it offers a dreamy one-stop shop of bushwalks, kayaking, swimming and a day spa, all on top of experiencing some of the region's best cuisine. You could do the whole shebang on a day trip, but luxurious all-mod-cons apartments overlooking the water make an overnighter pretty irresistible.

Marlborough Sounds
TOMAS PAVELKA/SHUTTERSTOCK

WHY I LOVE THIS TRIP

PETER DRAGICEVICH, WRITER

Slurping greenshell mussels and sipping sauvignon blanc in the summer sun is such a quintessentially Kiwi thing that it surpasses 'classic' and borders on 'iconic'. This drive takes you to the primary sources of both, and adds to the mix beaches, mountains, a lake, the gloriously fiddly coastline of the Marlborough Sounds and some of the country's most predictably sunny weather. Cheers and pass a napkin!

beach spread along its entire 8km length. A pine forest provides shade to the cyclists on the Great Taste Trail (p148), which passes through. You're very likely to see weka here, inquisitive flightless birds similar to kiwi but with much shorter beaks.

THE DRIVE: Head through Māpua village and take the Ruby Coast route to Motueka via Aranui Rd, Stafford Dr, Aporo Rd and the Coastal Hwy. In the distance you'll see the beech-forest-clad Mt Arthur in Kahurangi National Park.

07 Motueka

Motueka (pronounced maw-tu-eh-ka and meaning 'Island of Weka') is a bustling agricultural town that doubles as an ace visitor destination due to its ample accommodation, decent cafes and shops, and marginally salty setting along the shore of Tasman Bay. The town's buzzy aerodrome gives rise to several hair-raising activities, including skydiving in one of NZ's most scenic drop-zones. **Skydive Abel Tasman** *(skydive.co.nz)* will spiral you up to 16,500ft and throw you out of a plane strapped to a professional adrenaline junkie, at which point – if you can keep your eyes open – you can see Abel Tasman, Nelson Lakes and Kahurangi National Parks, and as far away as the North Island. Fancy the thrill without the spill? Skydive's front lawn is a lovely spot to spectate while soaking up some sun.

THE DRIVE: Motueka Valley Hwy is clearly signposted from High St, heading down College St towards the aerodrome. Follow the highway 54km inland until its final juncture at SH6, turn right, and drive 39km to Kawatiri. Head left on SH63 following the Buller River to St Arnaud, 25km away. In all, this scenic drive into the mountains should take around 90 minutes.

DETOUR

Abel Tasman National Park

Start: 07 Motueka

Blanketing the coast and hill country between Tasman and Golden Bays, NZ's smallest national park is famed for its picture-perfect arcs of golden sand lapped by seas of shimmering blue. Slightly less likely to make the postcard rack are its myriad other natural features such as limpid lagoons, sculpted granite cliffs and gorges, and spectacular karst caves concealed in its rugged interior.

Kerr Bay, Lake Rotoiti

PHOTO OPPORTUNITY

The jetty at Kerr Bay, Lake Rotoiti.

TOBIN AKEHURST/SHUTTERSTOCK

Hiking the **Abel Tasman Coast Track** is by far the most popular activity in the park, as is evident by the hordes that troop along it in high season. It's hardly a seething mass of humanity, however, with disadvantages limited largely to chock-a-block hut and campsite bookings, and the occasional risk of a photobomb.

Boat cruises galore are offered from Kaiteriteri, the built-up holiday resort 16km from Motueka, making it possible to undertake day walks on the usually three- to five-day track. If you're up for paddle power, however – arguably the best way to experience the park – bypass Kaiteriteri and head instead for Mārahau, a mere 3km further away, where **Kahu Kayaks** *(kahukayaks.co.nz)* can launch you on your way to glorious Anchorage beach, from where you can walk south along the Coast Track back to base.

08 Nelson Lakes National Park

Located at the northern end of the Southern Alps, Nelson Lakes National Park is a glacier-carved landscape of rugged greywacke mountains, ancient beech forest, and two picturesque lakes – Rotoiti and Rotoroa ('Small Lake' and 'Long Lake', respectively, in Māori). St Arnaud, the tiny national park village, lies alongside the shore of Rotoiti.

The national park's visitor hub is the **DOC Nelson Lakes Visitor Centre** *(doc.govt.nz)*, well worth a visit for its informative displays on the park's ecology and history. It will also pay to call in to check the forecast and track conditions if you're venturing out onto the park's trails. Changeable weather

ROLF_52/SHUTTERSTOCK

Wine tasting, Blenheim

MARLBOROUGH WINE REGION

Marlborough is NZ's vinous colossus, producing around three-quarters of the country's wine. At last count, there were 244 sq km of vines – which is even more extraordinary when you consider that the modern industry only really kicked off in 1973 when the Yukich family expanded their West Auckland operations to here.

Sunny days and cool nights create the perfect conditions for cool-climate grapes: world-famous sauvignon blanc, top-notch pinot noir, and notable chardonnay, riesling, gewürztraminer, pinot gris and bubbly. Drifting between tasting rooms and dining among the vines is a quintessential South Island experience. The big annual event is the one-day **Marlborough Wine & Food Festival** *(wine-marlborough-festival.co.nz;)*, held at Renwick Domain in mid February.

The **Marlborough Wine Trail** map – available from **Blenheim i-SITE** *(marlboroughnz.com)* and online at wine-marlborough.co.nz – lists 35 wineries that are open to the public. Some wineries charge a small fee for tasting, normally refunded if you purchase a bottle.

Top picks include **Allan Scott Family Winemakers** *(allanscott.com)*, **Wither Hills** *(witherhills.co.nz)*, **Forrest Wines** *(forrest.co.nz)* and **Wairau River** *(wairauriverwines.com)*; all except Forrest also have excellent restaurants. **Brancott Estate** *(brancottestate.com)*, under previous name Montana Wines, was the trailblazer of the wine region. The cellar door is no longer open to the public, but you can find its wines at most supermarkets. For a certified organic wine experience, check out Te Whare Rā's **cellar door** for classic Marlborough sauvignon blancs, among other varietals.

and tough terrain certainly make for some serious wilderness-hiking country, but numerous day walks offer more achievable options. Easy nature trails head off hither and thither from Lake Rotoiti's **Kerr Bay**, offering a chance to smell sweet beech trees and eyeball the birdlife. Reasonably fit walkers, however, could aim higher; a good pick is the five-hour **Mt Robert Circuit Track**, which circumnavigates the mountain, with an optional side trip along Robert Ridge offering staggering views into the heart of the national park.

THE DRIVE: The 92km drive down the Wairau Valley to Renwick is pretty as a picture, complete with shingle peaks, a braided river, and golden paddocks that eventually give way to the endless rows of grapevines dominating the lower plains.

09 Renwick

Not so long ago an unremarkable dot, the little town of Renwick now occupies an enviable position at the centre of Marlborough's growing wine industry. An island in a sea of vines, with more than 20 cellar doors in its ambit – along with an increasing amount of accommodation and traveller services – it's a pleasant and convenient base for exploring NZ's premier wine country. To cut straight to the wine chase, hire a bike from **Bike2Wine** *(bike2wine.co.nz)*, whose friendly staff will happily advise on the best two-wheeled tour for your schedule, fitness and inclinations.

THE DRIVE: Drive east on SH6 for 13km to Blenheim, passing Marlborough Airport after around 4km. If you can't see vines, vines, vines all the way after that, you're lost, very lost.

10 Blenheim

Servicing the viticultural endeavours that carpet most of the Wairau Plains between the Wither Hills and Richmond Ranges, Blenheim is a bustling town with a fairly farmy, workaday feel. In recent years, however, town beautification projects and wine industry spin-offs (such as decent places to eat and pubs you can take your children to) are inching Blenheim closer to a fully fledged tourist town. Threatening to blow the wine out of the water is the brilliant **Omaka Aviation Heritage Centre** *(omaka.org.nz)*. It houses a collection of original and replica Great War and WWII aircraft, brought to life in a series of lifelike dioramas (created by associates of *The Lord of the Rings* director, Peter Jackson, who also owns the centre's Great War collection), depicting dramatic wartime scenes such as the demise of the Red Baron. Budding aces can take to the skies on vintage biplane flights.

THE DRIVE: Head north on SH1 for 28km to return to Picton. After leaving the wide Wairau Plains, the views narrow as you head up the Tuamarina Valley and past the Para Wetlands towards the Marlborough Sounds.

FOOD GLORIOUS FOOD

Nelson's belt almost bursts with the weight of its restaurants and cafes, plumped up with fresh regional produce. Fortunately, the city's regular markets allow visitors to readily source some of this produce for themselves, too.

The must-do on Saturday morning is a meander through **Nelson Market** *(nelsonmarket.co.nz)*. 'Bustling' ain't the half of it, so tightly packed is this weekly affair with fresh fruit and veggies, food stalls, artisan cheese and pickles, not to mention an array of art, craft and homespun fashions.

The much smaller midweek **Nelson Farmers' Market** *(nelsonfarmersmarket.org.nz)* is an abundant alternative selling seasonal produce from asparagus to zucchini, with bread, chocolate and other commendable edibles filling the gaps.

For a healthy blend of drinking, eating and exercise – with a supersized helping of scenery on the side – hire a bike to ride the Tasman's Great Taste Trail (p148). Mainly off-road and accessible from various points around Nelson and Motueka, this cycle route can easily be sliced and diced into an assortment of adventures.

The Moutere Hwy is a scenic and fruitful drive or ride, particularly in high summer when roadside stalls are laden with fresh produce.

Vineyard, Blenheim

MATTHEW MICAH WRIGHT/GETTY IMAGES

15

MARLBOROUGH & NELSON

TASMAN & GOLDEN BAYS

DURATION: 3-4 DAYS

DISTANCE: 183KM / 114 MILES

GREAT FOR: FAMILIES AND NATURE

BEST TIME TO GO: PLENTY OF WINTER SUN MAKES THIS A GREAT YEAR-ROUND TRIP

This trip skirts two big bays at the top of the South Island. Centred on artsy Nelson, Tasman Bay is sprinkled with relaxed coastal settlements and swathed in seaside fun. It's a winding drive over Tākaka Hill to Golden Bay, a smaller and quieter region blending rural charm with enviable beaches. Abel Tasman National Park and Farewell Spit round out this trip in wild style.

LINK YOUR TRIP

14 Sunshine & Wine
Continue east from Nelson into the Marlborough Sounds for coastal views and excellent wine before heading south to the rugged Nelson Lakes National Park.

03 Kaikōura Coast
From Picton, 107km east of Nelson, you can head down the east coast visiting more wineries and spotting the odd whale along the way.

01 Nelson

Competing every year to be NZ's sunniest centre, Nelson's a great place for outdoor adventure. With three national parks and numerous other scenic reserves within easy reach, it offers land-based adventure galore, although its location along sandy Tasman Bay makes the seaside the first port of call for playtime. Number one in the popularity stakes is Tahunanui Beach, less than 10 minutes' drive from the centre of Nelson. It's a big one alright, with the bonus of pretty dunes and a large, grassy reserve alongside. The beach's vast, sandy shallows make for safe swimming, while offshore conditions favour kitesurfing and stand-up paddle boarding. **Moana SUP** *(moananzsup.co.nz)* is on hand to get you out on the water. If you'd rather stay dry there's also a playground, an espresso cart, go-karts, a roller-skating rink and a model railway.

THE DRIVE: From Nelson (or Tahunanui), head southwest

NEW ZEALAND TRANSITION/GETTY IMAGES

★ BEST FOR

LANDFORMS

Take a tour around the otherworldly dunes of Farewell Spit.

Sand dune, Farewell Spit Nature Reserve

along SH6 through Stoke, and alongside Waimea Inlet to Richmond, before turning onto SH60 signposted for Motueka. The 47km journey between Nelson and Motueka takes around 50 minutes.

02 Motueka

Although it's not obvious from the town centre, Motueka is just a stone's throw from the coast. To get the lay of the land, walk or cycle to the muddy estuary. What it lacks in sandy beaches, it more than makes up for in seabirds, saltwater baths and even a shipwreck. Continue on foot along the **Motueka Sandspit**, an important habitat for birds such as oystercatchers, terns, shags and godwits. The latter are known to migrate between here and Alaska's Yukon Delta in less than a week, flying nonstop. To find everything, just follow your nose or pick up a town map from the **i-SITE** *(nelsontasman.nz)*, where you can also get the **Motueka Art Walk** pamphlet, pinpointing sculptures, murals and occasional peculiarities around town. The last major town before Abel Tasman National Park (p140) and Golden Bay, Motueka is also a good place to stock up on supplies.

THE DRIVE: Motueka's main drag, High St, also happens to be SH60. Head north, cross the Motueka River, and before you know it you'll be in Riwaka.

03 Riwaka

Riwaka is a small settlement at the heart of fertile plains planted with orchards, vineyards and hops. If you're peckish, there's a couple of roadside cafes and, in season, a stall selling cherries. Pop in for craft-beer tasting at **Ailment Brewery** *(alimentbrewing.co.nz)* and pick up a flagon to go. It's well worth taking a 6km detour to the end of Riwaka Valley Rd where a 10-minute walk through native bush leads to the peaceful **Riuwaka Resurgence** (in Māori Te Puna o Riuwaka, meaning 'The spring of Riuwaka'). In this pocket of Kahurangi National Park, the Riuwaka River emerges from the base of Tākaka Hill in a crystalline pool set within a ferny glade. This *wāhi tapu* (sacred place) was once used by the local Te Ātiawa and Ngāti Rārua people for cleansing and healing rituals. The brave or foolhardy can swim at the bitterly cold Crystal Pool along the way, but not at the spring itself.

THE DRIVE: Continue along SH60, which turns sharply to the left and then the right before hitting a T junction. Turn right to drive the winding 6km to Kaiteriteri.

04 Kaiteriteri

This seaside hamlet is a holiday resort popular with both locals and overseas tourists who flock here during summer for its golden-sand beach, pretty lagoon playground and proximity to Abel Tasman National Park. It could be argued that Kaiteriteri has jumped the shark with a crowded camping ground complex now dominating the waterfront, but by lolling about on your beach towel – facing outwards – you should have little trouble conjuring up a chilled-out, seaside vibe. Lined up in the aforementioned camping ground complex are a bunch of tour operators itching to get you out into Abel Tasman National Park (p140), just around the corner. Long-standing **Wilsons** *(abeltasman.co.nz)* runs an excellent cruise-walk combo starting with a scenic boat trip to pretty **Medlands Beach**, followed by a four-hour walk through lush coastal forest and across a lofty swing bridge. The walk finishes at **Anchorage**, one of the park's finest beaches, where you can enjoy a spot of swimming before being collected for the cruise back to Kaiteriteri.

THE DRIVE: From the beach, head up and over the hill along meandering Kaiteriteri–Sandy Bay Rd for 6km then turn right onto Sandy Bay–Mārahau Rd. After tracing the shore of the pretty Otuwhero Inlet for 2km you'll arrive at Mārahau.

05 Mārahau

Less developed than Kaiteriteri, Mārahau is the main walking and kayaking gateway for Abel Tasman National Park and a laid-back place to while away a day or two. Three respectable dining options and a good horse-trekking outfit should fill up any downtime, as will Mārahau's rather lovely beach.

Revealed at low tide, the sand

Wharariki Beach (p149)

PHOTO OPPORTUNITY

Otherworldly rock formations of Wharariki Beach..

MICHAEL SCHWAB/GETTY IMAGES

flats and knee-deep pools conceal a delicious local delicacy – tuangi (cockles). If such seafood tickles your fancy and you don't mind sand under your fingernails (and quite possibly in your pants), you can readily gather a dinner's worth in the shallows a couple of hours either side of low tide. Be sure to collect only what you need, heeding daily limits posted beside the beach. Cockles marinières or cockles casino – what's it to be?

THE DRIVE: From Mārahau it's 9km along Riwaka–Sandy Bay Rd to the junction with SH60, where you turn right and climb over Tākaka Hill, reaching the summit after 10km, with panoramic views of Kahurangi National Park and Golden Bay. The steep, winding drive over Tākaka Hill will take around an hour. From here, Tākaka is 33km away.

06 Tākaka

Boasting a high concentration of conscious consumers and alternative lifestylers, Tākaka is Golden Bay's 'big' centre and a lovable little town to boot. You'll find most things you need here, and a few you don't, but we all have an unworn pair of yoga pants in our wardrobe, don't we? It's certainly easy to get sucked into a spot of recreational shopping along Tākaka's parade of interesting, independent businesses with a colourful, crafty bent. If you've a hankering for an old-school hardware store or a pottery shop stocking free-range eggs, you may just have found retail nirvana. Tākaka's great for a chow-down, too, with kale and quinoa not quite the only game in town by the time you've factored in pizza from **Dangerous Kitchen**

LH11/SHUTTERSTOCK

Canaan Downs Scenic Reserve

KARST IN STONE

Golden Bay may look pretty bushy but closer inspection reveals a remarkable karst landscape formed by millions of years of erosion and weathering, which dissolved the marble rock. Its smooth beauty is revealed on the one-hour drive over Tākaka Hill, a precipitous, serpentine route punctuated by spectacular lookout points and a smattering of other interesting stops.

Around 4km shy of the Tākaka Hill summit are the **Ngarua Caves** *(ngaruacaves.co.nz)*, a rock-solid attraction where you can see myriad subterranean delights including hundreds of stalactites and stalagmites, and skeletal displays of moa, NZ's extinct giant bird. Access is restricted to tours – you can't go solo spelunking.

Reached at the end of an 11km gravel road, signposted just before Tākaka Hill summit, is **Canaan Downs Scenic Reserve**. This area stars in both *The Lord of the Rings* and *The Hobbit* movies, but **Harwoods Hole** is the most famous feature here. It's one of the largest *tomo* (caves) in the country at 357m deep and 70m wide, with a 176m vertical drop – although you can't really see much from ground level. The 30-minute walk from the car park passes interesting limestone formations and an impressive lookout over the valley. The cave is off-limits to all but the most experienced cavers.

Mountain bikers with intermediate-level skills can venture along a couple of loop tracks, or head all the way down to Tākaka via the titillating **Rameka Track**. Also close to the top, the **Tākaka Hill Walkway** is a 2½-hour loop through marble karst rock formations, native forest and farmland. For more walks, see DOC's brochure *Walks in Golden Bay* (*www.doc.govt.nz*).

(the-dangerous-kitchen.menu-world.com), and a burger (and perhaps a local craft beer) at hip **Roots Bar** *(rootsbar.co.nz)*.

THE DRIVE: Four kilometres north of Tākaka, follow the signpost left for Te Waikoropupū Springs, another 3km further on.

07 Te Waikoropupū Springs

Commonly known as Pupu Springs, this hidden gem is the largest freshwater spring in the southern hemisphere, and reputedly the clearest in the world except for that beneath Antarctica's frozen Weddell Sea – measurements indicate a visibility of over 60m! The colourful little lake is refreshed with around 14,000L of water per second surging from underground vents. A 45-minute forest loop takes in the waters, which are *tapu* (sacred) and therefore off-limits for a plunge.

THE DRIVE: From the springs turn-off on SH60, it's an 11km, predominantly rural, drive to the Mussel Inn at Ōnekakā, albeit with glimpses of ocean seaward and bush-clad hills inland.

08 Mussel Inn

One of the country's most beloved brewery-taverns can be found sitting largely alone amid farmland in **Ōnekakā**, halfway between Tākaka and Collingwood. **The Mussel Inn** *(musselinn.co.nz)* is rustic NZ at its most genuine, complete with creaking timbers, a rambling beer garden with a brazier, and hearty, homemade food. Try the signature 'Captain Cooker', a brown beer brewed naturally with mānuka. If you can, coincide your visit with one of its immensely entertaining, regular live-music or open-poetry nights. The Mussel Inn is a firm favourite with touring musos, so don't be surprised if you see one of NZ's best or up-and-coming acts playing here. Also be prepared for the possibility of dancing on tables and other sundry merry-making.

THE DRIVE: Should you exercise self-control at the Mussel Inn, continue driving north on SH60, passing the turn-off for Tukurua after 3km. Around halfway to Collingwood (12km) you will pass the pretty Parapara Inlet, while grand mountain vistas open up to the southwest as you look up the Aorere River valley.

09 Collingwood

Far-flung Collingwood (population 240) is the last town in Golden Bay and exudes a real end-of-the-line vibe. It's also the bay's oldest town, and boomed so big during the late 1850s gold rushes that a few roosters suggested it become the nation's capital. Such stories are retold in the town's twin historical repositories, on the main street. **Collingwood Museum** fills a tiny, unstaffed corridor with an idiosyncratic collection of saddlery, moa bones, shells, sewing machines and old typewriters, while the adjacent **Aorere Centre** has an on-rotation slide show featuring the works of the wonderful pioneer photographer Fred Tyree.

THE DRIVE: From Collingwood, SH60 follows the coast north for most of the 24km to the Puponga Farm visitor centre at the base of Farewell Spit, just past the settlement of Puponga. On the way, you'll pass the pretty village of Pakawau, sited handsomely on a long and oft-deserted beach.

10 Farewell Spit

Bleak, exposed and positively sci-fi, Farewell Spit is a wetland

THE GREAT TASTE TRAIL

In a stroke of genius inspired by good weather and easy topography, the Tasman region has developed one of New Zealand's most popular cycle trails. Why is it so popular? Because no other is so frequently punctuated by stops for food, wine, craft beer and art, as it passes through a range of landscapes from bucolic countryside to estuary boardwalk.

The most popular and diversion-filled section of the **Great Taste Trail** *(heartofbiking.org.nz)* stretches 77km from Nelson to Kaiteriteri. While it can be ridden in full over a few days, staying in accommodation en route, it lends itself even better to day trips tailored to suit various interests and levels of ability.

Nelson, Motueka and Kaiteriteri are all good places to set off from, with numerous bike-tour companies offering bike hire, maps and advice. Highlights include wine touring around the Waimea area, Rabbit Island's easy forest trails, and the particularly scenic section from Motueka to Kaiteriteri traversing a fun mountain-bike park along the way.

PETE BAXTER/SHUTTERSTOCK

Te Waikoropupū Springs

of international importance and a renowned bird sanctuary – the summer home of thousands of migratory waders, notably the godwit, Caspian tern and Australasian gannet. Walkers can explore the first 4km of the spit via a network of tracks (see DOC's *Farewell Spit & Puponga Farm Park* brochure; doc.govt.nz). Beyond that, point access is limited to trips with the brilliant **Farewell Spit Eco Tours** *(farewellspit.com)*, scheduled according to the tide. Operating for more than 70 years and led by passionate local guides, this company runs memorable tours ranging from two to 6½ hours. Departing from Collingwood, tours take in the spit, the lighthouse, and up to 20 species of bird. Expect ripping yarns aplenty. The spit's 35km beach features colossal, crescent-shaped dunes, from where panoramic views extend across Golden Bay and a vast low-tide salt marsh.

THE DRIVE: From Puponga, it's 7km along the unsealed Wharariki Rd to the Wharariki Beach car park.

11 Wharariki Beach

The 20-minute walk across undulating farmland is a welcome build-up to the grand reveal of one of NZ's most windswept and interesting beaches. Desolate Wharariki Beach is quite the introduction to the wild West Coast, with a seal colony at its eastern end and otherworldly rock formations scattered about, including, just offshore, the extraordinary **Archway Islands**. As inviting as a swim may seem, just forget it. There are strong undertows here, making swimming incredibly dangerous. For a different perspective, befitting of the area's frontier feel, saddle up with **North West Horse Treks** *(ridegoldenbay.co.nz)* for its 3.5-hour trip taking in the beach.

STAY AWHILE

TĀKAKA

BY ASHLYN OSWALT

The Tākaka Hill's infamously curvy drive is worth it for the creative little town that lies below. The hairpin bends over the hill are a small price to pay for landing in this sunny, free-spirited paradise – the gateway to Golden Bay and Abel Tasman National Park.

I start my day in Tākaka by hopping between coffees and breakfast nibbles at the **Dangerous Kitchen** *(the-dangerous-kitchen.menuworld.com)* and **Wholemeal Café** *(wholemealcafe.co.nz)*, conveniently located next to one another. As a gluten-free vegetarian, I like to indulge when I can.

Next up are the sacred **Te Waikoropupū Springs** *(doc.govt.nz)*, the largest cold-water springs in the southern hemisphere that also have some of the clearest water anywhere. The fully accessible 45-minute loop track meanders along and partly over the springs, but make sure you look and don't touch – contact with the water is forbidden.

Golden Bay's beaches tend to be less crowded than those on the other side of the hill (another reward for that drive!). They're also postcard-worthy – swim or kayak off the golden sands of **Tata Beach** or explore the rock pools in **Ligar Bay** at low tide. A whole day can be spent lazing around either.

A trip to Tākaka isn't complete without a stop at **Mussel Inn** *(musselinn.co.nz)*, 15 minutes north of town. This brewery, restaurant and gig space is an institution tucked among the bush, and its Captain Cooker beer pairs well with all that Golden Bay sunshine. A plate of fresh steamed mussels cures any hunger woes, too.

LINK YOUR TRIP

Tākaka is halfway along the 15 **Tasman & Golden Bays** road trip.

Right: Tākaka Hill
Left: Tata Beach

LEFT: K M HARGREAVES/SHUTTERSTOCK; RIGHT: DONVICTORIO/SHUTTERSTOCK

PLACES TO STAY

- **Shady Rest B&B**
This boutique accommodation is set in a historic doctor's residence on Tākaka's main drag and makes a great place to appreciate the town's creative nature. There are private spa baths in many rooms. *(shadyrest.co.nz)*

- **Waitapu Springs B&B**
Eclectically decorated rooms set among a private garden could hardly be more relaxing, until you add in a spa and sauna. Peaceful and affordable, it's only a 20-minute walk into town. *(waitapusprings.com)*

- **Annie's Nirvana Lodge Backpackers**
Centrally located and wonderfully artsy, with a serene outdoor garden. Shared bathrooms and kitchen space. *(annies-nirvana-lodge-golden-bay-yha.southislandnz.net)*

16

★ BEST FOR

BIRDLIFE

Trees all a-twitter in Nelson Lakes National Park.

Nelson Lakes National Park

MARLBOROUGH & NELSON

GOING WEST: FROM PICTON TO WESTPORT

DURATION: 2-3 DAYS

DISTANCE: 290KM / 180 MILES

GREAT FOR: FOOD AND DRINK, CULTURE

BEST TIME TO GO: SPRING THROUGH AUTUMN FOR LEAFY VINEYARDS AND ALPINE ADVENTURES

This coast-to-coaster is a journey of contrasts. The dry Wairau Valley – its lower plains lined with grapevines and the upper valley blanketed in golden meadows – looks like a different planet compared to the lush, forested mountain country surrounding the Buller Gorge. Between the two, Nelson Lakes National Park is reason enough to travel this route, but wineries and pioneer history should clinch the deal.

LINK YOUR TRIP

17 West Coast Road
Westport is the starting gate for the classic journey down the wild West Coast.

19 Two Passes
From Westport, head south for 102km to Greymouth for the scenic circuit over Arthur's and Lewis Passes.

01 Picton

Sitting prettily at the head of Queen Charlotte Sound, the ferry port of Picton was first settled by Māori who collected *kaimoana* (seafood) in the area. Once Captain James Cook sailed through, whalers and sealers soon followed.

Dial back to such salty old stories at the **Edwim Fox Maritime Museum** *(edwinfoxship.nz),* home to purportedly the world's ninth-oldest surviving ship. Built near Calcutta (modern Kolkata) and launched in 1853, the *Edwin Fox* carried troops to the Crimean War, convicts to Australia and immigrants to New Zealand. Here it's displayed in dry dock alongside the museum, which houses related maritime exhibits.

THE DRIVE: Following SH1, it's a quick 28km zip to Blenheim through the Tuamarina Valley and Para Wetlands, into the broad Wairau Valley.

BENJAMIN_Y/SHUTTERSTOCK

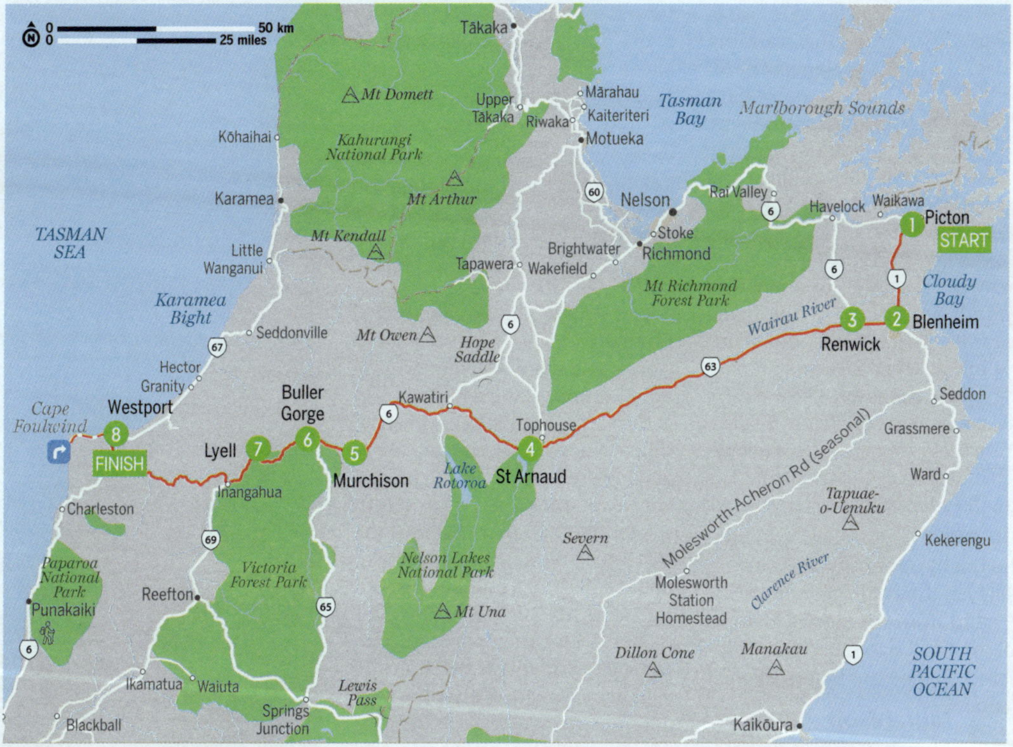

02 Blenheim

Workaday Blenheim is majorly preoccupied with servicing the 170-odd wineries that carpet most of the Wairau Plains between the Wither Hills and Richmond Ranges. In a town as flat as a pancake, 11-sq-km **Wither Hills Farm Park** provides rare views. Around 60km of walking and mountain-biking trails survey the Wairau Valley and Cloudy Bay. Signposts on Redwood St and Taylor Pass Rd lead to two of several entrances, where there are toilets and ample parking. A rewarding 6km loop starts at Redwood St and follows Sutherland Stream up to **Covenant Loop Track**, which takes in the summit of Mt Vernon (422m).

THE DRIVE: Drive west on SH6 for 13km to reach Renwick, passing Marlborough Airport sandwiched between endless rows of vines.

03 Renwick

This small town occupies an enviable position at the centre of Marlborough's wine-touring area, surrounded by more than 20 cellar doors. A satisfying way to explore it is on two wheels; hire a bike from Bike2Wine (p142) and follow the roadside paths and back roads among the vines. Pick up a copy of the *Marlborough Wine Trail* map (wine-marlborough.co.nz) to avoid getting lost. Good wineries to visit near Renwick include **Bladen** *(bladen.co.nz)*, **Forrest** *(forrest.co.nz)* and **Framingham** *(framingham.co.nz)*.

THE DRIVE: SH63 follows the Wairau Valley 92km up to St Arnaud through scenic wine country and sheepy upper reaches. Drive time is around 1¼ hours.

04 St Arnaud

Nelson Lakes National Park, as the name suggests, is dominated by bodies of water, in particular its two main lakes – Rotoiti and Rotoroa. It's also a mountainous and forested haven for birdlife and hikers. Near Rotoiti's northern shore, the small village of St Arnaud is home to the helpful DOC Visitor Centre, a smattering of locals, and warm hospitality at the long-standing lodge. The park has plenty of hardcore country, but you don't have to go far to survey its splendours. From Kerr Bay, just 500m from the village, take the easy Bellbird and Honeydew Walks through lakeside beech forest. You'll likely hear the sweet song of tūī and bellbirds and enjoy the attentions of inquisitive fantails and tomtits – the fruits of local conservationists' labours.

While at **Kerr Bay**, snap a photograph from the jetty – the classic Nelson Lakes shot. Below it, slithering eels will soon scarper should you brave a leap into the drink. The sandflies, however, won't be so kind.

THE DRIVE: Follow SH63 down the bushy upper Buller River valley to Kawatiri, 25km from St Arnaud. Turn left onto SH6 and follow it 45km to Murchison, situated on the Four Rivers Plain.

05 Murchison

Murchison is a hub for trout anglers and white-water addicts who converge on the area's many waterways, including the Buller, which runs alongside the town. It's a small and quiet place, frequented by passing travellers since the 19th century. In 1929 a magnitude 7.8 earthquake rocked the town, killing 17 people and triggering landslides that left Murchison stranded for several months. This and other local tales are recounted in the old-fashioned **Murchison Museum** *(visit murchison.nz)*. The butchery a few doors down sells properly cured bacon and local honey.

THE DRIVE: SH6 heads west through farmland before the valley walls close in. At the SH65 junction, around 11km along, continue right on SH6; Buller Gorge is another 4km on.

06 Buller Gorge

The wild drive along SH6 through the densely forested Buller Gorge, following the course of the broad, tannin-stained Buller River, is the scenic highlight of this trip. Chances are it might be wet, misty or otherwise mysterious, but inclement weather somehow only adds to the drama. Pull over at one of the rest areas along the highway to breathe in the pure, unadulterated freshness of it all.

There's also the opportunity to put some extra splash and dash into your drive with the **Buller Canyon Jet** *(bullercanyonjet.co.nz)*. It's one of NZ's most scenic and best-value jetboat trips – 40 minutes of zipping and spinning along the beautiful river, starting near NZ's longest swing bridge.

THE DRIVE: SH6 continues down the bushy Upper Buller Gorge for 19km to the Lyell historic reserve.

07 Lyell

The once-bustling gold-rush town of Lyell has long gone, but the historic reserve in its place is a popular camping and rest stop.

Wither Hills Farm Park (p153), Blenheim

WONG CM/SHUTTERSTOCK

PHOTO OPPORTUNITY

Endless views from Wither Hills Farm Park.

A short walk through beech forest takes you to overgrown **Lyell Cemetery** – a magical place of rest. Lyell is also the start of one of NZ's gnarliest new backcountry trails, the 85km **Old Ghost Road** *(oldghostroad.org.nz),* which follows a miners' track that was started in the 1870s but never completed as the gold rush petered out. It takes three to five days to walk or cycle its full length, but an easy, 4km return walk still provides plenty of interest, including rusty relics of the remote gold-mining settlements Gibbstown and Zalatown.

THE DRIVE: Head west on SH6, which crosses the Buller via an impressive old iron bridge after 3km. Ignore the Reefton turn-off (SH69), and soak up the splendid scenery of the Lower Buller Gorge. At the SH67 junction, 57km from Lyell, turn right towards Westport, 7km away.

08 Westport

Westport is the gateway to Karamea and the rest of the northern coast's less-visited, totally underrated reaches. The town itself is lined with low-rise heritage buildings. There's also an atmospheric old wharf ripe for redevelopment, and the **Coaltown Museum** *(coaltown.co.nz),* a modern affair that should stoke your interest for a couple of hours. **North Beach** is a great place for a stroll; start at the Buller River mouth and walk to the end of the massive breakwater. If there's a big swell, keep an eye out for local fishing boats trying to cross the treacherous bar, battling menacing, rolling waves. Walk north along the driftwood-strewn beach to peaceful **Orowaiti Lagoon**. Bird life here includes herons, ducks and dotterels, joined in spring and summer by one of the great distance aviators, the bar-tailed godwit.

DETOUR

Cape Foulwind

Start: 08 Westport

Along SH67A, 14km from Westport, you'll find Omau and the start of the **Cape Foulwind Walkway** *(doc.govt.nz),* a wonderful 3.4km (each way) amble traversing coastal hills between Omau and Tauranga Bay. Towards the southern end is the seal colony where – depending on the season – up to 200 kekeno (NZ fur seals) loll about on the rocks. Tauranga Bay (4km by road from the Omau car park) is popular with surfers who dodge its rocky edges.

Dutch explorer Abel Tasman was the first European to sight the cape, in 1642, naming it Clyppygen Hoeck (Rocky Point). However, it was re-christened by James Cook in 1770, who clearly found it less than pleasing. If you visit on a bad day, the name change will make perfect sense.

Cape Foulwind, Westport

NORTH DEVON PHOTOGRAPHY/SHUTTERSTOCK

Farewell Spit
Kahurangi Point
Collingwood
Tākaka
Kahurangi National Park
Motueka
Karamea
Mt Arthur
Nelson
Picton
Richmond
Mt Owen
Mt Richmond Forest Park
Blenheim
Westport
Cape Foulwind
Murchison
Lake Rotoroa
St Arnaud
Victoria Forest Park
Nelson Lakes National Park
Reefton
St Bernard
Punakaiki
Mt Unu
Hanmer Springs Forest Park
Mt Haast
19
Kaikōura
Greymouth
Hanmer Springs
TASMAN SEA
Lake Sumner Forest Park
Hokitika
Jacksons
Arthur's Pass National Park
Arthur's Pass
Gore Bay
18
Waipara
17
Mt Whitcombe
Ōkārito
Lake Coleridge
Whataroa
Franz Josef Glacier
Lake Heron
Belfast
Fox Glacier
Mt Hutt
Christchurch
Aoraki/Mt Cook National Park
Aoraki/Mt Cook
Methven
Lyttelton
Knights Point
Mt Cook Village
Lake Ellesmere
Akaroa
Lake Tekapo
20
Haast
Ashburton
Mt Ward
Tekapo
Lake Pukaki
Mt Aspiring National Park
Fairlie
Canterbury Bight
Temuka
Lake Ohau
Twizel
Mt Aspiring
Lake Benmore
Timaru
Lake Hāwea
Lake Wānaka
Ōmarama
22
21
Kurow
Wānaka
Waimate
SOUTH PACIFIC OCEAN
Queenstown
Cromwell
Ōamaru
Clyde
Alexandra
Palmerston
0
100 km
0
50 miles
Raes Junction
Otago Peninsula
Dunedin

WESTEND61/GETTY IMAGES

Lake Wānaka (p201)

CANTERBURY & THE WEST COAST

EXPLORE

CANTERBURY & THE WEST COAST

The Southern Alps, which form the spine of the South Island, are one of the most dramatic landscapes in New Zealand, making the drives in their shadow and through their passes some of the country's finest excursions. This natural barrier separates two very distinct regions. To the east are the golden Canterbury Plains and the rolling hills of Central Otago, while on the West Coast dense bush abuts weather-buffeted stretches of sand. The logical starting point for most of these routes is Christchurch, New Zealand's second-largest city, where the recovery from last decade's devastating earthquakes continues apace.

Kaikōura

Kaikōura is a pretty peninsula town backed by a picturesque snow-capped mountain range, but its main claim to fame is as a globally significant hot spot for marine wildlife. In 2016 the area was struck by a severe, magnitude-7.8 earthquake that lifted sections of the coastline by 8m, but it's now back in business. There's a large New World supermarket by the beach at the northern end of town, and a scattering of cafes, restaurants, bars and bakeries spread along the highway and the West End shopping strip.

Christchurch

Traditionally the most English of NZ's cities, Christchurch's heritage heart was all but hollowed out following the 2010 and 2011 earthquakes that left 186 people dead. Today, Christchurch is in the midst of an epic rebuild that's completely reconstructing the city centre, where over 80% of the

WHEN TO GO

The Canterbury Plains are one of NZ's driest areas, known for their crisp, cold winters and scorching summers. It's a different story altogether on the West Coast, which experiences a serious amount of rainfall (in places, up to 5m annually). The summer months of January and February are the peak season on both sides of the Alps.

buildings had to be demolished after the quakes. Scaffolding and road cones will be part of the city's landscape for a while yet, but don't be deterred. Exciting new buildings are opening all the time, and most sights are open for business. If you need to stock up on anything from outdoor equipment to groceries, you'll find everything you need here. A good option for fresh produce and multiple restaurants is the daily Riverside Market in the city centre. Other multivenue dining complexes include Little High Eatery, Welder and Tannery. For a bistro dinner, try 5th St in Sydenham or Earl in the central city.

Ōamaru

Ōamaru is offbeat regional NZ at its very best. Rattling around inside its enormous and ramshackle Victorian warehouses are oddballs, antiquarians and bohemians of all stripes who make art and dress up at the drop of a top hat. As the largest town in North Otago, it has plenty of supermarkets and a good array of restaurants and bars. Top options include Star & Garter, Last Post and Cucina

Hokitika

Hokitika is the archetypal West Coast town, positioned between a surf-battered beach and the snow-capped Southern Alps. It's the most appealing settlement on the West Coast by far, with grand old buildings surviving from its gold-rush past and a thriving community of local artisans filling them with their wares. Good eating options include the Hokitika Sandwich Company in the town centre and the restaurant at the Stations Inn, 4km out of town. For supplies, hit the New World supermarket on Revell St.

TRANSPORT

Christchurch is the transport hub of the South Island, with a busy international airport and buses heading to major cities and towns. Scenic train services connect it to Greymouth (TranzAlpine) and Picton (Coastal Pacific). Car or campervan hire is easily arranged. Kaikōura, Westport and Hokitika also have airports with limited domestic connections.

WHERE TO STAY

On the coast and the Canterbury Plains, accommodation types and choices are many and varied, but it's worth booking in advance in summer and when you head into the mountains, where options are more limited. Atmospheric hostels include Jailhouse Accommodation or the Drifter (Christchurch), Dolphin Lodge Backpackers (Kaikōura), Mountain House YHA (Arthur's Pass), Ōamaru Backpackers and Bazil's Hostel & Surf School (Westport). Memorable campgrounds include Lakes Edge Holiday Park (Lake Tekapo), Ross Beach Holiday Park and Fox Glacier Top 10. If you're looking for a boutique hotel, try The Observatory (Christchurch) or The Vicarage (Geraldine).

RESOURCES

- **kaikoura.co.nz**
  Visitor information for the Kaikōura District.
- **christchurchnz.com**
  Official tourism website for the city.
- **waitakinz.com**
  Portal for Tourism Waitaki, with in-person visitor information dispensed from Kurow Museum and Ōamaru & Waitaki Visitor Information Centre.
- **isitehokitika.nz**
  Website for the excellent Hokitika i-SITE, based in the town centre on Weld St.

WHAT'S ON

- **World Buskers Festival**
  Hits the streets of Christchurch every January.
- **Wildfoods Festival**
  One-day festival of daredevil eating in Hokitika in early March.
- **NZ Cup & Show Week**
  In November Christchurch's Addington Raceway hosts two days of harness racing, fashion and entertainment.
- **Ōamaru Victorian Heritage Celebrations**
  Ōamaru indulges in dress-ups, penny-farthing races and a grand fete in November.

17

CANTERBURY & THE WEST COAST

WEST COAST ROAD

DURATION: 6–7 DAYS

DISTANCE: 530KM / 329 MILES

GREAT FOR: FAMILIES, CULTURE AND HISTORY

BEST TIME TO GO: MARCH THROUGH MAY SEES GENERALLY SETTLED WEATHER AND FEWER CROWDS

A serious contender for NZ's most scenic road trip, the end-to-end journey along the West Coast offers deep immersion in the rich wilderness that covers 90% of the region. Nature is interrupted by a series of rustic, old gold- and coal-mining towns, dotting the highway and nestling into nooks in the mountain ranges. Along the way, the wild Tasman Sea beats an ever-present rhythm.

LINK YOUR TRIP

16 Going West: From Picton to Westport
Westport bookends the cross-island journey to the interisland ferry port of Picton.

22 Southern Alps Circuit
The section from Hokitika to Haast is part of this broader loop traversing the Southern Alps.

01 Westport

Flinty Westport typifies the towns of the West Coast, its fortunes waxing and waning on the output of its mines. The coal that has kept it stoked up for much of its existence is on the way out, but it leaves behind a legacy of low-rise heritage buildings, an old wharf precinct ripe for rejuvenation, and myriad industrial curios both in town and beyond. Lovers of gritty history will dig Westport.

A good introduction to the area's life and times is the **Museum of Kawatiri/Westport** *(pounamupathway.com/kawatiri)*, a thoroughly modern affair with well-composed yarns and evocative photographs. The Denniston displays are a highlight, illuminating one of the coast's most beguiling ghost towns, famous for its fantastically steep 'incline', down which hurtled fully laden coal wagons and the occasional coffin. Around 25km north of Westport, **Denniston Plateau** *(doc.govt.nz)* is now a captivating historic reserve with rusty relics galore.

PETER UNGER/GETTY IMAGES

★ BEST FOR

WILDERNESS

Ōpārara's freaky forest and limestone arches.

Moria Gate Arch, Ōpārara Basin

THE DRIVE: Heading south along SH6, swing into Mitchell's Gully Goldmine, 22km south of Westport, to meet a pioneer's descendants and the odd trap-door spider, before continuing another 5km to the unassuming village of Charleston.

DETOUR

Ōpārara Basin

Start: 01 Westport

The 111km stretch of highway heading north of Westport is much less travelled than the southerly route. Skip it and you miss a stack of spectacular sights including one of the West Coast's true gems, Ōpārara Basin.

Lying within Kahurangi National Park, this is a natural spectacle of the highest order – a remote valley concealing limestone arches and strange caves within a dense forest of massive, moss-laden trees that tower over Dr Seuss-esque undergrowth in every imaginable hue of green.

The valley's signature sight is the 200m-long, 37m-high **Ōpārara Arch**, spanning the picturesque Ōpārara River – home to the endangered, super-cute blue duck (whio) – reached on an easy, 2km (return) walk. The smaller but no less stunning **Moria Gate Arch** (43m long, 19m high) is reached via a divine forest loop walk (4km).

Just a 200m walk from the second car park is the **Box Canyon Caves**. Take your torch to enter a world of weird subterranean forms and rare, leggy spiders. Spiders, caves, darkness...sound like fun?

Beyond this point are the superb **Honeycomb Hill Caves and Arch**, accessible only on guided tours run by the **Karamea Information & Resource Centre** *(oparara.co.nz)*. From Karamea, the coast's northernmost settlement, it's 10km to the Ōpārara turn-off at McCallum's Mill Rd, and another 14km into the basin itself.

02 Charleston

It's hard to believe that Charleston, now little more than a clutch of buildings, was a boom town during the 1860s gold rush, complete with 80 hotels and three breweries. The town's thirsty miners staked their claims inland along the Nile River, which winds through a forested valley on the edge of Paparoa National Park. Nowadays the valley is the setting for trips deep into the **Nile River Caves**, run by **Underworld Adventures** *(caverafting.com)*. The limestone formations set the imagination into overdrive, making out odd creatures, strange faces, angel wings and organ pipes. A galaxy of glowworms twinkles overhead as you make your way towards the subterranean river, then raft towards the exit on a rubber tyre. The cave rafting tour begins with a fun ride on the narrow gauge 'rainforest railway' – it's worth a trip in itself, even if you don't fancy heading underground. The caving crew will give you the low-down at their basecamp cafe on Charleston's main road.

THE DRIVE: The 30km to Punakaiki is packed with staggering panoramas of lowland pakihi scrub and lush green forest alongside a series of bays dramatically sculpted by the ocean's relentless fury. Pull over at the designated viewpoints for safe snaps

03 Punakaiki

A small settlement beside the rugged **Paparoa National Park** *(doc.govt.nz)*, Punakaiki has a claim to fame in **Dolomite Point**, where a layering-weathering process called stylobedding has carved the limestone into what looks like piles of pancakes (hence its nickname **Pancake Rocks**). The thoughtfully landscaped walkway that meanders around the point affords various views of the rocks as well as epic ocean lookouts, but the X-factor relies entirely on time and tide. If possible, visit at high tide on a big sea, when the waves surge into caverns and boom menacingly through blowholes. Even better, aim for a high tide at sunset, when the pancakes turn mellow yellow and the fluttering flax flickers with light.

THE DRIVE: Part of the aptly named Great Coast Road, the 45km stretch between Punakaiki and Greymouth is flanked by white-capped waves and rocky bays on one side and the steep, bushy ranges of Paparoa National Park on the other.

♥ WHY I LOVE THIS TRIP

PETER DRAGICEVICH, WRITER

Dramatic scenery is a hallmark of New Zealand, but there's something positively operatic about the way that surf and land collide on the West Coast. It helps that this stretch is 90% conservation land, with only 1% of NZ's population living here. Along much of its length, the mountains dip their feet in the Tasman Sea, wearing a cloak of lush rainforest. It's a truly spectacular route.

04 Greymouth

Welcome to the West Coast's 'Big Smoke', crouched at the mouth of the imaginatively named Grey River and known to Māori as Māwhera. This is a town with hidden charms, some so well hidden that you may question their very existence. But by the time you've checked out the unpretentious town centre, wandered along the **Flood Wall Walk**, and followed the river to its mouth at the wild breakwater where waves come crashing in, you might just find yourself bitten by the Greymouth bug. The town is actually home to one of the coast's biggest tourist attractions, **Shantytown** *(shantytown.co.nz)*, a recreated pioneer village assembled from an array of original gold-rush buildings. It offers a pretty good history lesson on the coast's early settlement, enhanced with sweeteners such as gold-panning, steam-train rides, holographic movies and period-costume photo shoots in the old saloon. The squeamish may wish to skip the iron lung and other gory hospital exhibits.

THE DRIVE: The 39km drive to Hokitika hugs the coastline most of the way, passing the turn-off to Arthur's Pass around the halfway point, at Kumara Junction. Keep on trucking south on SH6.

05 Hokitika

The setting for numerous NZ novels – including Eleanor Catton's 2013 Man Booker award-winner, *The Luminaries* – Hokitika is yet another West Coast town founded on gold. Today it is the stronghold of indigenous *pounamu* (greenstone/jade), fashioned into pendants and other personal

Punakaiki

KAVRAM/SHUTTERSTOCK

treasures. Master carvers jostle for position alongside jewellers, glass-blowers and various crafts-people, making Hokitika a hub for craft lovers. The town also has some admirable historic buildings, including the 1908 Carnegie Building housing **Hokitika Museum** *(hokitikamuseum.co.nz)*. It has intelligently curated and wide-ranging displays covering such topics as Māori and their use of pounamu, the gold-rush era, and the region's natural and social history. Ten minutes' walk from the town centre is Sunset Point. A spectacular vantage point at any time of day, this is – as the name suggests – the primo place to watch the light fade. Seagulls, drifting sands and fish and chips: this is New Zealand.

THE DRIVE: From central Hokitika, drive inland on Stafford St, then follow the signs to Lake Kaniere Scenic Reserve, 20km away.

06 Lake Kaniere

At the foot of Mt Tuhua, and surrounded by classic West Coast rainforest, **Lake Kaniere** *(doc.govt.nz)* is a tranquil place even in high season. The reserve's hub is grassy **Hans Bay** where there are campsites, toilets and a jetty to jump off should you wish to avoid the tortuous tiptoe in. There are also numerous bush walks including a 650m amble to Canoe Cove.

THE DRIVE: Continue clockwise around the lake and then head back towards the coast on a gravel road (not suitable for campervans) to the small settlement of Kokatahi. From there zigzag on rural back roads signposted for the Hokitika Gorge. Total driving distance is 37km.

07 Hokitika Gorge

Through this ravishing granite ravine flow unbelievably turquoise waters, tinted by glacial 'flour'. The surreal scene can be photographed from various angles via a short forest walkway, complete with swing bridge, and a toe may be tentatively dipped in the drink.

THE DRIVE: Return to Hokitika via Kaniere–Kowhitirangi Rd, then head south on SH6 where you'll encounter the historic Mananui Tramline, which is definitely worth a wander. The rest of the drive to Whataroa (136km in total) passes a mixture of pasture and forest with teasing glimpses of the snowcapped Southern Alps.

Lake Matheson (p168)

YINGNA CAI/SHUTTERSTOCK

PHOTO OPPORTUNITY

Capture Aoraki/Mt Cook's reflection in mirrorlike Lake Matheson.

08 Whataroa

A dot of a town strung out along SH6, Whataroa is the departure point for tours to the sanctuary that is NZ's only nesting site for the *kōtuku* (white heron), which roosts here between October and February. The only way to visit the nesting site is with **White Heron Sanctuary Tours** *(whiteherontours.co.nz)* on an enjoyable 2½-hour tour involving a gentle jet-boat ride and a short boardwalk to a viewing hide. Observing scores of birds perched in the bushes is a magical experience, whether you're a seasoned twitcher or just a general nature lover.

THE DRIVE: Following the highway south for 14km, you'll reach the turn-off to the Forks, which branches west for 10km to Ōkārito. If it's raining down here in glacier country (and it often is), don't be surprised if the clouds open up as you reach the coast – just one reason we love Ōkārito.

09 Ōkārito

The sweet, seaside hamlet of Ōkārito sits alongside **Ōkārito Lagoon**, the largest unmodified wetland in NZ and a superb place for spotting birds including rare kiwi and the majestic kōtuku. There are numerous walks to enjoy, from the easy Wetland Walk (20 minutes) to the 3½-hour Three Mile Pack Track, which includes an invigorating (but tide-dependent) amble along Ōkārito's wild beach (a superb sunset spot, with the possibility of a beach bonfire). If you're even remotely into kayaking, a paddle on the lagoon is a must-do. **Okarito Kayaks** *(okarito.co.nz)* will kit you up and recommend a suitable adventure – most commonly a noodle across the lagoon's open waters and up into

ATOSAN/SHUTTERSTOCK

Fox Glacier

GLACIERS – THE COLD, HARD FACTS

Franz Josef and Fox Glaciers are peculiar – in no other place at this latitude do glaciers come so close to the ocean. Buzzing above them on an aerial sightseeing tour or walking on the ice, you'll be greeted not just by a snowy, mountainous spectacle, but also by panoramic views of the Tasman Sea and the lush rainforest that cloaks the alpine foothills and lowlands to the west.

The glaciers' existence is largely due to the West Coast's weather systems. A surfeit of snow falls in the glaciers' broad accumulation zones fuses into clear ice at around 20m deep and begins creeping down the steep valleys.

During the last ice age (15,000 to 20,000 years ago), the twin glaciers reached the sea. In the ensuing thaw they may have crawled back even further than their current positions, but in the 14th century a mini ice age caused them to advance to their greatest modern-era extent around 1750. Terminal moraines (debris marking the end of a glacier) from this time are still visible.

Climate change, however, has brought a consistent retreat over recent years, drastically reducing opportunities for viewing these glaciers on foot. The only way to get close to or on to the ice safely is with a guided helicopter tour.

luxuriant rainforest channels where all sorts of feathered creatures hang out. A more passive but equally memorable excursion is a bird-spotting boat trip with **Okarito Boat Eco Tours** *(okaritoboattours.co.nz)*. Their 9am two-hour eco tour offers a broad insight into this remarkable natural area.

THE DRIVE: Return to SH6. The 18km stretch of highway south to Franz Josef Glacier winds past pretty Lake Mapourika, where you can stop for an obligatory jetty photo, or even a quick dip, if a sandfly bite doesn't bother you.

10 Franz Josef Glacier

Franz Josef and its twin glacier, Fox, are the biggest drawcards of **Westland Tai Poutini National Park**. How close you get to either of them will depend on your budget.

In the case of Franz Josef, the cheapest option is an independent walk up the glacier valley. From the small but bustling Franz Josef village, it's 5km to the trail car park. From here you can take a 10-minute stroll to **Sentinel Rock**, or a 5.4km (return) stroll along the **Franz Josef Glacier/Kā Roimata o Hine Hukatere Walk**, which leads you up the glacier valley to the best permissible view of the terminal face, an elusive 750m away. If this removed view doesn't cut the mustard, consider an aerial sightseeing trip with one of the swarm of operators lined up on the village's main road. Alternatively, take a hike on the ice with **Franz Josef Glacier Guides** *(franzjosefglacier.com)*. Its tours require a helicopter to hop on and off the ice; the easier 'Heli Hike' combines a 10-minute flight with around two hours on the ice in the glacier's upper reaches.

THE DRIVE: The serpentine 23km drive between the Franz Josef Glacier and Fox Glacier townships could well be NZ's most scenic half-hour drive. As you near Fox, the valley reveal is the icing on the cake.

11 Fox Glacier

Compared to Franz Josef, Fox Glacier village is relatively small and sedate, with a more farmy feel and open aspect. Its glacier viewing options also include scenic flights (with operators lined up in the same fashion along the main road) and on-the-ice glacier hikes requiring a helicopter trip, offered by **Fox Glacier Guiding** *(foxguides.co.nz)*. Sadly, landslides in 2019 have permanently closed the roads leading towards its terminus, but you can get a decent, albeit distant, view from the roadside **Peak Viewpoint**. There are another couple of notable natural wonders in Fox Glacier's ambit. From the village it's just 6km down Cook Flat Rd to forest-fringed **Lake Matheson**, the famous 'mirror lake' in which the Southern Alps (including Aoraki/Mt Cook) are reflected, when conditions are ideal. Another 15km further down Cook Flat Rd you will hit the Tasman coast at black-sand **Gillespies Beach** *(doc.govt.nz)*. Interesting walks from here include a five-minute zip to the old miners' cemetery and the 6.8km return walk to **Galway Beach**, home to herds of seals.

THE DRIVE: Allow 90-minutes to reach Ship Creek Tauparikākā, 103km away along a scenic stretch of highway chopped through lowland forest and occasional pasture, with views inland to sheer-sided valleys, and intermittent but grand views seaward. This section of highway only opened in 1965, as commemorated at Knights Point lookout, 6km beyond Lake Moeraki. Stop there for awesome Tasman Sea views

12 Ship Creek Tauparikākā

Ship Creek Tauparikākā, 14km northeast of Haast River, is a terrific place to stretch the legs. It boasts two great short walks with fascinating information panels: the **Dune Lake Walk**, all sand dunes and stunted forest, leading to a surprising view; and the unsurprisingly boggy **Kahikatea Swamp Forest Walk**, featuring sections of handsome boardwalk.

THE DRIVE: This 18km stretch of the SH6 clings to the coast before cutting inland to cross the mighty Haast River on NZ's longest single-lane bridge. Just after it is Haast Junction, the turn-off for Jackson Bay; 3km further along is Haast township from where SH6 leads southeast to Central Otago via Haast Pass.

13 Haast

The Haast region bookends the West Coast road. It's a vast and rich wilderness of kahikatea and rātā forests, wetlands, sand dunes, seal and penguin colonies, birdlife and sweeping beaches, all aiding its inclusion in Te Wāhipounamu–South West New Zealand World Heritage Area. There's not a huge amount to see and do in the Haast township itself, with the exception of dropping into the **Department of Conservation Visitor Centre** *(doc.govt.nz)* and having a meal at one of the pubs.

Haast is the gateway to one of NZ's best off-the-beaten-track drives – the dead-end road leading south to Jackson Bay/Okahu.

YINGNA CAI/SHUTTERSTOCK

Ship Creek Tauparikākā

DETOUR

Jackson Bay Road

Start: 13 Haast

In fine weather, this is an intensely scenic journey between the Southern Alps and the wild coast, passing farms settled by some of the hardiest souls the South ever saw. Cemeteries and other heritage sites betray the settlers' wrangles on land and sea.

Wilderness, however, has always reigned supreme here, as is evident in the vast World Heritage Area that blankets the inland ranges. It's largely impenetrable to all but hardy hunters and super-keen hiking types, but a unique perspective is offered by **Wayne's Waiatoto River Safaris** *(riversafaris.co.nz)*. One of NZ's best backcountry jetboat tours, the two-and-a-half-hour trip takes passengers upriver deep into pristine forest, then all the way back down to the salt-misted river mouth. Magical.

Without stops, it's less than an hour to drive the entire 51km from Haast to the fishing village of **Jackson Bay/Okahu**, the only natural harbour on the West Coast. With good timing you'll arrive when **Cray Pot** *(thecraypotnz.com)* is open. This place is just as much about the dining room (a caravan) and location (looking out over the bay) as it is about the honest seafood, including fish and chips, crayfish, chowder and whitebait.

Walk off your fries on the **Wharekai–Te Kou Walk** (1.6km return) to tiny, boulder-strewn **Ocean Beach**, pounded by waves and lined with interesting rock pools. DOC's *Walks and Activities in the Haast Area* pamphlet *(doc.govt.nz)* details this and other jaunts along Jackson Bay Rd.

STAY AWHILE

HOKITIKA

BY ASHLYN OSWALT

I haven't really made it to the West Coast until I walk along Hokitika's driftwood-strewn beach, on the rugged coast of the Tasman Sea, getting soaked by sideways rain. While Hokitika's inclement weather can feel like a drawback, it's what makes the native bush lush and green.

Founded in 1864 during the gold rush, the town is also known for its other natural resource: *pounamu* (jade). A treasured stone for Māori, jade is traditionally carved into tools, weapons and jewellery. Browse the galleries that dot the main streets selling handmade wares, or take a three-hour guided walk along the Arahura River with **Te Rua & Sons** *(teruaandsons.com)* to learn about foraging and the significance of pounamu.

It's practically obligatory to stop at the **Hokitika Gorge** *(doc.govt.nz)* to take in views of the turquoise pools of water. Walk the easy 2km loop track that takes you across suspension bridges and through the forest. Many other walks in the area meander through old gold mining sites; check online to verify track conditions.

I like to end my day with a pizza from **Fat Pipi's** *(fatpipipizza.co.nz)* – try the whitebait flavour if you want a real taste of the West Coast. If the weather cooperates, I'll take it to watch the sunset at nearby, and aptly named, **Sunset Point**. From this spot, it's easy to see why so many shipwrecks transpired at this treacherous river mouth. With shipwrecks at the forefront, the driving rain and stinging sandflies feel insignificant.

LINK YOUR TRIP

Facing the Tasman Sea, Hokitika is halfway along the 17 West Coast Road road trip.

LEFT: WAN KUM SEONG/SHUTTERSTOCK; RIGHT: NARROW WINDOW PHOTOGRAPHY/SHUTTERSTOCK

Left: Hokitika Beach
Right: Hokitika Gorge

PLACES TO STAY

- **Hokitika Fire Station Boutique Accommodation**
  Luxury hotel set in the beautifully restored Hokitika Fire Station, a historic landmark. Centrally located, the spacious apartments are the perfect base for exploring Hokitika and the surrounding area. *(hokitikafirestation.co.nz)*

- **Beachfront Hotel Hokitika**
  Mere steps from the sand with a dining patio overlooking the water, this hotel is a great spot to take in the dramatic vistas of Hokitika from your cosy and warm room. *(beachfronthotel.co.nz)*

- **Pioneer Hotel**
  Offering tidy rooms with shared bathrooms, this is a budget-friendly, basic and central option. There's an on-site restaurant serving classic pub food. *(pioneerhotel.co.nz)*

18

CANTERBURY & THE WEST COAST

ALPINE PACIFIC TRIANGLE

★ BEST FOR

RELAXATION

Hanmer Springs' therapeutic hot pools.

DURATION: 3-4 DAYS

DISTANCE: 465KM / 289 MILES

GREAT FOR: NATURE, FAMILIES AND CULTURE

BEST TIME TO GO: ALL YEAR ROUND; SOME OF THE BEST WHALE-WATCHING IS IN WINTER

Hanmer Springs Thermal Pools (p174)

Travellers making a beeline for Kaikōura may be interested to find they can turn A to B into a terrific triangle. The highway behind the Seaward Kaikōura Ranges adds not only a quiet journey through quintessential inland Canterbury countryside, but also the hot pools of Hanmer Springs, various outdoor pursuits and the spectacular Molesworth high-country farm.

LINK YOUR TRIP

19 Two Passes
Join this scenic circuit over Arthur's and Lewis Passes at Christchurch, Waipara or Hanmer Springs.

22 Southern Alps Circuit
Christchurch is also the start and end point of an epic loop around NZ's majestic alpine scenery.

01 Christchurch

Christchurch boasts a host of urban attractions such as museums, galleries and restaurants, and it's a great place to stretch your legs on a walking tour. Don't miss the **Botanic Gardens**, a peaceful oasis in the heart of the city occupying 30 blissful hectares of arboreal and floral splendour. Beach bums, however, will also find satisfaction along the Pacific Ocean coast. The seaside superstar is **Sumner** – a perennially popular hot spot for its vibrant little village and holiday vibe. Closer to the city centre is **New Brighton**, with its distinctive pier reaching 300m out to sea. Our pick, however, is **Waimairi**, a little further north; it's a fine place for a swim or bodyboard between the flags.

THE DRIVE: Head north on Manchester St, then Cranford

CKTRAVELS.COM/SHUTTERSTOCK

St until you meet Main North Rd. Keep driving north for 2km then turn left onto Styx Mill Rd, following the signs to Willowbank, a 12km journey in total, which should take 20 minutes out of peak times.

02 Willowbank Wildlife Reserve

This family-friendly **wildlife reserve** *(willowbank.co.nz)* focuses on native NZ critters, heritage farmyard animals and hands-on enclosures with wallabies, deer and lemurs. The Natural New Zealand experience combines some of the country's precious native birdlife with some of their introduced predators, but luckily not in the same enclosure. Among a fleet of birds are four varieties of kiwi, plus the speedy NZ falcon and the muscular takahe – the heaviest rail in the world. For an up-close and personal experience, book one of the daily capybara or lemur encounters. The on-site cafe is a great spot to recount your experiences and quench your thirst.

THE DRIVE: From Willowbank, follow signposts 750m to SH1, then follow it north 52km to Waipara through the flat Canterbury Plains and across the braided Waimakariri and Ashley Rivers. The Hurunui hills appear before you around Amberley.

03 Waipara Valley

Waipara Valley may be the pint-sized cousin of heavyweight Marlborough to the north, but it certainly punches above its weight when it comes to knockout wines, with some of NZ's champion pinot noir, riesling and gewürztraminer produced here. **Waipara Springs** *(waipara springs.co.nz)*, 3km northeast of the township, is one of the valley's oldest vineyards. Its riesling can be enjoyed in the charming garden cafe, which serves platters and hearty salads. A further 2km along the highway, **Black Estate** *(blackestate.co.nz)*, occupying an architecturally striking black barn overlooking the valley, presents excellent wines alongside cuisine championing local producers. As well as common Waipara varieties, sniff out its interesting pinot-chardonnay rosé and seductive chenin blanc. The valley's 16 or so other producers can be found on the **North Canterbury Wine Region Map** *(northcanterburywines.co.nz)*.

THE DRIVE: Drive northeast on SH1 through Omihi and Greta Valley. Around 12km on, turn right onto the Gore Bay Tourist Drive (Hurunui Mouth Rd) to head over the hills to the coast, 59km from Waipara.

04 Gore Bay

Gore Bay is a great place to get out of the car and amongst the waves, with the southern end sandy and good for swimming, when conditions are conducive. One of Canterbury's better surfing breaks lends the little holiday village a touch of **Point Break** vibe. There are no shops here – just a camping ground – so pack a picnic and enjoy the serene views without the crowds. The Bay, however, is probably best known for its peculiar gully with walls sculpted by the elements to resemble church organ pipes. **Cathedral Cliffs** are located at the top of a bun-tightening 10-minute climb at the southern end of 'town'.

THE DRIVE: Head northwest along Gore Bay Rd 8km to reach SH1 at Cheviot. Follow the rural highway north, then over the Hundalee Hills to reach the coast at Oaro, 46km from Cheviot. SH1 hugs the craggy coast for the remaining 23km to Kaikōura.

05 Kaikōura

According to Māori lore, the Kaikōura Peninsula (Taumanu o te Waka o Māui) is where the demigod Māui placed his feet when he fished up the North Island. Kaikōura's people have maintained strong links with the sea – firstly Māori who prized the area for its *kaimoana* (seafood), and latterly European settlers who hunted the southern right and sperm whales that frequented the coast. These days Kaikōura's resident and visiting whale populations are targeted by tourists' viewfinders on world-famous whale-watching tours. An abundance of other marine tours runs the gamut from albatross-spotting to swimming with seals. Yes, you heard right. While seals can readily be seen lolling slothfully at various Kaikōura coastal colonies, NZ fur seals (kekeno) can also be observed on two-hour snorkelling trips with **Seal Swim Kaikōura** *(sealswimkaikoura.co.nz)*.

THE DRIVE: Head back on SH1 for 5km, then take SH70 inland to Waiau. Around 14km further on, turn right into Flintoft Mouse Point Rd, right again at the SH7 junction, then right again at SH7A. The 130km drive to Hanmer Springs should take two hours, tops.

06 Hanmer Springs

This pretty little mountain town is famous for its hot springs resort, **Hanmer Springs Thermal Pools** *(hanmersprings.co.nz)*, a large, pleasantly landscaped complex with pools aplenty, a day spa and a cafe, plus the super-exciting Conical Hill waterslide, the biggest in NZ. More relaxation can be found by way of nature-based activities. The town's primary outdoor playground is **Hanmer Forest Park** *(visithurunui.co.nz)*, less than 10 minutes' walk from the centre. The signature hike is the 1½-hour round trip up to Conical Hill Lookout. Mountain biking is also popular, not only around the park but through the town's quiet streets and cruisy Dog Stream trails. Bike hire is readily available around town; the **i-SITE** *(visithanmersprings.co.nz)* stocks a *Forest Park Walks* booklet and a mountain-biking map.

THE DRIVE: Head back along SH7A for 9km to rejoin SH7, and continue south through the Waiau River valley, staying on SH7 to the junction with SH1; then drive south for 10km to Amberley. It's 87km from Hanmer Springs to Amberley and should take just over one hour.

Cathedral Cliffs, Gore Bay
PI-LENS/GETTY IMAGES

DETOUR

Molesworth Station

Start: 06 Hanmer Springs

Spread over 1807 sq km of high country between Hanmer Springs and Blenheim, Molesworth Station is NZ's biggest cattle farm, ranging across a landscape so special it is protected by the Department of Conservation. Cutting through the station is the spectacularly scenic **Acheron Rd**, starting 8km from Hanmer via Jacks Pass Rd. A return day trip is a highly memorable outing.

Molesworth Station is a geolgy-lovers' dream, sporting more glacial features than you can lob a rock at. It's also ecologically significant, inhabited by dozens of threatened plant species competing with the beautiful but unwelcome briar rose. Amid many heritage farm buildings are two cob cottages, including the 1862 Acheron **Accommodation House** near the Hanmer end, which houses historic displays.

The Acheron Rd – via which it's possible to reach Blenheim, 207km (six hours) away – is usually only open from November to early April, weather permitting, with the gates open 7am to 7pm. Overnight camping is permitted in certain areas. For more information, see DOC's *Molesworth Station* brochure, available at the Hanmer Springs i-SITE.

Guided tours are available from Hanmer Springs with **Molesworth Tours** *(molesworth.co.nz)* and **Molesworth Tour Company** *(molesworthtours.co.nz)*.

07 Amberley

The Waipara Valley's 'other town', Amberley is home to a delightfully diminutive brewery, **Brew Moon** *(brewmoon.co.nz)*. Bedecked with striking street art, its out-of-this-world creations include the nicely balanced Hophead IPA and the hoppy Wolf of Washington American Pale Ale. Stop in to fill a rigger (flagon) to take away, or sip an ale with a platter or a pizza.

THE DRIVE: Drive for 47km south along SH1, across stranded rivers and the Canterbury Plains, then through the outer suburbs before hitting Christchurch. Just after the Ashley River, around 16km from Amberley, look for Cocoa Black cafe in Waikuku if you're feeling peckish.

Molesworth Station cattle farm

SANNEPHOTO/SHUTTERSTOCK

19

CANTERBURY & THE WEST COAST

TWO PASSES

★ BEST FOR

HISTORY

Reefton – NZ's answer to the *Bonanza* set.

Maruia Springs

DURATION: 4-5 DAYS

DISTANCE: 592KM / 368 MILES

GREAT FOR: NATURE, FAMILIES AND CULTURE

BEST TIME TO GO: SUMMER FOR ALPINE HIKES; WINTER FOR SNOWY PEAKS

These two Southern Alps passes provide a richly rewarding loop between the distinctly different east and west coasts. Debate rages about which pass is more beautiful – the lusher Lewis Pass or crag-tastic Arthur's. In and around them are lakes, braided rivers and a very odd rock garden, plus a series of small, interesting towns including the hot-pool resort of Hanmer Springs.

LINK YOUR TRIP

18 Alpine Pacific Triangle
At Hanmer Springs you can hop on to this inland and coastal spin between Christchurch and Kaikōura.

20 Inland Scenic Route
Linking Christchurch and Queenstown, this journey meanders along alpine foothills and traverses the iconic Mackenzie Country.

01 Christchurch

Welcome to a vibrant city in transition, coping creatively with the aftermath of NZ's second-worst natural disaster. Over a decade after the 2011 earthquake, Christchurch is being re-energised by new urban developments like the laneways of the **High St** precinct and the foodie haven that is the **Riverside Market**. As you'd expect, there are notable buildings, old and new. There are museums and galleries, too, along with the splendid **Botanic Gardens** and adjacent **Hagley Park**. There's also exciting dining and nightlife. This is a city full of surprises – street art and sculpture, pocket parks and pop-up performance spaces, much of it transient, tongue-in-cheek and downright fun. A walking tour is a great way to explore the city on foot; taking to the streets with a local will deepen your experience. **Āmiki Local Tours** *(amikitours.com)* offers insightful excursions taking in the city's Māori history and contemporary food scene.

NARUEDOM YAEMPONGSA/SHUTTERSTOCK

THE DRIVE: Exit Christchurch north on SH1, which stop-starts through a series of settlements on the Canterbury Plains. Just under an hour into the journey you'll reach the up-and-coming Waipara Valley wine region where you can stock up on a bottle before turning right, inland on SH7, towards Hanmer Springs via the pretty Weka Pass and Culverden. Total distance is 133km.

02 Hanmer Springs

This tree-lined town's raison d'être is the Hanmer Springs Thermal Pools (p174), a large complex forming the heart of the town. Unless you're made of sugar, or other circumstances forbid it, a visit is all but obligatory. There is, however, heaps more to Hanmer than just the pools. The mountain-ringed basin in which the town sits is the setting for all sorts of adventures, starting with the walking and mountain-bike trails throughout Hanmer Forest Park (p174), handily located on the edge of town. Other hiking and biking opportunities abound, but if you're looking to up the adrenaline buzz, head to **Hanmer Springs Attractions** *(hanmerspringsattractions.nz)*, where you can jetboat up and down the Waiau River or bungy jump off its bridge. The river's gentle flows also host family-friendly rafting or inflatable kayak trips.

THE DRIVE: Follow SH7A back to SH7 and turn right, following the river-lined road deep into the virgin beech forest of Lewis Pass Scenic Reserve. As the road enters the Buller District, it gets tight and winding before topping out at the pass proper (864m) and dropping down to Maruia Springs 6km away, just under an hour's drive (78km) from Hanmer Springs.

03 Maruia Springs

Right on the highway, perched on a riverbank surrounded by dense beech forest, **Maruia Springs** *(maruiahotsprings.nz)* is a well-regarded Japanese-inspired hot-spring resort. Much smaller and more relaxing than Hanmer – sandflies notwithstanding – it's an atmospheric spot for a therapeutic soak. Maruia's waters, peppered with black mineral flakes known as 'hot spring flowers', are pumped into a series of outdoor rock pools and private pools. New owners have invested in the property with improvements including additional outdoor bathing pools and private spas. Comfortable accommodation and tasty cafe fare is also on offer.

THE DRIVE: Continuing westwards from Maruia Springs, it's another 7km of forest-lined highway to Marble Hill, less than 10 minutes away.

04 Marble Hill

Located within Lewis Pass Scenic Reserve, **Marble Hill** *(doc.govt.nz)* is home to one of NZ's most beautiful DOC camping grounds – a row of sites tucked into beech forest, overlooking a grassy meadow, encircled by forested mountains. This special place represents a landmark victory for NZ's conservation movement. Back in the 1970s, this significant forest was saved from the chop by a 341,159-signature petition known as the 'Maruia Declaration', which played a part in the Department of Conservation's establishment in 1987. A more concrete feature of the reserve is **Evison's Wall**. A highly unsuccessful geological experiment started in 1964, the 24m-long wall was built along the Alpine Fault to establish how the fault was in fact moving. Such measuring methods have clearly been superseded, so now it's just a straight-as-a-die wall in an out-of-the-way place. For a spot of exercise, head out on the **Lake Daniells Track**. You don't have to go all the way – it's four to six hours return – but even a short foray will reveal all sorts of native flora such as matagouri, mistletoe and sweet-smelling beech trees.

THE DRIVE: The highway soon encounters Springs Junction, with the right fork (SH65) leading north towards Nelson Lakes. The two passes journey, however, continues along a northwest track towards Reefton through the stunning mountainous forest of Victoria Forest Park. The drive will take around 40 minutes (49km).

05 Reefton

For generations, Reefton's claims to fame have been mining (gold and then coal) and the town's early adoption of hydro-electric power generation (1888) and street lighting (1923) – hence the tag line, 'the town of light'. However, it's now gaining a reputation as an appealing base for mountain bikers and hikers. With charming old buildings and a slight sniff of the Wild West, it's a fascinating place for an amble. Pick up the *Walks and Tracks of Reefton* leaflet, available from the **Reefton i-SITE** *(reefton.co.nz)*, which details the Golden Fleece Walk (15 minutes), Bottled Lightning Powerhouse Walk (30-minute loop) and other easy strolls. Every gold-rush town needs a still, and Reefton's got a goodie in the form of the **Reefton Distilling Co** *(reeftondistillingco.com)*, which makes use of foraged botanicals and spring water sourced from the surrounding mountains. Book an hour-long tour or call in for a free tasting of their signature gin, vodka and berry liqueurs.

THE DRIVE: From Reefton, head southwest out of town on SH7. At the small farming settlement of Ikamatua (26km), turn right down Atarau Rd, signposted to Blackball, and follow it along the broad Grey River. Eventually another right turn onto Main Rd leads to the village. The drive takes around 45 minutes in total (57km).

06 Blackball

Blackball was established in 1866 to service gold diggers, with coal mining happening between 1890 and 1964. The town is often touted as the birthplace of the NZ Labour movement, after a successful miners' strike in 1908 led to the formation of a national Federation of Labour. You can read all about it at the open-air **Blackball Museum of Working Class History** *(blackballmuseum.org.nz)*. It's positioned right alongside the hub of the town. Formerly the **Blackball Hilton** *(blackballhilton.co.nz)*. This old pub has Labour-related memorabilia galore, hot meals, cold beer and bedrooms upstairs. Competing with the erstwhile Hilton in the fame stakes is **Blackball Salami Co** *(blackballsalami.co.nz)*, manufacturer of tasty salami, and sausages ranging from chorizo to black pudding. Blackball's other claim to fame is as the southern end of the **Paparoa Track**. This 55km Great Walk is a three-day hike (or two-day mountain-bike ride) through Paparoa National Park to Punakaiki on the coast.

THE DRIVE: Back at the Blackball turn-off, head west towards Greymouth on the Taylorville–Blackball Rd. Cross the Grey River to Stillwater and rejoin SH7, which follows the south side of the river past the historic Brunner Mine Site. It's a short, 30-minute (24km) drive in all.

07 Greymouth

Known to Māori as Māwhera, Greymouth is the West Coast's utilitarian administrative hub and the western terminus for the world-famous TranzAlpine scenic rail journey. Despite its monotone moniker there are some colourful sights to be seen in this workaday town, especially at the **Left Bank Art Gallery** *(leftbankartgallery.nz)*. Deposited within a dashing 95-year-old former bank are contemporary NZ prints, paintings, photographs and ceramics. Directly across the road is the **Flood Wall Walk** *(Māwhera Quay)*, which follows the Grey River towards its mouth along the top of the town's flood barrier.

THE DRIVE: Head south on SH6 for 17km to Kumara Junction; from here, head inland on the Great Alpine Hwy (SH73) to Kumara, another 7km away.

DETOUR

Lake Brunner

Start: 07 Greymouth

Lying inland from Greymouth, Lake Brunner is the largest of the West Coast region's many lakes and a tranquil spot for hiking, bird spotting and various water sports including boating and fishing. The

Marble Hill (p179)
HANS WISMEIJER/SHUTTERSTOCK

PHOTO OPPORTUNITY

Otira Viaduct in Arthur's Pass, possibly photobombed by parrots.

local boast is that the lake and Arnold River are 'where the trout die of old age', which implies that the local fish are particularly clever or the fisherfolk need to tighten their lines. **Greymouth i-SITE** *(westcoasttravel.co.nz)* can hook you up with a guide if you fancy an angle.

There are several short walks, as detailed in DOC's *Walks in the Lake Brunner/Moana Area* pamphlet (doc.govt.nz). A couple of these start at **Moana**, the main lakeshore settlement, and showcase ravishing rainforest complete with mighty miro and rimu trees. Moana's marina area is also great for a swim.

Moana has a couple of places to eat, including a cafe opposite the train station where the **TranzAlpine** *(greatjourneysnz.com)* train pulls in, and a pub with a sunny deck overlooking the lake. There are also numerous accommodation options, the best of which is the motor camp near the lake, in the Moana township. There are two reasonably equidistant routes to Lake Brunner from the Two Passes trip. From Greymouth, head east on SH7 for 13km to Stillwater and follow Arnold Valley Rd for 22km to Moana. Alternatively, detour north to the lake from the Great Alpine Hwy at Jacksons, from where it's 32km to Moana.

08 Kumara

Kumara, a wee dot on the Great Alpine Hwy, is yet another West Coast gold town that ground to a screeching halt. However, it has been greatly reenergised in recent years, largely due to the development of the **West Coast Wilderness Trail** *(westcoastwildernesstrail.co.nz)*, the 133km, multiday cycleway between Greymouth and Ross. Arguably the best day-ride section is between Kumara and Hokitika. The town's star is the **Theatre Royal Hotel** *(theatreroyalhotel.co.nz)*, which has undergone a major and sympathetic restoration and now showcases some of the best accommodation on the West Coast. Kumara's glittering history is entertainingly retold in the information panels opposite the hotel, while some of the town's boom-time relics can be viewed on short walks around town. There's also a glowworm dell in the bush behind the Theatre Royal's miners cottages. At the SH73 end of the track you'll find the historic baths, which in the town's heyday formed the largest swimming pool in NZ.

THE DRIVE: SH73 winds east through the mountains of Arthur's Pass, 71km (one hour) away. The actual pass is signposted (920m above sea level), after which you should stop for the obligatory snap of the Otira Viaduct and a possible encounter with the world's only alpine parrot, the kea.

09 Arthur's Pass National Park

The South Island's first national park, established in 1929, Arthur's Pass straddles the Southern Alps and thus befits its Māori name of Ka Tiriti o te Moana – steep peak of glistening white. The human heart of the park is **Arthur's Pass Village**, home to a permanent population of around 60 and existing almost entirely as a base for visitors venturing out on various outdoor adventures. While there are plenty of short walks from the village, the park's mountains and valleys are also a hub for multiday hikers. The **Goat Pass Track**, starting at Greyneys Shelter, 5km south of the village, is a popular option for those new to pass hopping and route finding. The two-day hike takes you over the 1070m Goat Pass, and along much of the easy-to-follow route that snakes beside the Mingha and Deception Rivers. The highlight is a night spent at Goat Pass Hut.

THE DRIVE: SH73 continues south and east through the Bealey and Waimakariri Valleys with their braided river beds, terraced meadows, and scree-scarred greywacke peaks. The Craigieburn Range rises impressively to your right as you approach Castle Hill/Kura Tāwhiti, 52km (around 45 minutes' drive) from Arthur's Pass.

10 Castle Hill/ Kura Tāwhiti

These otherworldly rocky outcrops, some up to 12m tall, were named Kura Tāwhiti (treasure from a distant land) by Ngāi Tahu Māori. European settlers saw them in a different light, likening them to the crenellations or battlements of a castle, hence the area's two names. Whichever way you look at them, they're a beguiling sight, and a spectacular place to explore. The karst (eroded limestone) formations, with the craggy Craigieburn and Torlesse Ranges serving as dramatic backdrops, offer some of the most interesting landscapes.

THE DRIVE: Follow SH73 east, leaving the mountainous folds of the Big Ben and Torlesse Ranges, over Porter's Pass down to the Canterbury Plains. It's 96km (90 minutes) to Christchurch.

Left: Otira Viaduct in Arthur's Pass

20

★ BEST FOR

STARGAZING

Super-bright stars of the Aoraki Mackenzie Dark Sky Reserve.

CANTERBURY & THE WEST COAST

INLAND SCENIC ROUTE

DURATION: 4-6 DAYS

DISTANCE: 639KM / 397 MILES

GREAT FOR: OUTDOORS, FOOD AND DRINK

BEST TIME TO GO: LATE SPRING WHEN BLOOMING LUPINS ADD A PASTEL PALETTE TO MACKENZIE BASIN

Aoraki Mackenzie Dark Sky Reserve (p189)

They don't called it 'inland' and 'scenic' for nothing, although 'spectacular' is a more fitting description. Yes, the most over-used superlative in the world of travel writing finds its nirvana here – on a road trip that sidles across the Canterbury Plains, around and over the Southern Alps' foothills, through the legendary Mackenzie Country, ending in totally over-the-top Queenstown.

LINK YOUR TRIP

23 Milford Sound/ Piopiotahi Majesty
Take in jaw-dropping lake, mountain and forest scenes virtually all the way from Queenstown to Milford Sound/Piopiotahi – the jewel in NZ tourism's crown.

26 Otago Heritage Trail
Drive 30km on SH8, from Cromwell to Alexandra, to experience more of Otago's flinty history and big-sky scenes.

01 Christchurch

Following Canterbury's devastating earthquakes, a surge of creativity and colour has sprung up in the cracks. **The Christchurch Art Gallery** *(Te Puna o Waiwhetū; christchurchartgallery.org.nz)*, located in the aptly named Arts Centre, takes pride of place in the city's cultural scene, presenting a broad but primarily NZ-focused range of exhibitions.

The bustling streets beyond the gallery fizz with upbeat inventiveness captured in colourful street art, pocket parks, upcycled sculpture, and pop-up performance spaces. Street art brightens the laneways around High St, and the city's chefs are equally bold. Roam through the main artery of the city, pedestrianised Cashel St, for high-street shops and take in the new developments emerging around the recently opened Te Pae convention centre and Te Kaha stadium.

THE DRIVE: From Christchurch drive 47km west on SH73

MATT MAKES PHOTOS/SHUTTERSTOCK

through the Canterbury Plains to Darfield. Continue west, this time on SH77 (Route 72), signposted for Mt Hutt, for the remaining 41km to Rakaia Gorge, the Southern Alps looming ahead.

02 Raikaia Gorge

The Rakaia is one of NZ's most voluminous braided rivers, fed by the rains and melting snows of the Southern Alps. On its 150km journey to the Pacific coast, it gradually widens and separates into strands over a gravel bed. At Rakaia Gorge, milky-blue waters are confined to a narrow chasm, crossed by twin bridges along SH72. A car park by the bridge is the start of the well-graded **Rakaia Gorge Walkway** *(doc.govt.nz)*, which traverses the river's terraces upstream into the upper gorge. Highlights of this half-day outing include native forest, old coal mines and the historic ferryman's cottage, but the grand finale is the view at the walkway's end. A speedier, more exhilarating alternative is to take a blood-pumping 45-minute ride through the gorge on the **Discovery Je**t *(discoveryjet.co.nz)*, based downstream of the bridge.

THE DRIVE: After crossing the twin bridges, continue along SH72 with the alps to your right and classic patchwork fields to your left. The Staveley Store is 25km from the gorge.

03 Stavely

Situated in a tiny village amid Canterbury countryside, the cute **Staveley Store & Cafe** *(staveleystore.co.nz)* sells top-notch coffee, tasty lunch rolls, delectable cakes and locally sourced groceries, including homemade preserves.

THE DRIVE: A further 9km southwest on SH72 is the village of Mt Somers.

04 Mt Somers

The small settlement of Mt Somers sits on the edge of the Southern Alps, beneath the mountain of the same name. The biggest drawcard to the area is the **Mt Somers track** (26km), a two-day hike circling the mountain, linking the popular picnic spots of Sharplin

Falls and Woolshed Creek. The track's western end can be explored from Woolshed Creek. A great five-hour return walk climbs to the abandoned **Blackburn Coal Mine** and along a ridge to the roaring **Woolshed Creek Canyon**, with excellent views at Trig R along the way. Try to spot local avian residents, including the melodious bellbird, the teeny rifleman and the super-swift NZ falcon.

THE DRIVE: Drive south on SH72 for 50km to sweet Geraldine through classic Canterbury pastoral and agrarian landscapes.

05 Geraldine

Consummately Canterbury in its dedication to English-style gardening, pretty Geraldine has a village vibe and an active arts scene. Be sure to duck behind the war memorial on Talbot St to the **River Garden Walk**, where green-fingered locals have gone completely bonkers planting abundant azaleas and rhododendrons – utterly splendid in spring. Information about trails in nearby **Talbot Forest** is available from the **visitor information centre** *(southcanterbury.org.nz)*. Geraldine boasts a terrific butchery and numerous artisan producers in Four Peaks Plaza. Check out **Geraldine Cheese Company** *(facebook.com/geraldinecheeseco)* before making a beeline for delicious cafe fare and preserves at **Barker's Foodstore & Eatery** *(barkersfoodstore.nz)*. On summer Saturdays, the town kicks into foodie gear with a farmers market in St Mary's Church car park.

THE DRIVE: Drive 46km west on SH79 through increasingly hilly terrain as it heads to rural Fairlie and the junction with SH8.

WHY I LOVE THIS TRIP

BRETT ATKINSON, WRITER

Fans of NZ mountain scenery, this is the trip you've been looking for. Depart from the flat environs of Christchurch, and the journey soon segues through alpine foothills to soaring and majestic peaks. Night skies are perfect for stargazing; alpine lakes are cerulean blue; and the world-class wines and adrenaline-fuelled fun of Queenstown and Central Otago provide the perfect conclusion.

DETOUR

Peel Forest

Start: 05 Geraldine

Tucked away between the foothills of the Southern Alps and the Rangitata River, Peel Forest is a small but significant remnant of indigenous podocarp (coniferous) forest, lined with various walking trails. Many of the totara, kahikatea and matai trees here are hundreds of years old and are home to an abundance of birdlife including riflemen (tītipounamu), wood pigeons (kereru), bellbirds (korimako), fantails (pīwakawaka) and grey warblers. A cafe, a DOC camping ground and other accommodation options encourage an overnight stay.

Continuing inland from the forest, a quiet, country road leads to Mesopotamia, the run of English writer Samuel Butler in the 1860s. It also passes the tour base of **Rangitata Rafts** *(rafts.co.nz)*, which runs one of the most exhilarating rafting trips in NZ. The three-hour adventure begins in the stupendously beautiful Rangitata River valley before heading into the maelstrom of the gorge's Grade V rapids.

Another way of soaking up the magnificent scenery is in the saddle with **Real Kiwi Horse Trekking** *(realkiwihorsetrekking.com)*. Trips through lush forest, up the flanks of Mt Peel and along the Rangitata River range from one-hour jaunts to multiday expeditions.

To reach Peel Forest, turn off SH72 on to Peel Forest Rd at Arundel, around 15km north of Geraldine. It's 8km off the highway.

06 Fairlie

Proclaimed 'Gateway to the Mackenzie', tree-lined Fairlie actually feels a world away from the tussocky Mackenzie Country lying beyond over Burkes Pass, but there are two fine reasons for a pit stop. Meat pies have fuelled many a NZ road trip, and the delicious salmon and bacon pie from **Fairlie Bakehouse** *(fairliebakehouse.co.nz)* is a savoury classic. Next, head to **Fairlie Heritage Museum** *(fairlieheritagemuseum.co.nz)*, a dusty but fascinating window into Canterbury's history with farm machinery, model aeroplanes, quirky

Raikaia Gorge (p185)
CURTIS WATSON/SHUTTERSTOCK

dioramas and random ephemera, including a homespun gyrocopter.

THE DRIVE: SH8 leads north over the relatively low Burkes Pass (709m), rounding Dog Kennel Corner into the Mackenzie Country, a land of golden tussock and surreal turquoise lakes, for a total driving distance of 43km.

07 Lake Tekapo

The expansive basin before you, from which the scenic peaks of Aoraki/Mt Cook National Park escalate, was named the Mackenzie Country after the legendary rustler James 'Jock' McKenzie, who ran his stolen flocks in this then uninhabited region in the 1840s. When he was finally caught, other settlers realised the potential of the land and followed in his footsteps. One of the area's few settlements, Lake Tekapo township was born of a hydropower scheme completed in 1953. Facing out across the opalescent, turquoise lake to a vast alpine backdrop, it's no wonder it has proven a hit with passing travellers. The prime focus for tour groups is the **Church of the Good Shepherd**, the interdenominational lakeside church built of stone and oak in 1935. A picture window behind the altar frames a distractingly divine view of lake and mountain majesty. Come early in the morning or late afternoon to avoid the masses.

THE DRIVE: Drive west then south over the Mary Range on SH8. On a fine day the views north will be dominated by NZ's highest peak, Aoraki/Mt Cook. After 47km you'll reach the lookout at the foot of Lake Pukaki.

08 Lake Pukaki Lookout

The largest of the Mackenzie's three alpine lakes, Pukaki is a vast jewel of totally surreal colour. At its southern end, just off the highway, Lake Pukaki Lookout is a well-signed and perennially popular spot affording picture-perfect views across the lake's waters all the way up to Aoraki/Mt Cook and its surrounding peaks. Beside the lookout, eat fresh sashimi from **Mt Cook Alpine Salmon** *(alpinesalmon.co.nz)*, the highest salmon farm on the planet, which operates in a hydropower canal system some distance away. Nearby, the **Punatahu Visitor Centre** presents the historical, geological and Māori cultural background of the lake and the region. Don't miss the superb lake and mountain views from the centre's windows.

Church of the Good Sherpherd, Lake Tekapo

PHOTO OPPORTUNITY

Church of the Good Shepherd and Lake Tekapo.

ATOMICZEN/GETTY IMAGES

THE DRIVE: Drive west for 2km along the base of Lake Pukaki then turn right up SH80, signposted for Aoraki/Mt Cook. This 55km drive, sidling alongside the lake with NZ's loftiest peaks looming ever larger, is totally distracting; pull over at lookouts to take it all in.

09 Aoraki/Mt Cook National Park

The 700-sq-km Aoraki/Mt Cook National Park forms part of the **Te Wāhipounamu–South West New Zealand World Heritage Area**, along with Fiordland, Aspiring and Westland Tai Poutini National Parks. The park is super-peaky. Nineteen of NZ's 23 mountains over 3000m high are found within its boundaries. It is also, of course, home to the nation's tallest mountain – **Aoraki/Mt Cook** (3724m). A series of vista-filled short walks can be enjoyed in conditions both claggy and clear. The most popular are the **Hooker Valley**, **Kea Point** and **Sealy Tarns** tracks, all starting from Mt Cook Village. In the heart of the village, the excellent DOC Visitor Centre dispatches vital information on hiking routes and weather conditions, plus houses extensive displays on the park's natural and human history. Most local activities can be booked here.

THE DRIVE: Drive back down SH80 to the junction with SH8, then turn right and continue for 9km to Twizel. The total distance from Mt Cook Village to Twizel is 64km and the trip should take just under an hour.

10 Twizel

Pronounced 'Twy-zel', thelittle town of Twizel gets the last laugh. Built in 1968 to service construction of the nearby hydroelectric power station, it was slated for obliteration in 1984 when the project was complete. But there was no way the locals were upping their twizzlesticks and relinquishing their relaxed, mountain-country lifestyle, so Twizel resolutely stayed put.

Today the town is thriving, and has almost all one might need. Stock up on supplies, have a craft beer at the **MoW Bar & Eatery** *(facebook.com/ministryofworksbarandeatery)*, and plan an adventure, such as tramping in Ruataniwha Conservation Park or riding the Alps 2 Ocean Cycle Trail.

THE DRIVE: The scenic splendour continues as SH8 cuts through the Mackenzie Country

BEERPIXS/GETTY IMAGES

Milky Way view , Church of the Good Shepherd

AORAKI MACKENZIE DARK SKY RESERVE

If you think the Mackenzie Country is dashing during the day, just wait until you see it at night.

On cloud-free nights, prepare to be blown away by the brilliance of stars. So exceptional are the viewing conditions here that, in 2012, the area was declared an International Dark Sky Reserve, one of only 16 in the world. If you check out the street lights in Lake Tekapo township you'll notice that they cannily shine down and not up, minimising light pollution.

You can stargaze easily and for free. But for truly out-of-this-world views of the Milky Way, nebulae, planets and moon craters, go on a tour with the **Dark Sky Project** *(darkskyproject.co.nz)* up to the University of Canterbury's observatory on the summit of Mt John, alongside Lake Tekapo. Book ahead, especially if the weather forecast is looking clear.

flats to the small town of Ōmarama, and over Lindis Pass Alpine Hwy. Drive down through the Morven Hills and into Central Otago to reach Cromwell. This 140km drive should take around two hours.

11 Cromwell

Cromwell's historic town centre was flooded when the Clyde Dam was completed in 1992, erasing 280 homes, six farms and 17 orchards. Fortunately, many historic buildings were relocated to the pedestrianised **Heritage Precinct** *(cromwellheritageprecinct.co.nz)* at Lake Dunstan's southern end and set up as period museum pieces, while others house cafes, galleries and interesting shops. There's also a summertime weekly **farmers market**. Nearby, **Bannockburn** is one of Central Otago's finest winegrowing subregions. Of the wineries open to the public, Mt Difficulty (p220) combines plummy pinot noir and a terrific terrace restaurant.

THE DRIVE: This 48km drive along SH6 to Arrowtown through the Kawarau Gorge is packed with mountain scenery. At Kawarau Bridge pause to spectate or take the leap yourself. The turn off for Arrowtown is 6km after the bridge.

12 Arrowtown

Quaint Arrowtown sprang up in the 1860s following the discovery of gold glistening in the Arrow River. Today its pretty, tree-lined avenues retain more than 60 of their original gold-rush buildings. The town makes a great base for exploring the wider region, enabling you to enjoy its history, charm and excellent restaurants once the tour buses have moved on. The Lakes District Museum & Gallery (p223) is an excellent, kid-friendly introduction to the area's colourful gold-rush history – try your luck panning for gold in the Arrow River.

THE DRIVE: Drive southwest on SH6 past Lake Hayes and then towards Queenstown, with views of the Remarkables peaks on your left. Once past the airport, the road runs beside Lake Wakatipu for the remaining 6km into Queenstown, for a total hop of just 20km.

13 Queenstown

Framed by the jagged peaks of the Remarkables and meandering coves of Lake Wakatipu, Queenstown is a right show-off. Looking like a small town but displaying the energy of a small city, it wears its 'Global Adventure Capital' badge proudly, and most visitors take the time to do crazy things here that they've never done before. One of the most famous of these acts is bungy jumping, pioneered by AJ Hackett. Their original bungy base still operates from Kawarau Bridge, but you can take the leap much closer to town at the **Ledge** *(bungy.co.nz)* – a 47m-high leap from the slopes of Ben Lomond. The bungy platform is located atop the Skyline Gondola (p219). This iconic Queenstown lookout is home to a cafe and restaurant, a paragliding launchpad, and the outrageously fun luge.

Bungy jumping, Kawarau Bridge
NICRAM SABOD/SHUTTERSTOCK

ELECTRIC-BLUE VIEWS

The **Waitaki Hydro Scheme** encompasses seven hydro lakes, including mighty Lake Tekapo and Lake Pukaki, as well as several smaller ones within the Mackenzie Country and adjacent Waitaki Valley.

Imbuing the landscape with considerable colour and texture, the scheme's lakes and canals brim with surreal blue waters, contrasting starkly with the surrounding golden tussock and flinty grey ranges.

So, what gives these lakes and canals their blazing turquoise colour? The answer: tiny particles of rock – known as 'glacial flour' or 'rock flour' – ground down by glacial erosion and washed into the lakes. This sediment gives the water a milky quality and refracts the sunlight beaming down, hence the distinctive brilliant blue hue. Photoshop? Who needs it!

21

★ BEST FOR

CYCLING

Swap the car for a bike on the Alps 2 Ocean Cycle Trail.

CANTERBURY & THE WEST COAST

ALPS TO OCEAN

DURATION: 12-14 DAYS

DISTANCE: 1379KM / 857 MILES

GREAT FOR: NATURE, CULTURE AND HISTORY

BEST TIME TO GO: SPRING AND SUMMER IF YOU WANT TO HIKE OR SWIM IN THE LAKES

Alps 2 Ocean Cycle Trail (p197)

New Zealand's highest mountain – Aoraki/Mt Cook – may be the geographical pinnacle of this memorable trip, but when it comes to eye-popping highlights, it's merely the tip of the iceberg. Amid expansive landscapes lined with glacier-carved valleys, turquoise lakes, tussock-covered highlands and broad, braided rivers are several friendly towns and a series of fascinating hydropower structures.

LINK YOUR TRIP

20 Inland Scenic Route
At Aoraki/Mt Cook or Twizel, join this classic drive through the big-sky landscapes of the central South Island.

04 East Coast Express
From Ōamaru, experience the East Coast's wildlife, ocean scenes and rural charm, plus rejuvenating Christchurch.

01 Aoraki/Mt Cook National Park

Aoraki/Mt Cook National Park's peaks are among NZ's grandest, with 19 numbering in the country's 23 over 3000m. It should come as no surprise, then, that NZ's greatest adventurer, Sir Edmund Hillary, honed his craft here, ascending Aoraki/Mt Cook – Australasia's highest mountain – in 1948. The 3724m 'cloud piercer' (as it's known in Māori) was actually at least 10m higher when Sir Ed climbed it, but in 1991 the summit collapsed, sending 12 million cu metres of rock cascading down the mountain. Discover more of the national park's fascinating stories at DOC's splendid Aoraki/Mt Cook National Park Visitor Centre (doc.govt.nz). A couple of minutes' walk away, inside the huge Hermitage Hotel, the **Sir Edmund Hillary Alpine Centre** *(hermitage.co.nz)* pays fitting tribute through various displays, while a series of

ANDREW BAIN/GETTY IMAGES

movies screened throughout the day includes the rousing Mt Cook Magic 3D – a must-see if inclement weather means you can't see the mountain for real.

THE DRIVE: Drive for 55km south on SH80, sidling alongside Lake Pukaki, pausing at lookout points to appreciate the colourful landscape. At the junction with SH8 turn right; it's 9km to Twizel.

02 Twizel

Built in 1968 to temporarily house workers on the nearby hydropower scheme, Twizel has survived way past its use-by date thanks to locals who refused to leave their little slice of paradise. They were certainly on to something, for the Mackenzie Country is now one of NZ's most celebrated landscapes, with Twizel sitting pretty in the thick of it.

As well as being the primary hub for two-wheeled tours on the Alps 2 Ocean Cycle Trail, it's also a handy take-off point for scenic flights over Aoraki/Mt Cook National Park. **Helicopter Line** *(helicopter.co.nz)*, operating from Pukaki Airport, 3km north of town, and Glentanner Park on SH80, offers a variety of options from 25 minutes to an hour, with the wow-factor rising in parallel with trip prices. All but the shortest aerial adventures feature a snow landing.

THE DRIVE: SH8 heads south through mountain surrounds. After 25km, turn right into Quailburn Rd and continue for 4km to the sign for Cathedral Cliffs, located at the end of an 11km private, unsealed road.

03 Clay Cliffs Paritea

About as 'hidden gem' as you can get in an area rife with nosy tourists, these eerie pinnacles, ravines and ridges have been shaped by around two million years of erosion along the active Ostler fault. But you don't have to be a geology geek to appreciate their wacky lamellar form and aggregate tectonicity. Short trails lead around and between the forms to make you feel like an ant crawling in a sandcastle. The cliffs are on private land; be sure to pay the modest entrance fee at the honour box at the gate. Walk 10 minutes along the trail from the car park to get among them.

THE DRIVE: Return to SH8 via Quailburn Rd, and turn right towards Ōmarama, 5km away. The total distance is about 16km.

04 Ōmarama

This quiet little town lies at a significant junction on the Inland Scenic Route between Christchurch and Queenstown, while SH83 funnels travellers down the Waitaki Valley towards the Pacific Ocean.

Ōmarama's huge, pollution-free skies encourage stargazing, particularly from the private, wood-fired hot tubs at **Omarama Hot Tubs** *(hottubsomarama.co.nz)*. The concept is Japanese, but with the surrounding mountain ranges, the lakeside setting and a pristine night sky, you could only be on the South Island of NZ. Choose between a 90-minute soak or a two-hour session in a 'wellness pod', which includes a sauna. Summer thermals and alpine scenery have made Ōmarama a world-renowned gliding base.

THE DRIVE: Drive southeast along SH83 through the upper Waitaki Valley for 24km to Otematata, passing Lake Benmore, which can be admired from Sailors Cutting. At Otematata, follow the signpost left to Benmore Dam, 5km away.

05 Benmore Dam

Benmore is the first of three hydro lakes in the upper Waitaki Valley, and the largest artificial lake in NZ. Benmore Dam, at its southern end, is a beauty. Completed and filled in 1965, it's the largest earth dam in the land and holds back enough water to power around 298,000 homes. The road across the dam not only enables you to snap it from every angle, but also provides access to the scenic north-bank road that winds around the next arrestingly blue stretch of water, Lake Aviemore. The lakeshores here are popular camping grounds with basic facilities; some Kiwi families have been setting up in the same shady patch every summer for generations.

THE DRIVE: After crossing the dam, drive for 23km along Te Akatarawa Rd until you reach Aviemore Dam. A refreshing dip may be had along the way. Cross the dam and follow SH83 down the Waitaki Valley to Kurow, 15km away.

06 Kurow

One of the most appealing stops along the Waitaki Valley is tiny, lost-in-time Kurow, home town of All Blacks hero Richie McCaw. The town also boasts champion wines. They may have a long way to go to achieve the reputation enjoyed by their colleagues over in Central Otago, but some wonderful drops are produced from the tricky but propitious local terroir. Visit **River T Estate** *(rivertestate.co.nz)*, which offers over 40 local wines by the glass, including its own well-regarded pinot gris and chardonnay. Linger over a platter featuring local Waitaki Valley produce and dine overlooking the vines – you're encouraged to stroll around and sample the grapes when they're in season.

THE DRIVE: Drive southeast on SH83 until you reach Livingstone–Duntroon Rd, just past teeny weeny Duntroon. Turn right, drive for 4km, then turn left into Island Cliff–Duntroon Rd. Elephant Rocks are 1km further on the right, 29km from Kurow.

07 Elephant Rocks

Pop the trunk, pocket some peanuts, and wander into a geological wonderland you'll never forget – a series of huge limestone boulders lying like oddly cast, oversized knucklebones on a lush green paddock nibbled neatly by sheep. Such is the fantastical nature of this bizarre landscape that it appeared as Aslan's Camp in the *Narnia* movies. These rock stars started life at the bottom of the ocean more than 24 million years ago. Originally formed from the skeletal remains of marine organisms compressed into limestone, they were thrust upwards and subsequently sculpted by wind, rain and rivers. Enjoy your peanut picnic in the warm cradle of a boulder. It may even bring on a wee nana nap.

Hooker Valley (p189)

YUNSUN_KIM/SHUTTERSTOCK

PHOTO OPPORTUNITY

The pointy end of Aoraki/Mt Cook from the Hooker Valley.

THE DRIVE: Continue southwest along Island Cliff–Duntroon Rd, which becomes Tokarahi–Ngapara Rd and then Weston–Ngapara Rd, for a meandering 40km drive through rolling, pastoral landscapes to Ōamaru.

08 Ōamaru

Nothing moves very fast in Ōamaru. Tourists saunter, locals linger and even its resurrected heritage transport - penny-farthings and steam trains - reflect an unhurried pace and a wellspring of eccentricity bubbling under the surface.

Also taking their time every evening, the tykes from the Ōamaru blue penguin colony *(penguins.co.nz)* surf in and wade ashore, heading to their nests in an old stone quarry near the waterfront. Stands are set up on either side of the waddle route. General admission will give you a good view of the action but the premium stand (adult/child $63/37.50), accessed by a boardwalk through the nesting area, will get you closer. You'll see the most penguins (up to 250) in November and December. From March to August there may be only 10 to 50 birds.

Lake Ohau, Alps 2 Ocean Cycle Trail (A2O)

ALPS 2 OCEAN ON TWO WHEELS

One of the best Great Rides within the **New Zealand Cycle Trails** *(nzcycletrail.com),* the 'A2O' serves up epic vistas from the foot of the Southern Alps all the way to the Pacific Ocean at Ōamaru. In fact, the off-road trail parallels this road trip for much of the way.

Off-the-bike activities include wine tasting, scenic flights and soaking in alfresco hot tubs, and while the whole trail takes four to six days to ride, it can readily be sliced into shorter sections. Twizel is an excellent base for day trips, such as the five-to-six-hour big-sky ride from Tekapo to Twizel, or from Twizel out to the lodge at remote **Lake Ohau** for lunch or dinner.

Down-home hospitality, along with bike hire and shuttle companies, such as Twizel-based **Cycle Journeys** *(cyclejourneys.co.nz),* make for easy logistics and maximum enjoyment. The **A2O website** *(alps2ocean.com)* has comprehensive details; the trail is also showcased in Lonely Planet's *Epic Bike Rides of the World* book.

Elephant Rocks (p194)

22

★ BEST FOR

MOUNTAIN SCENERY

An aerial sightseeing trip around Aoraki/ Mt Cook.

CANTERBURY & THE WEST COAST

SOUTHERN ALPS CIRCUIT

DURATION: 4-5 DAYS

DISTANCE: 299KM / 186 MILES

GREAT FOR: FAMILIES, OUTDOORS

BEST TIME TO GO: WINTER SNOWS ENSURE THIS ISA STUNNER ALL YEAR ROUND

Aoraki/Mt Cook National Park (p204)

Nothing defines the South Island like the Southern Alps, the 500km-long series of ranges stretching from Nelson Lakes to Fiordland. This trip offers the chance to admire a vast swathe of them from all manner of angles on such quintessential New Zealand experiences as glacier ice hikes, scenic flights, cross-country bike rides and nature walks – or just staring out the car window, if you prefer.

LINK YOUR TRIP

23 Milford Sound/ Piopiotahi Majesty
Lakes, mountains and waterfalls decorate this super-scenic drive from Queenstown to Milford Sound/Piopiotahi via Te Anau.

26 Otago Heritage Trail
Drive 24km south on SH8 from Cromwell to Clyde for a history-laden circuit around Central Otago and to the Pacific coast.

01 Christchurch

Nowhere in NZ is changing as fast as post-earthquake Christchurch, and visiting the country's second-largest city during its rebuilding phase is both interesting and inspiring. What's more, the majority of Christchurch's prequake attractions are open for business, including the new **Te Kaha Christchurch stadium** (a new location from the previous stadium) and the historic **Arts Centre**. Christchurch has long been a regular departure point for travellers to Antarctica. Near the airport (and serviced by a free shuttle from the city), the **International Antarctic Centre** *(iceberg.co.nz)* offers an opportunity to learn about the icy continent, see live penguins and experience -18°C wind chill.

THE DRIVE: Head out of town on SH73 across the Canterbury Plains and head into the Southern Alps. The Big Ben, Torlesse

FRANCESCA TAYLOR/SHUTTERSTOCK

and Craigieburn Ranges are but a prelude to the mega-peaks of Arthur's Pass National Park, around two hours (148km) from Christchurch.

02 Arthur's Pass National Park

Straddling the Southern Alps, Arthur's Pass National Park encompasses a seriously rugged landscape, riven with deep valleys and ranging in altitude from 245m at the Taramakau River to 2408m at the top of Mt Murchison. It's popular with alpinists and back-country hikers, but its dramatic wilderness can readily be appreciated on brief forays close to the highway. There are multiple walking options from the village, including one of NZ's best day hikes. The strenuous 7km climb up Avalanche Peak (only for fit and experienced walkers) rewards with staggering views of the surrounding mountains, valleys and hanging glaciers. The village itself, home to a permanent population of around 60, sports a couple of cafes and the **Arthur's Pass Visitor Centre** *(doc.govt.nz)*. Pop in here for walking track information and local weather forecasts.

THE DRIVE: Continue west on SH73. Beyond the actual pass (920m), craggy mountain vistas give way to rural scenes as the highway winds down to meet SH6, the West Coast Rd. At Kumara Junction head south to Hokitika, 22km away for a total of 100km (around 90 minutes).

03 Hokitika

Just one of scores of West Coast towns founded on gold, Hokitika boasts an admirable array of historic buildings, including the 1908 Carnegie Building housing the Hokitika Museum (p166). Its wide-ranging displays cover such topics as the gold rushes, the region's natural and social history, and traditional Māori use of *pounamu*. Hokitika today is a stronghold of this indigenous and highly prized stone, judiciously gathered from nearby rivers and beaches. It's fashioned into pendants and other treasures by master carvers who jostle for position alongside jewellers, glass-blowers and other craftspeople. Art-lovers will find the town a delight. Keep your fingers crossed for a clear evening, because five minutes' walk from the town centre is **Sunset Point** – a great place to watch the light fade with a feed of fish and chips, seagulls circling, and big Tasman Sea waves crashing on the shore.

THE DRIVE: Cross the broad Hokitika River and head south along SH6, skirting coastal farms and the dense bush that obscures Lake Māhinapua. The rest of the 27km drive cuts inland through a mixture of pasture and forest before crossing the Totora River and arriving in Ross.

04 Ross

Ross became famous in 1909 when NZ's largest gold nugget (the nearly 3kg 'Honourable Roddy') was unearthed. The Goldfields Heritage Centre displays a replica, along with a scale model of the town in its glittering years, and offers the opportunity to go gold panning in Jones Creek. Starting near the museum, the Water Race Walkway (one hour return) passes old gold diggings, caves, tunnels and a cemetery. The 1866 Historic Empire Hotel is further testament to the town's bygone era. Breathe in the authenticity, along with a whiff of woodsmoke, over a beer and an honest meal.

THE DRIVE: The 131km, nearly-two-hour drive south to Fox Glacier meanders inland crossing numerous mighty West Coast river systems, cutting through dense rainforest and passing tranquil lakes. The 30-minute section between the Franz Josef and Fox Glacier townships will knock your socks off.

05 Fox Glacier

Fox Glacier is the smaller and quieter of the twin glacier townships, and is set in more rural surrounds. Both have their relative merits and, if your itinerary allows, you should linger in both. The glacier viewing options are a little different for each. In Franz Josef you need to hike up the glacier valley to a viewpoint 750m from the terminal face, whereas in Fox it's visible in the distance from Cook Flat Rd and the Peak Viewpoint on Gillespies Beach Rd. In both towns the very best (albeit hellishly expensive) option is a helicopter ride onto the glacier itself followed by a guided hike through crevices and blue-ice caves; in Fox, this is offered by Fox Glacier Guiding (p168). Otherwise, skydives and scenic flights are offered by a raft of operators.

Makarora River

CHARNCHAI WASINANONT/SHUTTERSTOCK

☑ TOP TIP

PESKY SANDFLIES

You will encounter sandflies on the West Coast. While they don't carry diseases, they are a pain in the bum, face, arm, leg, ankle or whatever else is exposed. Your best deterrent is to cover up, although effective DEET-free products such as Okarito Sandfly Repellent are also readily available. Thankfully sandflies do go to bed after dark, allowing you some respite.

THE DRIVE: Allow 90 minutes to reach Ship Creek Tauparikākā, 103km away along a scenic stretch of highway chopped through lowland forest and occasional pasture. Stop at Knights Point, 5km south of Lake Moeraki, a spectacular lookout commemorating the opening of this stretch of highway in 1965.

06 Ship Creek Tauparikākā

For a taste of the wilderness that qualifies the Haast region for inclusion in Te Wāhipounamu–South West New Zealand World Heritage Area, you can't go past Ship Creek Tauparikākā. The car park by the highway is the trailhead for two fascinating walks. We suggest starting with **Kahikatea Swamp Forest Walk**, a 20-minute amble through a weirdo bog, before heading on to the beach for the **Dune Lake Walk**. This salty, sandy amble is supposed to take half an hour but may well suck you into a vortex of beach-combing, seabirdspotting and perhaps a spot of tree- hugging in the primeval forest around the reedy lake.

THE DRIVE: After Ship Creek Tauparikākā, SH6 sticks close to the coast for around 30 minutes before crossing the Haast River on NZ's longest single-lane bridge to Haast Junction. A little further on is the turn-off to Haast township – the last chance to stock up on food and fuel before continuing through spectacular Haast Pass to Makarora. This 97km leg will take around 1½ hours.

♥ WHY I LOVE THIS TRIP

BRETT ATKINSON, WRITER

Welcome to quite possibly the best road trip in the country – a perfect journey for a couple of weeks or more. Highlights include venturing deep into the Southern Alps via the Arthur's and Haast Passes with a possible detour to Mt Aspiring National Park equally inspiring. Beyond the grandeur of the Alps, there's the contrasting but equally compelling landscapes of Canterbury and the West Coast.

07 Makarora

The first sign of life after crossing Haast Pass into Central Otago, middle-of-nowhere Makarora survives as a road-trip stop and a base for adventure into Siberia. No, not that Siberia. We're talking about the remote wilderness valley within **Mt Aspiring National Park**, reached on one of the South Island's signature adventure tours – the **Siberia Experience** *(siberiaexperience.co.nz)*. This thrill-seeking extravaganza combines a 25-minute scenic small-plane flight, a three-hour hike through the remote mountain valley and a half-hour jetboat trip down the Wilkin and Makarora Rivers. There may be better ways to spend four hours, but it's tough to think of any. This terrific valley can also be reached on the **Gillespie Pass Circuit** *(doc.govt.nz)*, a magnificent 56km, three- to four-day loop for experienced, well-equipped hikers. The side trip to Crucible Lake is one of our favourite day hikes.

THE DRIVE: Head south on SH6 for about 60km. Take the third exit onto SH84 at the roundabout, continuing before turning left onto Ballantyne Rd.

08 Wānaka

While certainly more laid-back than its amped-up sibling Queenstown, Wānaka is not a sleepy hamlet any more. Its lakeside setting is utterly sublime, its streets less cluttered and clogged with traffic. Combine this with a critical mass of shops, restaurants and bars, and you've got an arguably more charming (and slightly cheaper) rival. There's also an endless array of adrenalising and inspiring outdoor activities. Wānaka is the gateway to Mt Aspiring National Park, as well as Cardrona and Treble Cone ski resorts. Closer to town, however, are heaps of easier and more accessible adventures; see DOC's *Wanaka Outdoor Pursuits* pamphlet for a comprehensive run-down. A classic walkway hoofs it up to the summit of **Mt Iron** (527m, 1½ hours return), revealing panoramic views of Lake Wānaka and its mind-boggling surrounds. To get out on the lake, either dive right in or hire a kayak or SUP from waterfront **Paddle Wānaka** *(paddlewanaka.co.nz)*.

THE DRIVE: Head over to Queenstown via the well-signposted Crown Range, NZ's highest sealed road at 1121m. Pull over at designated lookout points to admire the view on the way down to the Wakatipu Basin, and at the junction with SH6 head right towards Queenstown (67km, one hour).

DETOUR

Mt Aspiring National Park

Start: 08 Wānaka

Verdant valleys, alpine meadows, unspoiled rivers, craggy mountains and more than 100 glaciers make Mt Aspiring National Park an outdoor enthusiast's paradise. Protected as a national park in 1964, and now part of **Te Wāhipounamu–South West New Zealand World Heritage Area**, the park blankets 3555 sq km along the Southern Alps. Lording over it all is colossal **Tititea/Mt Aspiring** (3033m), the highest peak outside the Aoraki/Mt Cook area.

While the southern end of the national park near Glenorchy includes better-known walks such as the Routeburn and Greenstone & Caples tracks, the Wānaka gateway offers an easier way in via Raspberry Creek, at the end of Mt Aspiring Rd, 50km from town – much of it along the lake shore. Well worth the drive in itself, even if you don't fancy hiking, the road is unsealed for 30km and involves nine ford crossings; it's usually fine in a 2WD, except in very wet conditions.

A good option for intermediate hikers, taking three to four hours return, **Rob Roy Track** is a chance to see glaciers, waterfalls and a swing bridge, among other landmarks. The West Matukituki Valley Track, meanwhile, heads up to historic Aspiring Hut, popular with overnight walkers.

Your first port of call for advice and resources about these or any of the many other national park hikes should be the **Tititea/Mt Aspiring National Park Visitor Centre** *(doc.govt.nz)* in Wānaka. Note, even these lower-altitude tracks can be troublesome in bad weather.

09 Queenstown

New Zealand's premier resort town is an extravaganza of shopping, dining and tour booking offices, packaged up together in the midst of inspiring mountain surrounds. If you're looking to let your hair down and tick some big stuff off your bucket list, Queenstown's a beaut place to do it. Ease your way into it with a stroll around major sites such as the **Sky-**

Lake Tekapo (p204)

BEYONDNOTE/SHUTTERSTOCK

PHOTO OPPORTUNITY

Lake Tekapo and the Mackenzie Country from Mt John's summit (p204).

line Gondola *(skyline.co.nz)* and **Steamer Wharf** *(steamerwharf.co.nz)*, and following Queenstown Gardens' lakeshore path, revealing ever-changing panoramas of Lake Wakatipu and the Remarkables. Add to this backdrop the region's other mountain ranges, tumbling rivers, hidden canyons and rolling high country, and it's not hard to see why Queenstown is the king of outdoor adventure. The options are mind-boggling, so allow us to suggest one of the classics – a blast on the **Shotover Jet** *(shotoverjet.com)*. Quite likely to be the most hair-raising boat ride of your life, this trip through a rocky canyon features famous 360-degree spins that may well blow your toupee clean off.

THE DRIVE: Drive on SH6A out of Queenstown past the airport and then onwards on SH6 beyond Lake Hayes and the turn-off for Arrowtown. There are numerous temptations on the way to Cromwell including Gibbston Valley wineries and the original AJ Hackett bungy jump. This dramatic 60km drive through the Kawarau Gorge will take around an hour.

10 Cromwell

The high-mineral soils around Cromwell account for its claim to fame as a fruit bowl – as celebrated in the town's giant, gaudy fruit sculpture. Just south of town, **Bannockburn** is one of Central Otago's finest wine-growing subregions. One of the area's best wineries, **Carrick** *(carrick.co.nz)* has an art-filled terrace restaurant, lush lawns and mountain views. Partner a tasting platter with wines including the flagship spicy pinot noir or rich chardonnay. Designated drivers can get their kicks

KYLE SPARKS/GETTY IMAGES

Snowboarding, Coronet Peak

GETTING ON THE PISTE

The South Island is an essential southern-hemisphere destination for snow bunnies, with downhill skiing, cross-country (Nordic) skiing and snowboarding all passionately pursued. New Zealand's ski season is generally June through September, though it varies considerably from one resort to another, and can run as late as October.

New Zealand's ski fields come in all shapes and sizes. Some people like to be near Queenstown's party scene, others prefer the quality high-altitude runs on Mt Hutt or less-stressed and cheaper club-skiing areas. These are some of our favourite South Island skiing and snowboarding spots:

Treble Cone *(treblecone.com)* The highest and largest of the southern lakes ski areas is in a spectacular location 20km from Wānaka, with steep slopes suitable for intermediate to advanced skiers.

Coronet Peak *(coronetpeak.co.nz)* At the Queenstown region's oldest ski field, snow-making and treeless slopes provide excellent skiing and snowboarding for all levels. There's night skiing Wednesday, Friday and Saturday in peak season.

Cardrona *(cardrona.com)* Around 34km from Wānaka, with several high-capacity chairlifts, beginners tows and a gondola cable car.

Mt Hutt *(mthutt.co.nz)* One of the highest ski areas in the southern hemisphere, located close to Methven. There are plenty of beginner, intermediate and advanced slopes.

Ohau *(ohau.co.nz)* This commercial ski area is on Mt Sutton, 42km from Twizel. There are plenty of intermediate and advanced runs, excellent snowboarding, two terrain parks and Lake Ohau Lodge.

at the **Highlands Motorsport Park** *(highlands.co.nz)*, a first-rate, 4km racing circuit offering go-karts, and blurred laps in a Ferrari 488 at 230km/h.

THE DRIVE: From Cromwell cross the bridge over Lake Dunstan and drive north on SH8 along the lake, through Tarras, and on to Lindis Pass before passing into Mackenzie Country. Around 9km after Twizel is the turn-off for Aoraki/Mt Cook on SH80. This 204km journey should take less than three hours.

11 Aoraki/Mt Cook National Park

The spectacular 700-sq-km Aoraki/Mt Cook National Park, along with Fiordland, Aspiring and Westland National Parks, forms part of the Te Wāhipounamu–South West New Zealand World Heritage Area, which extends from Westland's Cook River down to Fiordland. Fenced in by the Southern Alps and the Two Thumb, Liebig and Ben Ohau Ranges, more than one-third of the national park has a blanket of permanent snow and glacial ice. The highest *maunga* (mountain) in the park is mighty **Aoraki/Mt Cook** – at 3724m it's Australasia's tallest peak. Scenic flights are offered by **Helicopter Line** *(helicopter.co.nz)* and **Mount Cook Ski Planes** *(mtcookskiplanes.com)*.

THE DRIVE: Return along SH80, pausing at lookout points along the 55km stretch to soak up more of the mesmerising lake and mountain scenery. At the junction with SH8 turn left and drive a further 47km northeast over the Mary Range to Lake Tekapo.

12 Lake Tekapo

With spectacular alpine lakes, the mountain- ringed basin known as the Mackenzie Country is one of the South Island's most celebrated landscapes. Towards its northern boundary is Lake Tekapo township, born of a 1950s hydropower scheme. On the turquoise lake's shore, the 1935 Church of the Good Shepherd (p188) features a picture window framing divine views of the lake and snowcapped Southern Alps. Arrive early morning or late afternoon to avoid the crowds. From atop nearby **Mt John** (1029m), there is an epic 360-degree panorama. A winding but well-sealed road (a fee applies), or circuit walking track (2½ hours return) leads to the summit, home to astronomical observatories and **Astro Café**.

THE DRIVE: Climb away from the lake on SH8 over the relatively low Burkes Pass (709m) and on to the rural town of Fairlie, home of super-fine pies. From here, drive on SH79 through rolling countryside to Geraldine, the cheese-and-pickle capital of NZ. Total distance is 89km.

13 Geraldine

With a touch of quaint English village about it, Geraldine is a pleasant place to break a journey amid the rural Canterbury Plains. On the town's northwestern fringe, **Talbot Forest Scenic Reserve** *(doc.govt.nz)* is a good place to stretch your legs and hug some magnificent trees, including lofty kahikatea (white pine) and a massive totara estimated to be around 800 years old. The forest lends its name to one of Geraldine's signature attractions, **Geraldine Cheese Company** *(facebook.com/geraldinecheeseco)*. Across the road, Barker's Foodstore & Eatery (p186)

MĀORI GREENSTONE ROUTES

The South Island is known in Māori as Te Waipounamu – the waters of greenstone – which gives some idea of the stone's importance during the early days of Aotearoa's settlement. *Pounamu* is nephrite jade, bowenite or serpentinite, prized for its toughness and beauty and used to make weaponry, tools and jewellery.

Pounamu comes from only one place in New Zealand – the western side of the Southern Alps, particularly from rivers around Hokitika. It was the search for *pounamu* that saw Māori, from around 1300, forge routes from the more populated east coast through river valleys and over mountain passes. These were incredibly intrepid journeys through wild terrain made all the more frightening by New Zealand's volatile maritime climate. The navigational and survival skills of these Māori explorers was a boon for pioneering Europeans who relied heavily on their guidance when surveying the south during the 19th century.

Arthur's, Haast and Lewis Passes, Buller Gorge and the Milford Rd were once single-track pathways followed by Māori greenstone gatherers. Others, such as Mackinnon Pass (on the Milford Track) and Harper Pass, have remained passable only on foot.

YIUCHEUNG/SHUTTERSTOCK

Lake Tekapo

sells tasty pickles to complete your ploughman's lunch.

THE DRIVE: Drive north on SH72, crossing the braided Rangitata River after 6km, then passing through pastoral land along Roman-straight roads. Continue on SH72 as it traces around the eastern edge of the mountains. Turn left on to SH77, 72km from Geraldine, and drive the last 10km to Methven.

14 Methven

Methven is busiest in winter, when it fills up with snow bunnies heading to nearby Mt Hutt ski field. At other times tumbleweeds don't quite blow down the main street – much to the disappointment of the wannabe gunslingers arriving for the raucous October **rodeo**. Over summer it's a low-key and affordable base for explorations into the spectacular mountain foothills. The town itself can be explored on a **heritage trail** and the **Methven Walk/Cycleway**. Maps for these are available from the **i-SITE** *(mthutt.co.nz)*, which can also provide information about other activities in the area including horse riding, hot-air balloon trips and jetboat trips on the nearby Rakaia Gorge.

THE DRIVE: Drive north on Mt Hutt Station Rd and then turn right on to SH72, passing through Mt Hutt village before reaching the beautifully blue river at Rakaia Gorge, 16km from Methven.

15 Rakaia Gorge

One of NZ's most voluminous braided rivers, the Rakaia starts out deep and swift in the mountains before gradually widening and separating into strands over a gravel bed. The half-day **Rakaia Gorge Walkway** is a good opportunity to survey the river's milky blue waters and take in other sites, including the historic ferryman's cottage and old coal mines.

THE DRIVE: Drive east on SH72 (aka Route 77) for 41km to Darfield, leaving the mountains in the rear-view mirror as you reach the patchwork Canterbury Plains. Continue east on SH73, until the outskirts of Christchurch, then follow signs for the city centre. Total distance is 88km.

TASMAN SEA
Whataroa
Mt Arrowsmith
Fox Glacier
Franz Josef Glacier
Bruce Bay
Aoraki/ Mt Cook
Mesopotamia
Knights Point
Mt Cook Village
Haast
Jackson Bay/ Okahu
Mt Ward
Lake Tekapo
80
Lake Pukaki
Lake Tekapo
Fairlie
Te Wāhipounamu– South West New Zealand World Heritage Area
Lake Ohau
Ohau
Twizel
6
8
Mt Aspiring
Lake Hāwea
Ōmarama
Lake Wānaka
Lake Aviemore
Mt Tutoko
Wānaka
Centaur Peaks
Kurow
Waimate
Milford Sound/ Piopiotahi
82
Glenorchy
24
Tarras
Duntroon
Arrowtown
Lake Wakatipu
Queenstown
Cromwell
26
Ōamaru
Clyde
Alexandra
85
Fiordland National Park
Lake Te Anau
Jane Peak
23
87
Te Anau
Palmerston
Middlemarch
Roxburgh
Karitane
Manapōuri
94
8
Lumsden
Lake Mahinerangi
Dunedin
Takitimu Forest
Lawrence
Waihola
Hokonui Forest Park
Gore
1
Milton
Winton
Balclutha
Tuatapere
Te Waewae
Edendale
99
Catlins Conservation Park
Riverton
Invercargill
Owaka
Papatowai
25
Bluff
Oban
Stewart Island/ Rakiura
0 100 km
0 50 miles

KATIBUSNELLO/SHUTTERSTOCK

Lake Wakatipu (p211)

QUEENSTOWN & THE SOUTH

EXPLORE

QUEENSTOWN & THE SOUTH

Here is the New Zealand of your dreams – the epic mountains, towering fiords, pristine lakes and craggy coastlines of the deep south. In this dramatic landscape, seals loll on rocks, snow dusts jagged horizons, roads unwind through dappled forests and your phone loses connection. The centre of the action is NZ's adventure capital, Queenstown. From here you can traverse the golden-hued hills of Central Otago en route to the region's charming capital, Dunedin. Then there's the drive along the spectacular Milford Rd to the glacier-carved grandeur of Fiordland National Park, one of the world's great remaining wildernesses.

Queenstown

Queenstown's self-proclaimed 'adventure capital of the world' tag is only part of its appeal. It also occupies a glorious setting: beside a lake and ringed by mountains. Add to that world-class restaurants and a wine region on its doorstep, and you've got a place to relish even if you never feel the smallest inclination to break a sweat. Expect big crowds, especially in summer and winter, but also big experiences.

The town centre is packed with outdoor shops and has a few mid-size grocery stores, but the large supermarkets are near the airport in Frankton. For a cafe breakfast or lunch, try Bespoke Kitchen (near the gondola) or The Boat Shed (lakeside near Frankton). Fergburger is a Queenstown institution, but be warned: the queues can be extreme. Memorable dinner options include Sherwood Restaurant, the Bunker and Blue Kanu.

Wānaka

Like Queenstown, Wānaka is a beautiful lake-and-mountain resort town bristling with outdoor and adventure opportunities. It retains a laid-back, small-town atmosphere, though things get busy at the height of the ski season and in midsummer. Outdoor stores abound, and there's a large Woolworths supermarket in the town centre. On the touristy lakefront strip, Big Fig offers all-day eating, while The Catch

WHEN TO GO

Queenstown and Wānaka are year-round resorts. Snow activities dominate from June to September, but the towns are nearly as busy in summer, with visitors hitting the hiking and cycling trails. In winter you'll need to carry snow chains to drive some of these routes, and the high-altitude roads sometimes temporarily close in bad conditions.

is a good spot for fish and chips. For something a little fancier, try Francesca's Italian Kitchen, Kika, Bistro Gentil or Arc.

Dunedin

Two words immediately spring to Kiwis' minds when they think of Dunedin: 'Scots' and 'students'. The very name Dunedin is derived from the Scottish Gaelic name for Edinburgh, Dùn Èideann. The city is immensely proud of its Scottish heritage, never missing an opportunity to break out the haggis and bagpipes on civic occasions. Students from the University of Otago make their presence felt in the bars and live-music venues during term time.

Kick-start your day with a caffeine hit from The Perc, near the Octagon, Dunedin's eight-sided main 'square'. Nearby you'll find Bacchus Wine Bar and Pizza Bar, both good dinner options. If you feel like a seafood splurge, book in at Plato. For a fast and satisfying refuelling stop, grab a burger at Good Good. Shop for supplies in the Victorian-era town centre, and pick up fresh produce and culinary treats from the excellent Otago Farmers Market, held at the grand Dunedin Railway Station on Saturday mornings.

TRANSPORT

Queenstown has a busy international airport and there are domestic airports in Dunedin and Invercargill, plus tourism-focused airfields in Wānaka, Te Anau and Milford Sound/Piopiotahi. Intercity buses link the major towns, and Queenstown has its own bus network, which stretches out to include Frankton, Arrowtown and Lake Hayes. Queenstown also has the region's biggest fleet of rental cars.

WHERE TO STAY

Queenstown, Wānaka and Te Anau are tourist towns, with a broad range of accommodation of all kinds. The workaday cities of Dunedin and Invercargill also have plenty of options. Among the best hostels are Tahuna Pod Hostel (Queenstown), Adventure Queenstown and Southern Comfort Backpackers (Invercargill). Holiday parks offer budget and midrange choices, including Driftaway Queenstown, Arrowtown Holiday Park, Wānaka Top 10, Manapōuri Holiday Park and New Haven (Surat Bay). Luxury travellers are spoilt for choice, too, with the likes of Eichardt's Private Hotel (Queenstown), Stoneridge Estate (Lake Hayes), Arrowtown House (Arrowtown) and Edgewater (Wānaka).

RESOURCES

- **queenstownnz.co.nz**
  Official website of Discover Queenstown. The very helpful Queenstown i-SITE visitor information centre is located in the Clocktower Building.
- **lakewanaka.co.nz**
  Wānaka's i-SITE is also centrally located, near the lake.
- **dunedinnz.com**
  Dunedin City Council operates the i-SITE on the Octagon.

WHAT'S ON

- **Warbirds Over Wānaka**
  Vintage fighter planes take flight over the Easter weekend in even-numbered years.
- **Clyde Wine & Food Harvest Festival**
  Held on Easter Sunday on Clyde's main street.
- **Bluff Oyster & Food Festival**
  The nation's favourite seasonal bivalves are celebrated in this May festival.
- **Winter Pride**
  The South Island's biggest gay celebration brightens up Queenstown in late August and early September.

23

★ BEST FOR

WATERFALLS

Te Anau–Milford Hwy after a drop of rain or two.

QUEENSTOWN & THE SOUTH

MILFORD SOUND/ PIOPIOTAHI MAJESTY

DURATION: 3-4 DAYS

DISTANCE: 291KM / 181 MILES

GREAT FOR: NATURE, FAMILIES

BEST TIME TO GO: NOVEMBER TO MAY; THE HOMER TUNNEL CAN BE CLOSED DUE TO AVALANCHE RISK IN WINTER AND SPRING

Stirling Falls (p217)

A well-beaten path this may well be, but its bookends are nothing short of sublime – Queenstown, buzzing with adrenaline and fuelled up on fabulous food and wine; and at the other end Milford Sound/Piopiotahi, NZ's most famous sight. In between is a series of eye-popping, often untouched wilderness landscapes, with the lovely lakeside town of Te Anau a handy base for exploring them.

LINK YOUR TRIP

22 Southern Alps Circuit
From Queenstown, embark on this granddaddy of road trips taking in the best of the South Island's mountain scenery.

24 Central Otago Explorer
Queenstown is the start of a tour around this bountiful region's highlights.

01 Queenstown

A small town with a big attitude, Queenstown is synonymous with the outdoors and adventures such as bungy jumping, skydiving and jetboating. Then there's the other Queenstown – the one with the cosmopolitan restaurant and arts scene, excellent vineyards and seven world-class golf courses. For the best of both worlds, it's hard to beat. If that wasn't enough, Queenstown goes for gold with an utterly sublime setting along the frayed shore of Lake Wakatipu, framed by the jagged peaks of the Remarkables. To soak up the town's scenery, stroll along Steamer Wharf to **Queenstown Gardens**, the leafy peninsula at the town centre's very edge. The lakeside track through the gardens affords ever-changing panoramas of the lake and surrounds, while its lush lawns sport fine trees,

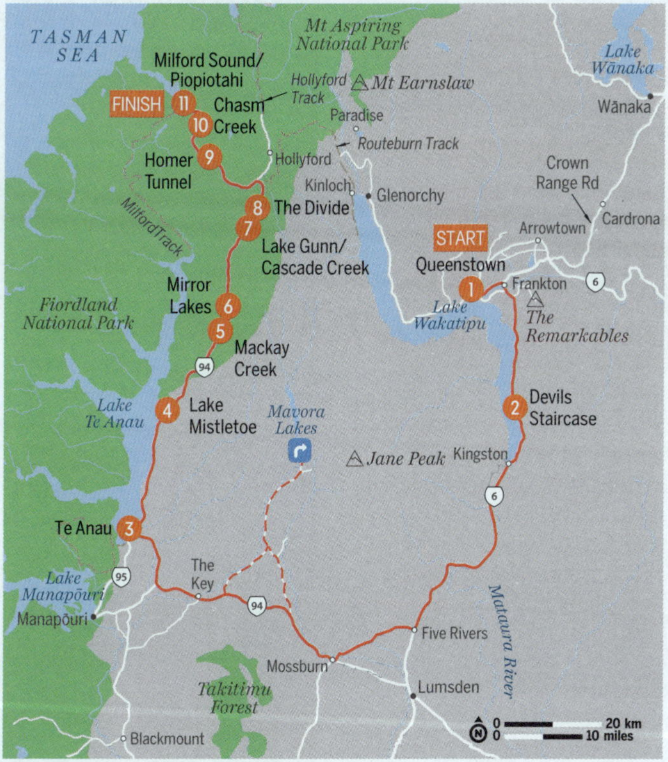

UWE ARANAS/SHUTTERSTOCK

rose gardens and occasional curiosities, including the fun and free **frisbee golf course** *(queenstowndiscgolf.co.nz)*.

THE DRIVE: Head east along SH6A to Frankton, then turn onto SH6 south, signposted for Te Anau. Skirting past the Kelvin Peninsula at the foot of the Remarkables, the road then follows the eastern shore of Lake Wakatipu with stunning alpine views either side of the highway. The distance from Queenstown to the Devils Staircase is 35km.

02 Devils Staircase

The views along the shores of **Lake Wakatipu**, NZ's longest and third-largest lake, are distractingly beautiful, with the Remarkables and Hector ranges rising to the east, Cecil Peak to the west, and the deep blue lake in between. This is a winding drive ripe for rubbernecking, so keep your eyes on the road and your hands upon the wheel. Look out for the Devils Staircase, the aptly named lookout point that punctuates a tortuous section of road that winds up, over and around the lake edge. Pull over, jump out, breathe in that clear mountain air and revel in the amazing views.

THE DRIVE: Continue along SH6. The topography flattens as you approach Five Rivers, 58km from the Devils Staircase. Turn right onto SH97 towards Mossburn. At Mossburn, turn right onto SH94. At the Key, 34km from Mossburn, the Fiordland mountains appear for the first time. This 136km drive should take around two hours.

> ☑ TOP TIP
>
> **MILFORD MAYHEM**
>
> To evade Milford's crowds, leave Te Anau early (by 8am) – tour buses from Te Anau and Queenstown aim to arrive for cruises between noon and 2pm. Be sure to fill up with petrol in Te Anau, and note that snow chains must be carried on icy or avalanche-risk days from May to November.

03 Te Anau

Picturesque Te Anau is the main gateway to Fiordland National Park and ever-popular Milford Sound/Piopiotahi. Bordering NZ's second-largest lake, the township has a smattering of good restaurants and places to stay, but it's much easier on the liver and wallet than attention- grabbing Queenstown. Lake Te Anau was gouged out by a huge glacier and has several arms that extend into the mountainous, forested western shore opposite the town. Hidden away on this side, accessible only by boat, are the **Te Anau Glowworm Caves** *(realnz.com)*. First described in Māori stories, this 200m-long cave system was lost in time until it was 'rediscovered' in 1948. It's filled with strange rock forms, whirlpools and waterfalls trickling and tumbling. Within the cave's innermost realms, masses of glowworms lure prey with their come-hither sparkle. The 2¼-hour guided tour reaches the heart of the caves via a lake cruise, walkway and a short boat ride.

THE DRIVE: Fill up with petrol and follow the signs to one of NZ's most scenic drives – the Te Anau–Milford Rd, which traces the lake edge north of Te Anau for most of the way to the Lake Mistletoe car park (28km).

DETOUR

Mavora Lakes

Start: 03 Te Anau

As the crow flies, **Mavora Lakes Conservation Park** *(doc.govt.nz)* is relatively close to the tourist honey-pots of Queenstown, Te Anau and the Milford Rd, but a long, slow gravel road and spartan facilities (long-drop toilets, water supply and fire-pits) mean that only the eager venture in.

The heart of the park is the sublime Mavora Lakes camping area, huge golden meadows sitting alongside two lakes – North and South Mavora – fringed by forest and towered over by the impressive Thomson and Livingstone Mountains with peaks rising to more than 1600m. Cloaked in beech, the valley walls pitch steeply skyward, terminating in ranges of rocky peaks that contrast starkly against the undulating blanket of golden grassland on the valley floor. North Mavora served as the cinematic location for Nen Hithoel in *The Lord of the Rings*.

If you're camping or in a campervan, this is a tranquil place to stay, although it can get busy during the school summer holidays (December to January).

Those short on time can still savour its serenity on one of a number of short walks, such as the 2½-hour **South Mavora Lake Track**, circumnavigating the smaller lake from the bridge near the North Mavora Lake camping area. On the western shore the track passes through mature beech forest; on the other side it traverses large grassy flats. There are two scenic, springy swing bridges, views galore and squadrons of birds – from honking flocks of waterfowl in the marsh to tiny riflemen and robins flitting through the forest.

From Te Anau, take SH94 towards Queenstown, then 14km before Mossburn, turn left onto Centre Hill Rd. From there, it's another 39km, heading north along a mostly unsealed road, to South Mavora Lake.

PHOTO OPPORTUNITY

Mitre Peak standing sentry above Milford Sound/Piopiotahi.

04 Lake Mistletoe

It's an easy amble through mānuka (tea tree) scrub and regenerating mountain beech forest to this compact and serene glacial lake (45 minutes return). Beside the lake, an excellent place for a picnic, there are great views of the mountain ranges that make up some of the vast Fiordland National Park. On the lake and among the surrounding rushes and flax you're likely to see resident scaup (ducks), and if you look really carefully you may spot native frogs hopping about. The frogs (known to Māori as pepeketua) are of the genus *Leiopelma*, a

Mitre Peak/Rahotu

FILIP FUXA/SHUTTERSTOCK

♥ WHY I LOVE THIS TRIP

PETER DRAGICEVICH, WRITER

Every part of this drive is magical, from its very beginning in bustling Queenstown, skirting the lake and the aptly named Remarkables mountain range. However, the natural beauty builds to a crescendo once you pass Te Anau. A succession of mirror lakes and bush walks provide a surfeit of 'wow' moments on the approach to the Homer Tunnel. Try and save some gasps for the spectacular finale: the view of Mitre Peak/ Rahotu reflecting in the waters of the fiord.

PURIPAT LERTPUNYAROJ/SHUTTERSTOCK

Chasm Creek

CRUISING THE SOUND

There's no getting around it: no visit to Fiordland is complete without a trip to Milford Sound/Piopiotahi, the first sight of which will likely knock your socks off (if the drive there hasn't already). Sheer cliffs rise out of still, dark waters, and forests clinging improbably to the near-vertical slopes sometimes relinquish their hold, causing a 'tree avalanche' into the deep. The spectacular, photogenic 1692m-high Mitre Peak/Rahotu rises dead above, one of few vistas truly worthy of the word 'iconic'.

The average annual rainfall of around 6.5m is more than enough to fuel cascading waterfalls and add a shimmering moody mist to the scene, while the freshwater sitting atop warmer seawater replicates deep-ocean conditions, encouraging the activity of marine life such as dolphins, seals and penguins.

A cruise is Milford Sound/Piopiotahi's most accessible experience, as evident from the armada of companies berthed at the waterfront cruise terminal. You can book here, but you're far safer to book in advance, especially in high season (November to April). Each company claims to be quieter, smaller, bigger, cheaper or in some way preferable to the rest. What really makes a difference is timing. Buses coming all the way from Queenstown aim for sailings between around noon and 2pm, so if you avoid that time of day there will be fewer people on the boat, fewer boats on the water and fewer buses on the road. Cruises outside this window are also around 30% cheaper. Overnight cruises are also available, giving you a chance to commune with nature when the tour buses are long gone.

primitive group of amphibians that have hardly changed over millions of years. All the nature walks lining the Te Anau–Milford Hwy are detailed in DOC's *Fiordland Day Walks* brochure, available online (doc.govt.nz) or from the Fiordland National Park Visitor Centre in Te Anau.

THE DRIVE: Continue north on SH94 for around 1km before the road cuts inland at Te Anau Downs and heads up the Eglinton Valley. After another 21km you will reach Mackay Creek.

05 Mackay Creek

One of many well signposted spots to pull over and soak up the Milford Rd's majesty, Mackay Creek offers an escape from the sweet confines of the beech forest lining the road to the open surrounds of the Eglinton Valley. There's little here except for basic camping, picnic benches and the wonderfully expansive views of the valley and vertiginous Earl Mountains, which provide a taste of what's to come. The creek is particularly photogenic in late spring when the lupins lining its banks are gloriously in bloom. Take care when pulling off or turning back on to the highway, as visibility is poor.

THE DRIVE: Drive for 7km along the Eglinton River valley flats and through beech forest until you see the DOC sign for Mirror Lakes.

06 Mirror Lakes

If the weather's fine, make sure you stop to take the five-minute boardwalk at Mirror Lakes through beech forest and wetlands. On a calm day the lakes perfectly reflect the Earl Mountains across the valley and the harakeke (flax) that fringes the water. If your arrival coincides with a tour bus, be prepared to jostle for space. The lakes area is also home to extensive birdlife, including the endangered mohua (yellowhead), with its colourful plumage and machine-gun-like chitter-chatter. There are around 5000 of these tiny insect-eating birds in the wild. Efforts are ongoing to bolster their population by introducing birds bred on predator-free island sanctuaries back into the valley. The bird features on New Zealand's 100-dollar bill.

THE DRIVE: Continue driving north mainly through red beech forest, with occasional glimpses of the valley and mountains. It's a 20-minute, 20km drive from Mirror Lakes to Lake Gunn.

07 Lake Gunn/ Cascade Creek

Cascade Creek is the closest campsite to Milford Sound/Piopiotahi and from here you can take the **Lake Gunn Nature Walk** (45 minutes return), which loops through tall red beech forest ringing with birdsong, with side trails leading to peaceful lakeside beaches.

This area, known to Māori as O Tapara, was a regular stopover for parties heading to Anita Bay in Milford Sound/Piopiotahi in search of *pounamu* (greenstone/jade).

THE DRIVE: Continue driving north for 7km to the Divide. You'll pass Lakes Fergus and Lochie along the way.

08 The Divide

Stunted silver beech predominates as you make your way up to the harsher environs of the Divide, the lowest east–west pass in the Southern Alps. This is a trailhead for the Routeburn, and Greenstone and Caples multiday hikes. A marvellous three-hour return walk can be had along the start of the Routeburn, ascending (in gut-busting fashion) through beech forest to the alpine tussockland above the bushline at **Key Summit**. The nature walk around the boggy tops, festooned with mountain flax, snow totara and dracophyllum, is a great excuse to linger, while on a good day the 360-degree panorama encompasses the Hollyford, Eglinton and Greenstone Valleys, and Lake Marian basin with pyramidal Mt Christina (2474m). The view is truly worth the effort, but in anything less than clear weather, don't even go there.

THE DRIVE: From the Divide, SH94 snakes west, passing Marian Corner where safety gates will be closed if there is a risk of avalanche further along. The road then climbs through the cascade-tastic upper Hollyford Valley to the Homer Tunnel. It's 16km from the Divide to the tunnel entrance.

09 Homer Tunnel

Framed by a spectacular, high-walled, ice-carved amphitheatre, the 1270m-long Homer Tunnel is the only road access point for Milford Sound/Piopiotahi. Begun as a relief project in the 1930s' Depression and finally completed in 1953, the tunnel is one way, with in-flows controlled by traffic lights. During the summer months, this can mean delays of up to 20 minutes while you wait for the lights to turn green, but when immersed in such a spectacular environment, who cares? Kea (alpine parrots) loiter in gangs around the tunnel entrance looking to mug tourists for scraps of food, but don't feed them as it's bad for their health.

Dark, rough-hewn and dripping with water, the tunnel delivers you to the head of the spectacular Cleddau Valley. Any spare 'wows' might pop out about now.

THE DRIVE: From the end of the Homer Tunnel to Chasm Creek is an 8km drive. If it's wet or has been raining, waterfalls cascading down the Cleddau Valley walls resemble brooding skies streaked with bolts of lightning.

10 Chasm Creek

The Chasm Walk is an easy 20-minute return walk from the car park and well worth a stop, come rain or shine, though check the DOC *(doc.govt.nz)* site to see if the bridge is still under repair. Pebbles caught in the frenetic currents of the Cleddau River have hollowed boulders into shapes reminiscent of a Salvador Dalí scene, while deep falls and thrashing waters give an unmistakeable glimpse of nature's might. A dip is definitely off the cards. Instead you can pick up a coffee at the espresso van here from November to April. Along the trail, look out for glimpses of Mt Tutoko (2723m), Fiordland's highest peak, above the beech forest.

THE DRIVE: The final 10km to Milford Sound/Piopiotahicontinues down the Cleddau Valley, passing over the Tutoko River suspension bridge at around the halfway point. Parking is $10 per hour in the main car park, but there's free parking on Deepwater Basin Rd, 1.5km before the sound. From there it's a 20- to 30-minute walk to the terminal.

11 Milford Sound/ Piopiotahi

The Grand Canyon, Uluru, Victoria Falls – **Milford Sound/ Piopiotahi** *(milfordsoundtourism.nz)* is up there with the best of them, which explains why it receives around a million visitors each year, many of them crammed into the peak months (January and February). Each summer, around 8000 arrive on foot via the **Milford Track**, which ends at the sound. Many more arrive via the multitude of bus tours. But don't worry: out on the water all this humanity seems tiny compared to nature's vastness. And getting out on the water is a must. Fortunately there are cruises galore, but kayak trips offer an even more mind-blowing perspective of this monumental landscape of kilometre-high cliffs. Te Anau–based **Rosco's Milford Kayaks** *(roscosmilfordkayaks.com)* offers guided, tandem-kayak trips including the 'Morning Glory', a challenging paddle running the full length of the fiord to Anita Bay, and the less strenuous 'Stirling Sunriser', which ventures beneath the 151m-high **Stirling Falls** for a 'glacial facial'. Although Milford Sound/Piopiotahi is best appreciated from the water or air, killer views of Mitre Peak/Rahotu can still be enjoyed from the 400m **Foreshore Walk**.

Waterfalls above Homer Tunnel (p215)
FILIP FUXA/SHUTTERSTOCK

POWEROFFOREVER/GETTY IMAGES

Hiking, Fiordland National Park

FIORDLAND NATIONAL PARK

Fiordland National Park is arguably New Zealand's finest outdoor treasure. In this landscape, the anxieties of modern life lose their grip and give way to the grand galleries of the natural world. Carved in epic battles between rock and ice, Fiordland can make you feel like a tiny speck in the face of nature in the very best way.

At 12,607 sq km, Fiordland National Park is the country's largest national park, making up half of the Te Wāhipounamu–South West New Zealand World Heritage Area. Jagged, mountainous and densely forested, it is cut through by numerous deeply recessed sounds (technically fiords) that reach inland like crooked fingers from the Tasman Sea. Formed during the glacial periods of the last ice age, its peaks are very hard and have eroded slowly, compared to the mountains of Mt Aspiring and Arthur's Pass, which are softer. Gentle topography this is not. It is raw and hard-core all the way.

High rainfall – delivered across the Tasman Sea – results in super-lush vegetation. Inland forests feature red, silver and mountain beech, while coastal forest is dominated by podocarp species such as matai, rimu and totara, as well as the red-bloomed southern rata. Fiordland is well known to bird-watchers as the home of the endangered flightless takahe, but more commonly spotted are kereru (NZ pigeons), riflemen, tomtits, fantails, bush robins, tui, bellbirds and kaka, as well as cheeky kea (alpine parrots) and rock wrens in high-altitude areas. If you wander around at night you might occasionally hear a kiwi.

It's around 85 million years since the snippet of land that became NZ split off from the supercontinent Gondwanaland; Fiordland makes it seem like just yesterday.

24

★ BEST FOR

FOODIES

Amisfield Bistro & Cellar Door, often voted New Zealand's top winery restaurant.

QUEENSTOWN & THE SOUTH

CENTRAL OTAGO EXPLORER

DURATION: 3-4 DAYS

DISTANCE: 210KM / 130 MILES

GREAT FOR: NATURE, HISTORY AND CULTURE

BEST TIME TO GO: ALL YEAR, BUT WINTER SNOWS SOMETIMES CLOSE CROWN RANGE RD

Cycling on the shore of Lake Wakatipu, Queenstown

Welcome to one of New Zealand's most popular outdoor playgrounds, vaunted for adrenalised pursuits such as skiing, hiking, mountain biking and skydiving, taking place in sublime alpine surrounds. Central Otago also drips with gold-rush history and brims with world-class wineries, and is home to the energetic lakeside town of Queenstown. This relatively short tour packs a helluva punch, but you'll want to stretch it out to take it all in.

LINK YOUR TRIP

22 Southern Alps Circuit
See some of the South Island's best mountain scenery by hopping on this circuit at Queenstown or Wānaka.

26 Otago Heritage Trail
Keep mining for gold history and gorgeous Otago scenery by jumping on this loop at Clyde, 24km from Cromwell.

01 Queenstown

Queenstown is the vortex of a whirl of wild adventures taking place in its inspiring mountain surrounds. If you're looking for some high-speed, free-fall, dizzying spins and head rushes, this racy town is just the ticket. The town, however, has a quieter side. Stop and smell the roses, play some frisbee golf and wander the lakeshore path as it reveals ever-changing panoramas of Lake Wakatipu and the Remarkables. Beyond the gardens, the path continues to Frankton and beyond, as part of the **Queenstown Trail** *(centralotagowine.co)*, best explored by bicycle – hire one from **Vertigo Bikes** *(vertigobikes.co.nz)* in the centre of town, or grab an ebike from **ChargeAbout** *(chargeabout.co.nz)*. Come evening, head to Queentown's cosmopolitan restaurants and bars, lingering over fine local food and world-class wine. Evenings are also a good time

LARKYPHOTO/GETTY IMAGES

to head up the **Skyline Gondola** *(skyline.co.nz),* when the crowds have thinned and the town lights twinkle below.

THE DRIVE: SH6A heads east out of town, past pretty Lake Hayes to Arrow Junction, where you should stay on SH6, signposted to Cromwell. It's less than half an hour (23km) to the Kawarau Bridge, gateway to the Gibbston Valley.

DETOUR

Glenorchy

Start: 01 Queenstown

Set in achingly beautiful surroundings, tiny Glenorchy is the perfect low-key antidote to Queenstown.

The 45-minute drive to reach it from Queenstown, along Lake Wakatipu's northern shoreline, is an absolute doozy. The further you go, the more gobsmacking the vistas become, as the jagged peaks of the Humboldt Range reveal themselves.

At Glenorchy itself, a small array of adventure operators can get you active on the lake and in nearby valleys by kayak, horse, helicopter or jetboat. If you prefer to strike out on two legs, the mountainous region at the northern end of Lake Wakatipu is also the setting for some of the South Island's finest hikes, including the **Routeburn and Greenstone Caples Tracks** *(doc.govt.nz).*

Those with sturdy wheels can explore the superb valleys north of Glenorchy. **Paradise** lies 15km northwest of town, just before the start of the Dart Track. If your idea of paradise is a paddock, you're in luck; otherwise just enjoy the gravel road here as it runs through beautiful farmland fringed by majestic mountains. You might recognise it from *The Lord of the Rings* movies as the approach to both Isengard and Lothlórien.

Glenorchy-based **Dart River Adventures** *(dartriver.co.nz)* runs one of NZ's most memorable jetboat trips into the heart of this spectacular wilderness. As well as some high-octane zipping along the beautiful braided Dart River, there's a short walk through pristine beech forest and breathtaking views of **Mt Earnslaw/Pikirakatahi**. Also on offer are jetboat rides combined with a thrilling river descent in an inflatable three-seater 'funyak'.

02 Gibbston Valley

As you enter Gibbston Valley, the most striking sight is the historic **Kawarau Bridge** beside the highway. Dangling from it is the world's first **bungy jump site** *(bungy.co.nz),* and therefore a fitting place to take the 43m plunge. Should that escapade not appear on your hit list, perhaps just pull in for a coffee and watch other muppets do it – it's the best free entertainment in town. This schist-lined valley is one of Central Otago's main wine subregions, accounting for around 20% of grape plantings. Get into the groove at **Gibbston Valley** *(gibbstonvalley.com),* less than 1km from Kawarau Bridge, where you can taste both wine and cheese, take an informative tour into NZ's largest wine cave, and hire bikes to pedal around the wineries along the Gibbston River on another section of the Queenstown Trail. Whether travelling by car, bike or on foot, don't miss **Peregrine** *(peregrinewines.co.nz)*, one of Gibbston's top wineries, producing excellent sauvignon blanc, pinot gris, riesling and pinot noir. Also impressive is the winery's architecture – a bunker-like building with a roof reminiscent of a falcon's wing in flight.

THE DRIVE: SH6 snakes through the Kawarau Gorge with its schist outcrops and wild briar roses. After around 20 minutes, it emerges into the dry, lumpy landscape of Cromwell Basin. Pearson Rd is well signposted to your right; follow it to Bannockburn Rd and turn right, where you will see signposts for various wineries. This drive will take around 30 minutes in total (35km).

03 Bannockburn

Two-thirds of Central Otago's grapes are grown within Cromwell Basin, and of the many subregions here, none is more famous than Bannockburn. Lying in the rain-shadow of the Carrick Range, its highly variable terroir lends itself to numerous varietals including riesling, chardonnay and pinot gris. Pinot noir, however, is king of the castle, with Bannockburn lauded as one of the best places outside of Burgundy for cultivating this notoriously fickle grape. A dozen or so wineries are open to the public, all within a very short drive. The pick of the crop is **Mt Difficulty** *(mtdifficulty.nz)*, whose genesis dates back to the early 1990s, when five growers collaborated to produce wine from the promising but unproven Central Otago region. Not only does it offer the chance to taste various wines at its welcoming cellar door, its spectacular perch overlooking the Cromwell Basin encourages a very long lunch. Sharp and modern, with scrumptious fare and alfresco dining on the terrace, it pays to book a table and sort out well in advance who's responsible for driving onward.

THE DRIVE: Head back on Bannockburn Rd, following it for 7km to Cromwell and all the way to the intersection with SH8B. Turn right to cross Lake Dunstan – formed when the mighty Clutha River/Mata-Au was dammed in the early 1990s – then turn left and follow SH8 as it skirts along the lake edge. The Bendigo Loop Rd to Bendigo Historic Reserve is signposted 15km from Cromwell at Crippletown, from where it's another 5km to the entrance, around 35 minutes from Bannockburn.

04 Bendigo Historic Reserve

Located high in the Dunstan Range, **Bendigo** *(doc.govt.nz)* is just one of 20 or so significant goldfield sites in Otago. Gold was first discovered here in 1862, mined from alluvial gravels. These easy pickings soon ran out, forcing hundreds of miners into the hard task of extracting the gold from quartz reefs. Relics from this era include mine shafts and tunnels, machinery, dams and water races, as well as the crumbled stone remnants of Crippletown, Logantown and Welshtown where the miners lived. Reaching the site is part of the adventure – it's up an extremely steep dirt road, accessible by 2WD, but only just. Don't attempt this in wet weather or if your car's a bit dodgy. From the upper car park, a fruitful wander can be had around ruined stone houses and the aurora stamping battery where quartz was crushed. If your will and the weather permit it, consider the five-hour **Kānuka Loop Track** punctuated by relics, craggy rocks and regenerating kanuka forest, and offering totally mind-boggling views over Lake Dunstan and the Upper Clutha Valley.

THE DRIVE: From the reserve's lower car park, continue north along Bendigo Loop Rd, which rejoins SH8 several kilometres from where you headed in. Turn right to continue on SH8 7km through farmland to the Wānaka–Lindis Pass junction. The road to Wānaka leads west, but it's worth driving the extra 1.5km north on SH8 to Tarras, all up 15km from Bendigo.

05 Tarras

An endearing stopping point on the Inland Scenic Route, blink-and-miss-it Tarras is in the middle of merino-sheep country, but it entices motorists with a country cafe and shops selling classic Kiwi treats like mini chocolate fish, fine wool garments (check out the 'merinomink' wool mix with snuggly possum fur) and stylish home-grown clothes designs. While you're here, be sure to stop into the House of Shrek and find out exactly what ovine hijinks are required to become NZ's most famous sheep. It's quite a yarn.

Wakatipu Basin (p222)

VARINTHORN NIYOMDUSADEE/SHUTTERSTOCK

PHOTO OPPORTUNITY

Wakatipu Basin from the Crown Range Rd.

THE DRIVE: Return the way you came, back 1.5km to the junction, and take SH8A signposted to Wānaka. The highway heads up the mountain-lined valley of the mighty Clutha River/ Mata-Au, which it eventually crosses to join SH6 heading to Wānaka. The 35km journey will take around 30 minutes.

06 Wānaka

What a peach! An enviable lakeside setting amid a sublime alpine landscape would be reason enough to linger in Wānaka. However, its outdoor adventure scene – although decidedly less flashy than over the hill in Queenstown – offers more than enough buzz and fun, plus there is easily enough dining, nightlife and cellar doors to satisfy the town types. As well as being the gateway to nearby **Mt Aspiring National Park** (and two winter ski resorts), there are numerous walks and bike rides closer to town; see DOC's *Wānaka Outdoor Pursuits* pamphlet *(doc.govt.nz)* for a comprehensive rundown. Among many family- friendly attractions is the eclectic **National Transport & Toy Museum** *(nttmuseumwanaka.co.nz)*, where small armies of Smurfs, *Star Wars* figurines and Barbie dolls share billing with a multitude of classic cars and a mysteriously acquired MiG fighter jet from the Polish Air Force. In all there are more than 60,000 items filling four giant hangars, so there are bound to be at least one or two that usher you down memory lane.

THE DRIVE: From the lakefront, head south on McDougall St, which swiftly becomes Cardrona Valley Rd. Follow it up the pretty, tussock-covered Cardrona Valley and in around 20 minutes you'll reach the Cardrona Hotel, 24km from Wānaka.

07 Cardrona

The cute settlement of Cardrona reached its zenith in the 1870s at the height of the gold rush when its population numbered over 1000. The heart of the village is the **Cardrona Hotel** *(cardronahotel.co.nz)*, an emblem not just of the village but of the nation, partly due to its appearance in an incredibly manly beer commercial back in the day. It's said to be the most photographed pub in NZ. Dating back to 1863, it seriously hits its straps après-ski, but its atmospheric interior, good restaurant and beer garden make it a worthy stop all year round.

THE DRIVE: Continue south on Crown Range Rd, which tops out in tussock-covered style at 1076m, making it NZ's highest sealed road. Pull over at designated lookout points to admire the view on the way down to the Wakatipu Basin, taking in a patchwork of fields within a ring of mountains and offering glimpses of distant lakes. At the intersection follow SH6 right for a few kilometres to Arrow

Wānaka

JANICE CHEN/SHUTTERSTOCK

Junction. Take the right turn towards Arrowtown, along McDonnell Rd, 31km (around 40 minutes) from the Cardrona Hotel.

08 Arrowtown

Established in the 1860s following the discovery of gold in the Arrow River, Arrowtown's pretty, tree-lined avenues retain more than 60 buildings dating from those glory days. The **Lakes District Museum & Gallery** *(museumqueenstown.com)* provides a comprehensive introduction to the area's colourful history, while just down the road you can see where Chinese diggers lived and worked along Bush Creek. NZ's best example of an early Chinese settlement, it features interpretive signs explaining the lives of Chinese miners during and after the gold rush (the last resident died in 1932), while restored huts and the only remaining Chinese store in the southern goldfields make the story more tangible. Subjected to significant racism, the Chinese often had little choice but to rework old tailings rather than seek new claims. Arrowtown makes a great base for exploring the Wakatipu Basin, especially if Queenstown's buzz might blow your circuits. One of Central Otago's signature wineries, in fact, is just 8km from town and can be reached by bicycle on the Arrow River Bridges Trail, part of the Queenstown Trail. As famous for its superb dining as it is for its wines, **Amisfield Bistro & Cellar Door** *(amisfield.co.nz)* is a must-visit for the travelling gastronome.

THE DRIVE: Take the alternative route back to Queenstown, via Malaghans Rd, crossing the Shotover River. It's a 20km journey taking around 20 minutes.

ROLF_52/SHUTTERSTOCK

Vineyard, Gibbston Valley (p219)

CENTRAL OTAGO WINE

Central Otago's wild landscapes make up the world's southernmost wine region and NZ's highest, ranging between 200m and 450m above sea level. Vineyards are spread throughout the deep valleys and basins of six subregions – Gibbston, Bannockburn, Cromwell Basin, Wānaka, Bendigo and Alexandra.

In all, Central Otago covers nearly 6% of the country's grape-growing area (although its wine output is less than 3%).

The industry is reasonably young, with the few vines planted back in 1864 an early forerunner of an industry that has only burgeoned since the mid-1990s. The scene remains largely in the hands of friendly boutique enterprises and winemakers still experimenting with terroir not yet fully understood. But don't let this fool you into thinking that the wines are in any way substandard. Diminutive Otago may lack history and might, but an intoxicating number of its wines are world-class.

Soils are varied but predominantly glacial, with a high mineral content, while various microclimates share a common theme of hot days, cold nights and low rainfall. These conditions have proven excellent for aromatics, particularly riesling and pinot gris, but Central Otago's hero is pinot noir, the best of which give Burgundian reds a run for their money. This varietal accounts for more than 75% of the region's plantings.

It would take a good two days' touring to get a comprehensive taste of the terroir, with around 30 wineries regularly open to visitors, and many more by appointment. If you're short on time you could focus on the Gibbston Valley (with cycle touring a possibility), but a much broader picture is revealed around Cromwell and Bannockburn, beyond the gates of the dramatic Kawarau Gorge.

Download the wine-touring maps from the **Central Otago Winegrowers Association** *(centralotagowine.co)* to plan your oenophilic odyssey.

25

QUEENSTOWN & THE SOUTH

SOUTHERN SCENIC ROUTE

★ BEST FOR

WILDLIFE

Otago Peninsula's albatross, penguins, fur seals and sea lions.

DURATION: 5-7 DAYS

DISTANCE: 554KM / 344 MILES

GREAT FOR: FOOD AND DRINK, OUTDOORS

BEST TIME TO GO: SUMMER AND AUTUMN, WHEN THE WEATHER IS MORE SETTLED

Fur seal, Otago Peninsula

This long, U-shaped noodle around NZ's deep south takes travellers from Fiordland's deep forest, lakes and Doubtful Sound/Patea, to the wildlife-rich Otago Peninsula. Unforgettable coastal landmarks include lonely beaches, cliffs, sea caves and other salt-crusted oddities, but there's plenty of pretty countryside inland, too. The trip to Stewart Island/Rakiura makes for the ultimate detour.

LINK YOUR TRIP

20 Inland Scenic Route
Pick up this classic trip at Queenstown, 171km northeast of Te Anau, and drive it in reverse.

04 East Coast Express
From Dunedin, continue up the east coast for a good slice of New Zealand history, plenty of seaside fun and some great food.

01 Te Anau

Lake Te Anau is NZ's second-largest lake, bound by the Takitimu Mountains to the south, the Livingstone Mountains to the east, and rugged Fiordland peaks to the north and west. Gouged out by a huge glacier, it has several arms that extend into the mountainous, forested western shore. The lake's deepest point is 417m, about twice the depth of Loch Ness. At its southern end is the Te Anau township, Fiordland National Park's low-key but likeable hub. As well as being the gateway for three Great Walks and trips to Milford Sound/Piopiotahi, it's a great launch pad for aerial adventures. Get a bird's-eye view of the lake, **Kepler Mountains** and the town's rural surrounds on a 30-minute chopper flight with **Southern Lakes Helicopters** *(southernlakeshelicopters.co.nz)*, or sample the Kepler Great Walk by flying to the first hut – alpine Luxmore – and back to town.

GUNTSOOPHACK YUKTAHNON/SHUTTERSTOCK

THE DRIVE: Head 22km south on SH95 to Manapōuri with the low pastoral hills of the Ramparts to the left and the forested foothills of the Kepler Mountains on your right. As you approach Lake Manapōuri, prepare yourself for another Fiordland 'wow' moment as the lake, its many islands and wild mountain backdrop come into view.

02 Manapōuri

In 1969, Lake Manapōuri was the focus of NZ's first major environmental campaign when hydroelectric dam plans proposed raising the lake level by 30m. A whopping 17% of voting-age citizens signed a petition against the idea, an action that also contributed to the downfall of the government at the following election. The West Arm power station was eventually built without any change to the lake level. The remote power station can be seen on cruises to Doubtful Sound/Patea, departing from Manapōuri. At three times the length and 10 times the area of Milford, and much, much less visited, Doubtful Sound/Patea is a must-see if you have the time and money. The day-long 'wilderness cruise' run by **Real Journeys** *(realnz.com)* includes a 3-hour cruise. Walkers can cross the Waiau River with **Manapouri Water Taxi** *(manapouriwatertaxi.co.nz)* to access the Circle Track (3½ hours), or Hope Arm (five to six hours return). Few visitors actually linger in Manapōuri, which is a shame as it has many merits including a better lakeside view than Te Anau.

THE DRIVE: Drive 5km east and then head south through rural Southland. At the 90km mark you will reach Te Waewae Bay having passed through Clifden (where the road becomes SH99) with its Victorian suspension bridge.

03 Te Waewae Bay

This long, moody, windswept stretch of beach sets a steely glare towards Antarctica. For travellers heading east, it provides a first glimpse of the snowcapped Southern Alps descending into the sea, framing the western end of the bay.

Stop at the spectacular lookout at **McCracken's Rest** and keep an eye out for the Hector's dolphins and southern right whales that are occasionally sighted here. Just past Orepuki is the turn-off for **Monkey Island**, a grassy islet just metres offshore and accessible at low tide.

THE DRIVE: Follow SH99 along the coast then cut across the headland to Colac Bay, and on to Riverton, 40km distant.

04 Riverton

Quiet little Riverton (known to Māori as Aparima) is worth a stop for lunch and a wander. Also, if frigid swimming takes your fancy, the long, broad sands of Taramea Bay are good for a bracing dip or a surf lesson with **Southland Surf School** *(facebook.com/surfingnz.co.nz)*. **Te Hikoi Southern Journey** *(tehikoi.co.nz)* is a fantastic little museum relaying local stories in clever and inspiring ways. Highlights include a fascinating 16-minute film about Pākehā (white) sealer Jack Price and his Māori wife Hinewhitia who were stranded on the Solander Islands, south of Fiordland. Oh, if only all small-town museums could be this good!

THE DRIVE: Drive east on SH99 over the flat agricultural terrain of southern Southland until you reach the junction with SH6 at Lorneville, 33km from Riverton. Turn right onto SH6 and follow the dead-straight road to Invercargill, 8km away. Invercargill's suburban sprawl starts around 5km north of the city centre.

05 Invercargill

Poor old Invercargill had lost much of its mojo lately with the closure of its **Invercargill Public Art Gallery** *(invercargillpublicartgallery.nz)* due to earthquake risks, but luckily, you can still visit exhibits at **He Waka Tuia** *(hewakatuia.nz)*. Thank goodness for its motoring attractions, which keep alive the legacy of Burt Munro. The local legend still holds the world land-speed record for an under-1000cc motorcycle, which he set in 1967 at the age of 68, riding a 47-year-old bike that he modified himself in Invercargill. See Munro's actual bike at **E Hayes & Sons** *(ehayes.co.nz)*, an unlikely stop, as it's a hardware store, but all the more fun for that. Munro's story is immortalised in the film *The World's Fastest Indian*, starring Sir Anthony Hopkins.

THE DRIVE: The drive to Bluff and Stirling Point is 30km. Head south on SH1, skirting around the New River Estuary to the west and then Bluff Harbour to the east. Across the harbour you'll see Tiwai Point, the site of an aluminium smelter – NZ's largest single consumer of electricity, for which the Lake Manapōuri power station was built.

♥ WHY I LOVE THIS TRIP

MONIQUE PERRIN, WRITER

This trip is the perfect blend of soul-cleansing wilderness and delightful encounters with quirky, chatty locals – people shaped by living in a landscape of humbling beauty. And oh, the road! Such a pleasure to drive as it meanders over undulating hills, revealing a new misty shoreline around every corner. Leave the highway to the checklist tourists – you'll be glad you took the scenic route.

DETOUR

Gore

Start: 05 Invercargill

Around 65km (roughly an hour's drive via SH1) northeast of Invercargill, the rural town of Gore is proud to be the 'home of country music' in NZ – celebrated with the annual **Gold Guitar Week** *(goldguitars.co.nz)* – and the focal point for an illicit moonshine-making history.

In the early 20th century, Gore's enterprising Scottish immigrants responded to 50 years of prohibition by distilling their own moonshine. The **Hokonui Moonshine Museum** *(gorenz.com)* shines a tongue-in-cheek light on some colourful characters and whisky-drenched escapades of the era. On display is fascinating home-made distilling apparatuses hidden for decades in the back of local sheds. Admission includes three tastes of the local tipple ranging from rough to polished – 'fast and furious', 'whisky wannabe' and 'dessert'. They're also available for purchase.

For something a little more refined, head across the road to the the century-old former public library which now houses

McCracken's Rest, Te Waewae Bay
NATWICK/SHUTTERSTOCK

McCRACKENS REST
60 km INVERCARGILL
TUATAPERE 18 km
PAHIA HILL
STEWART ISLAND
HUMP RIDGE 28 km
McCRACKEN'S REST

the **Eastern Southland Gallery** *(esgallery.co.nz)* – aka the 'Goreggenheim'. This significant collection of NZ art includes many works by Ralph Hotere. The also-amazing John Money Collection combines indigenous folk art from West Africa and Australia with works by esteemed NZ artist Rita Angus.

Wannabe WWI flying aces should buzz over to **Croydon Aircraft Company** *(croydonaviation.co.nz)*, 16km northwest of Gore. These aerophiles are world-famous for restoring vintage aircraft; they'll even take you up in a two-seater 1930s Tiger Moth biplane.

06 Bluff

Windswept and more than a little bleak, Bluff is Invercargill's port. The main reason folk come here is to catch the ferry to Stewart Island/Rakiura or to pose for a photo beside the Stirling Point signpost, which is often said to be the southernmost point of NZ. Sorry to disappoint you, but it isn't. Despite the oft-quoted phrase 'from Cape Reinga to Bluff' and the fact that SH1 terminates at **Stirling Point**, the South Island's southernmost point is Slope Point in the Catlins, with Stewart Island/Rakiura and remote dots of rock lying even further south. But let's not let the facts get in the way of a good story, or photo. **Bluff Hill** (Motupōhue) is another reason to visit. Accessed on foot from Stirling Point, or via Flagstaff Rd in the middle of Bluff, this wind-ravaged reserve boasts awesome views across Foveaux Strait to Stewart Island/Rakiura. If the wind isn't threatening to sweep you off your feet, follow the spiralling path up to the lookout.

> **PHOTO OPPORTUNITY**
>
> Stirling Point signpost at Bluff, the unofficial bottom of the South Island.

THE DRIVE: Drive back to Invercargill, then head east on Gorge Rd–Invercargill Hwy to Fortrose, 46km away. Continue east on SH92 for 31km then turn right towards Waikawa. Drive south for 12km, through Niagara (note the cafe) to Waikawa, then on to Curio Bay, 106km in all from Stirling Point.

Stirling Point signpost, Bluff

KATIBUSNELLO/SHUTTERSTOCK

DETOUR

Stewart Island/Rakiura

Start: 06 Bluff

Travellers who make the effort to reach NZ's 'third island' are rewarded with a warm welcome from both the local kiwi and the local Kiwis. A bushy island, 85% of which is designated **Rakiura National Park**, it is arguably the best place to spy the country's shy, feathered icon in the wild. With an estimated population of 20,000, they outnumber the locals by approximately 50 to one.

Stewart Island/Rakiura is a bird sanctuary of international repute, and even the most amateur of spotters are likely to be distracted by the constant – and utterly glorious – squawking, singing and flitting of feathery flocks. Guided by expert naturalists, **Ulva's Guided Walks** *(ulva.co.nz)* offers excellent half-day tours exploring Ulva Island in Paterson Inlet. There are also kiwi-spotting tours to Mamaku Point.

If the weather is unkind, step into **Rakiura Jade** *(rakiurajade.co.nz)*, Dave Goodin's atmospheric workshop suspended right over the water, to learn the skills of carving *pounamu*. Over 4½ hours Dave will guide you through selecting the right piece of stone, carving and polishing it, and even braiding the twine to hang it around your neck.

07 Curio

Named after a 19th-century whaling captain, the Catlins coast is a beguiling blend of fecund farmland, native forest, lonely lighthouses, empty beaches and wildlife-spotting opportunities. On a clear summer's day it's a beauty to behold. In the face of an Antarctic southerly, it's an entirely different story. Good luck. The beachy settlement of Curio Bay attracts a deluge of sunseekers in the summer months but is a sleepy hamlet at other times. Most of its accommodation lines up along **Porpoise Bay**, a glorious stretch of sand and water conducive to swimming, where Hector's dolphins and blue penguins come to rear their young. Incorporated in the **Curioscape** *(curioscape.co.nz)* centre is a pleasant cafe, visitor centre and the **Gateway**, a modern museum with a multiscreen film experience. From here you can walk to the **petrified forest** of Jurassic-era trees on the shore, visible for four hours either side of low tide. The walk is via a boardwalk over nesting grounds for endangered yellow-eyed penguin (hoiho). They waddle ashore at dusk; do the right thing and keep your distance (at least 50m).

THE DRIVE: Drive north for 12km back to the junction with SH92, turn right and head east through the forested foothills of the Maclennan Range to Papatowai. The total distance is 44km. The long solitary sweep of Tautuku Bay, just shy of Papatowai, is worth a quick stop.

08 Papatowai

Nestled near the mouth of the Tahakopa River, the village of Papatowai has perhaps a few dozen regular inhabitants but in summer it swells with holidaymakers, who are mainly drawn by the languid vibe, good bush walks and pretty picnic spot at the river mouth. One of the best reasons to stop here is the **Lost Gypsy Gallery** *(thelostgypsy.com)*. Fashioned from remaindered bits and bobs, 'organic mechanic' Blair Sommerville's intricately crafted automata are wonderfully irreverent. The collection in the bus is a teaser for the carnival of creations through the gate (young children not allowed, sorry...). The buzz, bong and bright lights of the organ are bound to tickle your ribs.

THE DRIVE: Drive north and then northeast for 26km along SH92 through forest and farmland to Owaka. Worthy stops en route (but off the main road) include McLean Falls, Matai Falls, Jack's Blowhole and especially Purakaunui Falls. Owaka provides a chance to stock up on petrol and groceries before you turn right and follow the signs for Pounawea, 4km away.

09 Pounawea

Pounawea, a beautiful hamlet on the edge of the **Catlins River Estuary**, is a delightful place to linger for a night or two, with accommodation there as well as at Newhaven, just across the inlet. Look out for the daft-looking royal spoonbill and listen to the roar of the waves coming over the bar. Within walking distance of Newhaven car park, **Surat Bay** is a serene spot, notable for the sea lions that laze around between here and **Cannibal Bay**, including pups in December and January. Give them a wide berth (that's the sea lions – and any cannibals too, of course).

THE DRIVE: Return to Owaka and then drive 7km northeast on SH92 to Ahuriri Flat. Turn right here, signposted for Kaka Point, and drive 8km to Molyneux Bay. Turn right and drive along the coast on the windy and sometimes steep and narrow road to the Nugget Point car park, 6km away. Total driving distance is 25km.

10 The Nuggets

The biggest attraction at the northern end of the Catlins is **Nugget Point/Tokatā**. This is the king of the region's viewpoints, made all the more interesting by the wave-thrashed cliffs and the toothy islets known as the Nuggets protruding from the surf. Seals and sea lions can often be spotted lolling about below and there's also plenty of birdlife, such as soaring shearwaters and spoonbills huddling from the breeze. A 900m walk leads from the car park to the lighthouse on the point itself.

Just shy of the Nugget Point car park is **Roaring Bay**, where a well-placed hide allows you to spot yellow-eyed penguins (hoiho) coming ashore (best two hours before sunset; viewing times are posted on a noticeboard at the car park). Obey all signs: as you can see, this is a pretty precarious existence.

THE DRIVE: Drive north along the coast through Kaka Point to the junction with SH1. Turn right and drive 81km northeast on SH1 through the rural Otago towns of Balclutha and Milton to the Dunedin suburb of Burnside. Turn right into Stevenson Rd, then Emerson St, then Blackhead Rd; Tunnel Beach Rd will be on your left. Total distance is 102km.

11 Tunnel Beach

A short but steep track (20 minutes down, 40 back up) accesses a dramatic, rocky stretch of coast where the wild Pacific has carved sea stacks, arches and unusual formations out of the limestone. The beach takes its name from a hand-hewn stone tunnel at the bottom of the track, which civic father John Cargill had built to give his family access to secluded beach-side picnic spots. The ocean may look inviting but strong currents make swimming here dangerous. The tunnel is cut off at high tide so check tide times online before you set off.

THE DRIVE: Return back to SH1 and head east following the signs for Dunedin city centre. Out of peak times, this 8km drive through the western suburbs and central Dunedin should take around 15 minutes.

12 Dunedin

Known as the 'Edinburgh of the South' due to its settlement by two shiploads of Scots in 1848, Dunedin is an atmospheric place with a creative community and more culture to explore than you'd expect in a petite city. Artists and makers abound, and in recent years Dunedin's streets have themselves become canvases for a growing contingent of international street artists. World-class walls have been added by artists from Poland, China, Italy, Puerto Rico, Australia and elsewhere, some of the walls three-storeys high. Explore for yourself to find these Easter eggs, or take the **Dunedin Street Art Walking Tour** with self- described 'senior entrepreneur' Victoria Gilliand, aka Street Kiwi, who is a huge street-art fan girl. For more institutional art, the **Dunedin Public Art Gallery** *(dunedin.art.museum)* is one of NZ's best. Its airy exhibition spaces principally present important works from the nation's back catalogue, but plenty of floor space is also set aside for contemporary shows.

DETOUR

Otago Peninsula

Start: 12 Dunedin

Right on Dunedin's doorstep, the Otago Peninsula is a hot spot for wildlife-watching, with species including fur seals, sea lions, albatrosses, penguins and a fleet of other seabirds. The rugged headland also boasts walking trails, beaches and interesting historical sites. The road is a stunner too, hugging the coast with dramatic views across the water.

Twitchers of any persuasion won't want to miss **Taiaroa Head**, the world's only mainland royal albatross colony, accessible on guided tours run by **Royal Albatross Centre** *(albatross.org.nz)*. The birds are present throughout the year, but the best time to see them is from December to March, when one parent is constantly guarding the young while the other delivers food. Watching these clumsy giants coming in to land is pretty hilarious.

Another rewarding way to encounter the peninsula's critters is with **Nature's Wonders** *(natureswonders.co.nz)*. The tours along the beautiful beaches of a coastal sheep farm, often guided by real Kiwi farmers, offer a chance to see yellow-eyed penguins and NZ fur seals, blissfully unfazed by the 'go-anywhere' Argo vehicles.

Tunnel Beach

HEAVENLYFLOWER/SHUTTERSTOCK

TOP TIP

A CATLINS CAPER

Many of the Catlins coast's splendid, often strange surprises – such as **Waipapā Lighthouse**, **Slope Point**, **Cathedral Caves** *(cathedralcaves.co.nz)* and **Purakaunui Falls** – await discovery down back roads, dead-end roads, gravel roads and other roads-less-travelled. If you have the time, it's definitely worth exploring with a copy of the local touring map *(catlins.org.nz)*.

26

★ BEST FOR

HERITAGE

Clyde's stone buildings dating from the 1860s.

QUEENSTOWN & THE SOUTH

OTAGO HERITAGE TRAIL

Oliver's (p239), Clyde

DURATION: 4-6 DAYS

DISTANCE: 450KM / 280 MILES

GREAT FOR: NATURE, CULTURE AND HISTORY

BEST TIME TO GO: CHANGING SEASONAL COLOUR PALETTES MAKE THIS TRIP STRIKING ALL YEAR ROUND

It was the discovery of gold in the 1860s that led to settlement of the rugged Otago region. Today, old miners' trails and an abandoned railway lead visitors through remote towns dominated by big skies in one of the country's most beloved cycling regions. The road takes in historic stone buildings, gold-rush stories, romantic old railway bridges, and offers plenty of chances to stretch the legs on a short walk or bike ride.

LINK YOUR TRIP

25 Southern Scenic Route
Head south from Dunedin to explore the wild, crazy Catlins coast, Stewart Island /Rakiura and the pretty, rural Southland.

04 East Coast Express
Travel north from Dunedin to experience the east coast's wildlife, ocean scenes, rural charm and rejuvenating Christchurch.

01 Dunedin

Dunedin is full of hidden surprises. This student city loves a laugh and a drink, and you'll find plenty to entertain and nourish you here, from a vibrant live-music scene to a smorgasbord of international restaurants. There's the famous **Speight's brewery** *(speights.co.nz)*, which has been churning out beer since the late 19th century and is the oldest operating brewery in NZ. On the street outside, a tap delivers the chemical-free spring water that feeds the brewery to passers-by. Meanwhile, indie choccy maker **Ocho** *(ocho.co.nz)* tickles sweet tooths with tours of its factory producing single-origin chocolate sourced from Papua New Guinea, the Solomon Islands and further afield. It's worth dropping into **Bay Road Peanut Butter** *(bayroad.nz)* next door

MARINA MATHEWS/OLIVERS

too. Dunedin's rich cultural tapestry is stitched together tidily at **Toitū Otago Settlers Museum** *(toituosm.com)*. Interactive and engrossing, it features a Māori section, an awesome car collection and a room devoted to a seminal New Zealand music production company, Flying Nun Records. Inside the Victorian portrait gallery, a host of early settlers stare out from behind whiskers and lace.

THE DRIVE: Head south on SH1. Around 57km along, just after Milton, turn right onto SH8 and follow it inland towards Lawrence – the scene of NZ's first gold rush in 1861. Continue to Raes Junction, after which it's around 10km to the Horseshoe Bend Bridge car park. Total journey time is around 90 minutes (127km).

02 Horseshoe Bend Bridge

This historically significant bridge was built in 1913 to replace a 'wire and chair' arrangement used to ferry early settlers over the Clutha River/Mata-Au – NZ's second-longest river. What a prospect! The mighty river's swift, swirling waters can be admired on the **Horseshoe Bend Track**, taking around 45 minutes each way. Beyond the handsome timber bridge, it's another 15 minutes or so to the **Lonely Graves**, one of the area's more poignant gold-rush relics. Sitting side by side in a fenced plot, their tale tells of the discovery of the body of a young man. Unable to be identified, the body was said to have been buried by a certain William Rigney in the company of other concerned citizens, and marked with the words 'Somebody's Darling Lies Buried Here'. When Rigney himself died in 1912, he was buried alongside.

THE DRIVE: Following the banks of the Clutha River/Mata-au, continue north on SH8 for 25km to Roxburgh.

03 Roxburgh

Surrounded by apple, apricot and other sweet-smelling orchards, the rural village of Roxburgh is a core member of Central Otago's fruit-growing set. The main attraction for passing travellers is a cycle ride along the Roxburgh Gorge or **Clutha Gold Trails** *(cluthagold.co.nz)*; these trails follow the ever-changing, highly scenic banks of the mighty Clutha River/Mata-Au and Lake Roxburgh, which pools against one of the river's dams. The twin trails offer a chance to survey many historic gold-mining relics, including water races and rock bivvies; the fragrance of wild thyme introduced by Chinese miners is often pervasive. **Highland Bike Hire** *(highlandbikehire.co.nz)* can provide bike hire and transport. But hang on, slam on the brakes! Roxburgh has another major attraction – **Jimmy's Pies** *(jimmyspies.co.nz)*, world-famous in New Zealand since way back in 1959. These buttery, calorific treats are best piping hot straight out of the oven. An apricot and chicken pie will give you a taste of the terroir.

THE DRIVE: SH8 winds along rugged, rock-strewn hills above the Clutha River/Mata-Au, passing a scattering of tiny towns, many of which date from the gold rushes. In season, roadside fruit stalls sell just-picked stone fruit, cherries and berries. It's 42km (30 minutes) to Alexandra.

04 Alexandra

Unless you've come especially for the Easter Bunny Hunt or the springtime Blossom Festival and NZ Merino Shearing Championships, the main reason to visit unassuming Alexandra is mountain biking. It's the major settlement along the Central Otago Rail Trail (NZ's original off-road cycling epic). The town offers more eating and sleeping options than the rest of the one-horse (or fewer) towns on the Rail Trail. It's also the predominant starting point of the **Roxburgh Gorge Trail** *(cluthagold.co.nz)*, some of the craziest bits of which can be explored on foot from the old Alexandra Bridge, or contact **Altitude Bikes** *(altitudebikes.co.nz)* who can set you up with a bike and information. There's also a rather spectacular walk around **Flat Top Hill Conservation Area** *(doc.govt.nz)*, 6km south of town (on the SH8 road to Roxburgh). A 40-minute loop features information panels explaining the significance of this 'block mountain' and its threatened ecosystems, and vast, panoramic views from the high points. Alex, as it's known to the locals, marks the southeastern corner of the acclaimed Central Otago wine region. Of the dozen wineries in the immediate vicinity, only a handful are open for tastings. These are detailed on the *Central Otago Wine Map*, available from **Alexandra i-SITE** (centralotagonz.com).

THE DRIVE: Follow signs along SH8 – which vaguely parallels the Clutha River/Mata-au – to Clyde, 8km away.

05 Clyde

Considerably more charming than his buddy Alex, Clyde looks more like a 19th-century gold-rush film set than a real town. Set on the banks of the emerald-green **Clutha River/Mata-Au**, Clyde retains a friendly, small-town feel, even when holidaymakers flood in during the peak summer season. A popular amble or cycle is the **Alexandra–Clyde 150th Anniversary Walk**, a fairly flat, one-way (three-hour) riverside trail with ample resting spots and shade. **Trail Journeys** *(trailjourneys.co.nz)* can set you up with cycles and transport.

THE DRIVE: From SH8, take Springvale Rd heading east out of town. At Springvale, around 11km from Clyde, head north-east on SH85 for 17km to the Ophir turn-off. It's another 1.5km or so to the town.

06 Ophir

Ophir (population 50) is one of Central Otago's true heritage gems. Gold was discovered here in 1863 and the town swiftly formed, adopting the name of the biblical place where King Solomon sourced his gold. By 1875, the population

OTAGO CENTRAL RAIL TRAIL

From the early 20th century to the 1990s, the Central Otago rail line linked small, inland goldfield towns between Dunedin and Clyde. After the 150km stretch from Middlemarch to Clyde was permanently closed, the rails were ripped up and the trail resurfaced. The result is a year-round, mainly gravel cycling and walking trail. Culverts, beautiful old rail bridges, viaducts, dramatic rock cuttings and spooky tunnels remove most of the ups and downs, making this a very accessible trail popular with families, older folks and weekend cyclists.

Running between Clyde and Middlemarch – thus paralleling part of this road trip – it offers opportunities to get out of your vehicle, don the walking shoes or hire a bike, and explore a historic route. It sports excellent facilities (toilets, shelters and information) and attracts well over 80,000 visitors annually; March is the busiest time. The entire trail takes three to four days to complete by bike (or a week on foot), and can be ridden in either direction. It is, however, easy to tailor day trips of various lengths, with plenty of bike hire and shuttle services available. Good bases for riding the trail include Clyde, Alexandra, Ranfurly and Middlemarch, with others such as Naseby and St Bathans easy detours. In person, any of the area's i-SITEs can provide advice on ride options, accommodation and refreshments. Comprehensive planning information is available at otagocentralrailtrail.co.nz and otagorailtrail.co.nz.

Taieri Gorge Railway (p237), Middlemarch
NIGEL JARVIS/SHUTTERSTOCK

hit over 1000 but when the gold disappeared, so did the people. Ophir's fate was sealed when the railway bypassed it in 1904, leaving its main street trapped in time. The most photogenic of Ophir's many heritage buildings is the still-functioning 1886 **post office** *(historic.org.nz)*. At the far end of town, the sealed road ends at the 1870s **Dan O'Connell Bridge** across the scenic Manuherikia River. Single-lane and built of schist and timber, it's a classic Central Otago suspension bridge.

THE DRIVE: Follow Ida Valley–Omakau Rd south, which parallels the Central Otago Rail Trail for part of the way, swinging left at Poolburn until you reach Oturehua, 32km from Ophir.

07 Oturehua

Perfect for a spot of rural time-travel, Oturehua boasts New Zealand's oldest continually operating shop, the nostalgic 1899 **Gilchrist Store** *(gilchriststore.co.nz)*, where floor-to-ceiling wooden shelves are still stocked with old boxes of soap powder, rolling tobacco and laxative tablets. Just out of town is **Hayes Engineering Works** *(hayesengineering.co.nz)*, where you can wander about the workshop filled with lathes, drills and pulleys where inventor and engineer Ernest Hayes manufactured all manner of useful farm devices, including his famous fencing wire strainer. His wife Hannah cycled from farm to farm to sell his labour-saving inventions. Together they raised nine kids in the little house that's now a cosy cafe, and retired to the much more comfortable 'big house' (1920), fitted with mod-cons from piped radio to electricity.

> **PHOTO OPPORTUNITY**
>
> Gilchrist Store's lost-in-time goods stock the shelves in NZ's oldest continually operating store.

THE DRIVE: Continue north on Ida Valley–Omakau Rd and turn right at the SH85 junction. Five minutes along is Wedderburn Goods Shed, made famous when Grahame Sydney painted it in *July on the Maniototo*

Gilchrist Store, Oturehua

GEOFF MARSHALL/ALAMY

(1975). Eleven kilometres along SH85 is the Ranfurly–Naseby Rd turn-off to Naseby, 26km from Oturehua. South of here, Waipiata makes a pleasant stop for the night.

DETOUR

St Bathans

Start: 07 Oturehua

A 17km detour north from SH85 (turning right onto St Bathans Loop Rd) heads into the foothills of the imposing Dunstan Mountains and on to diminutive St Bathans. This once-thriving gold-mining town of 2000 people is now home to only half a dozen permanent residents living amid a cluster of cutesy 19th-century buildings. There's not much in town but the historic **Vulcan Hotel** – an atmospheric (and famously haunted) spot to drink, eat or stay.

The **Blue Lake** is an accidental attraction: a large hollow filled with blue water that has run off abandoned gold workings. Walk along the sculpted cliffs to the lookout for a better view of the alien landscape (one hour return).

08 Naseby

Cute as a button, surrounded by forest and dotted with old stone buildings, **Naseby** *(nasebyinfo.org.nz)* is the kind of small settlement where life moves slowly. But typical of Central Otago's townships, these streets once ran hot with gold fever. At one time, Naseby was home to 4000 or so miners. After the rushes, the town was all but forgotten, leaving its 19th-century streetscape virtually intact. Heritage lovers will adore the village's old-world architecture, but it also boasts pleasant walking and cycling trails in the surrounding forest. The best time to be in town is undoubtedly winter. It gets mighty cold here but the long nights are perfect for star gazing. **Naseby Night Sky Tours** *(nasebynightskytours.wixsite.com/home)*, led by local astrophysicist Paul Bishop, pinpoints planets, star clusters and constellations. The town has also embraced its frosty weather with NZ's only year-round curling rink (sort of like lawn bowls on ice). If you've ever fancied giving it a whirl, slide on over to **Maniototo Curling International** *(curling.co.nz)*. From June to August the Southern Hemisphere's only **ice luge** *(maniototoadventurepark.co.nz)* opens up next door, where you can hurtle 360m down a hillside on a wooden sled.

THE DRIVE: Return to SH85 the way you came in. At the junction, follow SH85 left to reach Kyeburn, then turn right onto SH87 to reach Middlemarch, 65km (around 45 minutes) from Naseby.

09 Middlemarch

With the Rock & Pillar Range as an impressive backdrop, the small town of **Middlemarch** *(middlemarch.nz)* is famous in NZ for the **Middlemarch Singles Ball** – though now part of the Cavalcade Hoedown instead of a standalone event – where southern men gather to entice city gals to the country life. Oh, to be a fly on the wall, eh? Like its sibling towns throughout Central Otago, Middlemarch has many charming heritage buildings, including the railway station built when the Otago Central line reached town in 1891. Today Middlemarch is the eastern end of the Otago Central Rail Trail (p234); with two large cycle-hire companies on the main street, this is a great spot to get out for a ride to sample the trail. Heading south though, the tracks are still in place and the trains rumble on under the banner of **Taieri Gorge Railway** *(dunedinrailways.co.nz)*. Occasional trains travel between Middlemarch and Dunedin, but for most you must head down to Pukerangi, 20km south. The journey, in beautifully restored 1920s cars, takes in narrow tunnels, deep gorges, winding tracks, rugged canyons and viaduct crossings.

THE DRIVE: Continue south on SH87 for 65km until you reach SH1, which you should follow for the final 15km into central Dunedin. The journey time is just under an hour (80km).

STAY AWHILE

CLYDE

BY ASHLYN OSWALT

Alexandra may be the hub of Central Otago, but Clyde is most certainly its soul. Set along the Clutha River/Mata-Au, this tiny town looks like a set from a gold-mining movie and downtown can hum despite a population of only 1200.

Historic buildings, many from the late 1800s, line the streets. I like to take a self-guided walking tour, starting at the impressive **Clyde Dam**, completed in 1992, and meandering around the many stone buildings in town. **Olivers** *(olivers.co.nz)* is hard to miss – it features boutique accommodation, a fine-dining restaurant, cafe and brewery, with some of the buildings dating back to 1869. I enjoy resting my legs with a scone at its Merchant of Clyde Cafe.

Clyde is the beginning (or end) point for two popular cycling trails, the **Otago Central Rail Trail** *(otagocentralrailtrail.co.nz)* and **Lake Dunstan Trail** *(centralotagonz.com)*. I prefer the former for an easy, 152km amble along a rail trail, but the latter offers a more challenging 55km ride along Lake Dunstan and the Kawarau and Clutha rivers. Rent bikes from **Central Cycle Trail Co** *(centralcycletrail.co.nz)*.

All that activity always works up a thirst, so I'm sure to schedule in some time to indulge in the nearby wineries. **Monte Christo** *(montechristowinery.co.nz)*, established in 1864, is a grand estate complete with stone buildings and wine tastings. **Dunstan Road Wines** *(dunstanroadwines.com)* offers minimal intervention wines and good yarns – be sure to get in touch ahead of time if you want to drop in.

LINK YOUR TRIP

Smack in the middle of the South Island, Clyde is on the 26 **Otago Heritage Trail** road trip.

Left: Cycling, Otago Central Rail Trail
Right: Clyde

LEFT: JANICE CHEN/SHUTTERSTOCK; RIGHT: MARINA MATHEWS/OLIVERS

PLACES TO STAY

- **Olivers Lodge & Stables**
  Luxury accommodation in the heart of town, decorated with an elegant mix of original and modern. Freshly baked breakfast served every morning. *(olivers.co.nz)*

- **Dunstan House & Cafe Clyde**
  Built in 1898, this historic hotel housed miners in the gold-rush days but now welcomes cyclists and those looking to tour the area's fine wine. Charming cafe attached. *(dunstanhouse.co.nz)*

- **Monte Christo Cottages**
  Three modern cottages for soaking in the views of Monte Christo Winery, with luxurious amenities such as a wine fridge. You are at a winery, after all. *(montechristowinery.co.nz)*

TOOLKIT

ARRIVING

The overwhelming majority of travellers arrive by plane at Auckland, Wellington, Christchurch or Queenstown Airports, all of which are modern and easy to traverse. Entering New Zealand is a fairly straightforward affair and customs officials are generally friendly, provided you have all your paperwork in order and follow the rules around what you need to declare to maintain the country's biosecurity.

CAR RENTAL AT AIRPORTS

Major players such as Avis, Budget, Europcar, Ezi, Hertz and Thrifty all have desks in the International Arrivals area at Auckland, Wellington, Christchurch and Queenstown Airports.

Theoretically you can hire a vehicle on a walk-up basis, but it's the last thing you'll want if you've just come off a long flight (as most flights to New Zealand are).

You'll save time and money if you book in advance, and you're more likely to get the vehicle you want.

Plenty of other rental companies can arrange for a vehicle to be collected from the airport or can provide free shuttles to their nearby bases.

This includes the many motorhome and campervan rental companies, all of which have offices near the airports in Auckland and Christchurch. Some also rent out of Queenstown airports.

AIRPORT TO CITY CENTRE

	AUCKLAND	WELLINGTON	CHRISTCHURCH
RIDESHARE	30min **$55**	25min **$30**	20min **$30**
BUS	1hr **$17**	30min **$11.50**	30min **$4**
TAXI	30min **$75**	25min **$50**	40min **$25**
SHUTTLE	40min **$30**	30min **$20**	30min **$25**

AIRPORTS

Each of NZ's four main international airports has ATMs (cash machines), exchange bureaux, duty-free shopping, car hire, pay phones, free wi-fi, food outlets and well-maintained toilets.

VISAS

Most visitors to New Zealand will require either a visa or an NZeTA (NZ Electronic Travel Authority). The main exception are Australian citizens who can enter the country and stay indefinitely.

NZETAS

If you're from a visa-waiver country (immigration.govt.nz) you'll still need to arrange an NZeTA in advance, which allows stays of up to three months (six months for UK citizens).

DUTY FREE

New Zealand's duty-free alcohol allowance is three 1.125L bottles of spirits and 4.5L of wine or beer. The allowance for tobacco products is 50 cigarettes or cigars or 50g of tobacco.

GETTING AROUND

HIGHWAY CLOSURES

In recent years a series of extreme-weather events has resulted in landslides and slips affecting highways around the country. Cyclone Gabrielle in February 2023 caused major damage to the road network that may take years to repair. The worst-effected areas were Northland, the beaches to the west of Auckland, the Coromandel Peninsula, East Cape, the Gisborne/Tairawhiti region and Hawke's Bay. Waka Kotahi (the NZ Transport Agency) lists all highway closures on its website (nzta.govt.nz).

DRIVING INFO

Drive on the left.

All vehicle occupants must wear a seatbelt.

.05

Blood alcohol limit is 0.5g/L.

TRANSPORT CARDS

Most NZ cities have their own smart card for use on buses and trains, which means you'll need a separate one for each public-transport network. Plans are afoot to coordinate them into one system by 2027.

SPEED LIMITS

The speed limit is 50km/h in built-up areas, dropping to 30km/h in some suburban streets. On the open road and most highways the limit is 100km/h, except near some major cities where the limit is 110km/h.

PARKING

Pay close attention to parking signs in urban areas. Parking can usually be paid for by card or coins at a physical meter or by using an app. Increasingly, parking buildings are using number-plate-recognition technology rather than physical tickets.

DRIVING ETIQUETTE

New Zealanders can be impatient drivers and are prone to tailgating. If you're in a slow vehicle, keep to the left and consider pulling over to let others overtake you if you notice a queue forming behind you.

TRAVEL COSTS

Car rental
From $80 per day

Petrol
Approx $2.55 per litre

EV charging
69c per kWh

Some shopping centres, hotels and sights allow free (slow) EV charging.

ACCOMMODATION

HOW MUCH FOR A NIGHT IN A...

Bach
$175

Backpacker hostel
$35

Powered campsite
$40

BACH

In New Zealand, a holiday home is known as a bach (pronounced 'batch') or, in some parts of the South Island, a crib. Traditionally these were basic, family-owned cottages, but nowadays a bach can be anything from a rustic cabin to a luxury beach house. Prices vary widely depending on size and standard. Booking sites include bookabach.co.nz, bach-care.co.nz and airbnb.co.nz.

CAMPSITE & HUT

The Department of Conservation (DOC) manages hundreds of campsites and huts in conservation land around NZ. A standard campsite (with water source and long-drop toilet) costs around $10 per night, ranging up to $40 for a powered site in peak season. Hut prices start at around $15 a night for a basic plastic-covered mattress in a bunk room.

GREAT WALKS HUT

While most DOC accommodation doesn't require a booking, you'll need to book in advance for the Great Walks season (October to April). Great Walks huts tend to be of a higher standard. Prices start from $25 for a bunk in the shoulder season. Note, there is different pricing for international and New Zealand visitors.

HOLIDAY PARK

New Zealand's holiday parks are more than just campgrounds. Along with powered and unpowered tent and campervan sites, they generally also have a range of cabins (with or without kitchens and bathrooms) and plush self-contained motel-style units. The best ones have swimming pools, spa pools, playgrounds, games rooms, TV lounges, communal kitchens and small shops selling essential supplies.

HAPPY HOSTELS

New Zealand has some of the best hostels in the world, ranging from small, homestay-style affairs with just a handful of beds to refurbished hotels and purpose-built towers. As well as dorm rooms, they usually have a range of private rooms, some with their own en-suite bathrooms. A dorm bed will set you back $35 to $50.

MOTEL WOES

You'll find motels all over the country and, as you might expect, the quality varies greatly. However, during the COVID-19 pandemic, many were converted into emergency housing and some still double as temporary social-housing providers. Sadly, in some parts of the country (notably Rotorua and Hamilton) some residents have developed a reputation for violent and intimidating behaviour. There are still lots of exceptional motels out there, so don't be put off - but do your research and be sure to check recent reviews online.

CARS

CAR RENTAL

There are plenty of options for car rental in NZ, including the big international brands and some local operators. Names to look out for include Ace, Apex, Avis, Budget, Dollar, Enterprise, Europcar, Ezi, Go, Hertz, Omega, Pegasus, Sixt and Thrifty. If you're after a motorhome or campervan, you'll also be spoilt for choice, with brands such as Apollo, Britz, Escape, Hippie, Jucy, Maui, Mighty, Spaceships, Tui and Wilderness. Some specialise in luxury motorhomes, while others cater to back-packers. Mopeds are a fun way to get around Waiheke Island; there's a rental agency near the ferry terminal.

Your hotel may be able to help you book a rental, but it's highly unlikely that it'll rent cars of its own.

HOW MUCH TO HIRE A CAR?

Small petrol hatchback **$80 per day**

Hybrid sedan **$130 per day**

EV **$80 per day**

EVS

These days most of the larger car-rental companies offer electric vehicles, but you're likely to pay a premium for them.

The number of charging stations around the country is growing, but you may still need to do some planning ahead on a longer journey. Waka Kotahi, the NZ Transport Agency, has a map listing EV-charging stations on its website *(journeys.nzta.govt.nz/ev-chargers)*.

OTHER GEAR

Car-rental companies will provide all of the extra kit you may need, for an extra charge. If you have children requiring a booster seat, car seat or baby capsule, it's wise to book these in advance.
If you're travelling on high-altitude roads in winter, consider hiring snow chains.

SEITA/SHUTTERSTOCK

RESPONSIBLE TRAVEL

CLIMATE CHANGE & TRAVEL

Lonely Planet urges all travellers to engage with their travel carbon footprint, which will mainly come from air travel. While there often isn't an alternative, travellers can look to minimise the number of flights they take and use cleaner ground transport, such as trains.

One proposed solution – purchasing carbon offsets – unfortunately does not cancel out the impact of individual flights. While most destinations will depend on air travel for the foreseeable future, for now, pursuing ground-based travel where possible is the best course of action.

The **UN Carbon Offset Calculator** shows how flying impacts a household's emissions.

The **ICAO's carbon emissions calculator** allows visitors to analyse the CO_2 generated by point-to-point journeys.

Know Before You Go
doc.govt.nz
Department of Conservation (DOC) official website.

Protect The Forests
kauriprotection.co.nz
Information on protecting NZ's forests from kauri dieback disease.

Keep It Green
forestandbird.org.nz
New Zealand's leading independent conservation organisation.

BOATING

DOC has rules regarding how close boats can get to marine mammals such as dolphins and whales. Anyone in charge of a vessel (including skippers of tour boats) should abide by them.

FISHING

Fishing in NZ is highly regulated, with catch and size limits in place for different species and for the collection of other seafood such as shellfish and crustaceans. No fishing is permitted in marine reserves.

RĀHUI

From time to time a local tribe will impose a *rāhui* (prohibition) on fishing, gathering seafood or accessing an area. It's always done for a reason (often environmental) and should be respected.

SAFE TRAVEL

BEACH HAZZARDS

New Zealand's surf beaches regularly claim lives. If a beach is patrolled by lifesavers, always swim between the flags. Dangerous rips can sweep a person out to sea quickly. If you're not sure how to spot them or how to escape one if you do get caught, don't venture beyond waist depth at an unpatrolled beach.

EARTHQUAKES

New Zealand is known as the 'Shaky Isles' and earthquakes are a fairly common occurrence in some parts of the country.

If you feel an earthquake, the official advice is to 'drop' (down on your hands and knees, preferably under a strong table), 'cover' (your head and neck) and 'hold' (on to your shelter until the shaking is over).

TSUNAMIS

Signs draw attention to tsunami evacuation zones along the coast. If you're in one when an earthquake occurs, 'drop, cover and hold' until the shaking is over. If the earthquake lasts longer than a minute or is strong enough to make it difficult to stand, move quickly to the nearest high ground or as far inland as you can.

CAR BREAKDOWNS

Check with your rental company about roadside assistance and keep their phone number handy. If you're a member of an international automobile association (such as RAC UK), you may find you're eligible for reciprocal services from the AA in NZ. Call 0800 500 222 for the AA's roadside assistance; you can join at the roadside for $209.

GEOTHERMAL AREAS

In the North Island's many geothermal areas, be sure not to venture off the paths as the ground can be surprisingly thin, with scalding mud or water underneath.

Temperatures at natural hot springs, even those at popular Hot Water Beach, can vary widely. Test the heat before you plunge in, and keep an eye on the kids.

IN CASE OF EMERGENCY

111
Police

111
Ambulance

111
Fire Service

111
Coast Guard

On-water assistance call 500

VHF Channel 16

TOOLKIT

NUTS & BOLTS

GOOD TO KNOW

Time zone
NZ time zone GMT +12hr

Country code
+ 64

Emergency number
111

Population
5.3m

CURRENCY: NZ DOLLAR ($)

OPENING HOURS

Standard office hours are 9am to 5pm Monday to Friday. Most retail stores are open until 5pm or 6pm, with reduced hours at weekends. Larger supermarkets often remain open until 10pm or 11pm.

CURRENCY EXCHANGE

Changing foreign currency (and, to a far lesser extent, travellers cheques) is usually no problem at NZ banks or at licensed exchange bureaux in major tourist areas, big cities and airports. However, withdrawing directly from ATMs usually secures the most favourable rates.

ELECTRICITY

Type I
230V/50Hz

WAYS TO PAY

EFTPOS is extremely common in NZ, even for small amounts, and many people no longer carry cash. However, you may be charged a small surcharge (around 2%) if you use contactless payment or pay by credit card. Phone-based tap payments are still uncommon but are increasingly available.

TIPPING

Tipping is completely optional in NZ. There's absolutely no expectation of a tip in a restaurant, hotel or taxi. That said, staff are usually very grateful for a gratuity.

SMOKING

Smoking is prohibited in most indoor public places, including public transport, and some outdoor ones such as sports stadiums. It is illegal to smoke in a private vehicle carrying a child aged under 18.

TAP WATER

Generally, tap water is safe to drink. In some remote areas (including some DOC huts and campsites) you may need to boil water, but there's likely to be a warning sign if that's the case.

HOW MUCH FOR A...

Coffee
$5

Glass of wine
$12

Tap beer
$10

National park entry
Free

INDEX

Drives 000
Map pages **000** 000

M

N

O

P

THE WRITERS

This is the 4th edition of Lonely Planet's Best Road Trips New Zealand guidebook, updated with new material by Ashlyn Oswalt.

Writers on previous editions whose work also appears in this book are included below.

Ashlyn Oswalt

Ashlyn Oswalt is an American writer based in New Zealand, covering travel, food and the outdoors. She can be found campervanning her way around the South Island with her dog and husband, attempting to surf, or growing far too many tomatoes in her backyard.

Contributing writers

Brett Atkinson, Andrew Bain, Peter Dragicevich, Monique Perrin, Charles Rawlings-Way, Tasmin Waby

Send us your feedback

We love to hear from travellers - your comments keep us on our toes and help make our books better. Our well-travelled team reads every word on what you loved or loathed about this book. Although we cannot reply individually to your submissions, we always guarantee that your feedback goes straight to the appropriate writers, in time for the next edition.

BEHIND THE SCENES

This book was produced by the following:

Commissioning Editor Darren O'Connell

Coordinating Editor Brana Vladisavljevic

Production Editor Lucy Jones

Image Researcher Dominic Allen

Cartographer Mark Griffiths

Assisting Editors Gabrielle Stefanos

Cover Researcher Daisy Korpics

Thanks to Ronan Abayawickrema, Sofie Andersen, Melanie Dankel

Product Development Sofie Andersen, Melinda Anderson, Marc Backwell, Alison Killilea, Darren O'Connell, James Smart, Saralinda Turner, Robin Yule

Acknowledgments

Digital Model Elevation Data Contains public sector information licensed under the Open Government Licence v3.0 website nationalarchives.gov.uk/doc/open-government-licence/version/3/

Cover photographs

Front: Campervan, Lake Hāwea; Kieran Stone/Getty Images

Back: Kawarau Gorge Suspension Bridge; Adwo/Shutterstock

Visit **lonelyplanet.com/contact** to submit your updates and suggestions or to ask for help. Our award-winning website also features inspirational travel stories and news.

Note: We may edit, reproduce and incorporate your comments in Lonely Planet products such as guidebooks, websites and digital products, so let us know if you are happy to have your name acknowledged. For a copy of our privacy policy visit **lonelyplanet.com/legal**

lonely planet

Published by Lonely Planet Global Limited
CRN 554153
Digital Depot, Roe Lane off Thomas Street, Dublin
D08 TCV4, Ireland (EU authorised representative)
4th edition – Sep 2026
ISBN 9781837584543

10 9 8 7 6 5 4 3 2 1
Printed in China